Who Are the Russians?

Alla SERGUEEVA

WHO ARE THE RUSSIANS?

Translated from the Russian by Isabelle Deschamps

Max Milo Éditions, Paris, 2023
www.maxmilo.com
ISBN 9782315011551

Introduction

In recent years, there has been a growing interest in Russia and its people on the part of foreigners wondering about the "enigmatic Russian soul" and about Russians themselves. In the West, Russians are perceived as being as incomprehensible and unpredictable as their "Slavic soul". With the opening of borders, many Russians have moved abroad and, strange as it may seem, this has led them to "reflect" on themselves. More and more often, they ask themselves: "Why are we different from others?" It's a question that comes up in jokes and dinner-table discussions with friends, and even in prime-time TV debates. However, neither the brochures nor the "round tables" or TV debates on this theme provide a satisfactory answer; they only confuse the reader (the viewer), reinforcing his or her conviction that the character of the Russian remains elusive. In the heat of discussion, a lot of unjust and simply stupid things are said (and written) about Russians, their way of life and their mentality.

It's not a simple question. If we take out of context certain traits of the Russian character or certain aspects of his lifestyle and compare them with Western models, we can only wonder. For a long time now, Russians have been asking themselves: *How is it that, despite our vast territory and natural resources, we are poorer than the inhabitants of countries that call themselves civilized? Surely it's* not only the stupid and adored leaders who are responsible for this situation? And *why is Russia's economic development so jerky?* A leap forward followed by periods of inertia, and then collapse. Is this the result of absurd management, a lack of willpower, or the normal pace of development? Or is it linked to our tradition of "cigarette breaks" during work, to our *oblomovchtchina* ("Oblomov-style abulia"). Or is it something else?

More generally, is Russia *Eastern* or *Western*? What counts is not so much the country's geographical location as the Russians' *mentality*.[1] How can we distinguish between what is more "Western" and what is more "Eastern"? To what ethnic type is this mentality linked? For every Russian, "the East is a refined civilization", but what have we taken from it? We often criticize ourselves for lacking the subtlety and adaptability of the Orient. Can we find the "key" to the *Russian character*?[2] And if it does exist, haven't its traits changed under the influence of recent historical reversals in Russia? *Is it justified to call the Russian "sovkom"* ("soviet" in the pejorative sense)? Why do Russians aspire so much to the "art de vivre" of other countries, and make no secret of their admiration for "Western civilization"? They dream of doing business with a foreign firm, and many of them marry foreigners. And they happily leave their homeland, weary of the vicissitudes they encounter there. They have already populated a large part of the world. But, at the same time, they often find it hard to put down roots in their adopted country and avoid nostalgia for their homeland. It is also said that Russians are strongly imbued with a collectivist spirit. So why do they do so little to help each other abroad, and why don't they form "communities" like other expatriates around the world? Ultimately, are they *collectivists or individualists, patriots or stateless?*

And where do they get these *strange, typically Russian habits* in their daily behavior that shock foreigners? They are, *for* example, prone to *toska*, a kind of Russian "spleen", and have frowning faces, rarely brightened by a smile, while, more than anyone else, they like to party in the company of friends and the inevitable alcoholic beverages; they are then exuberantly cheerful in places where it would not occur to foreigners to relax. Among these peculiar

---

1. Mentality: characterizes people living in a concrete culture, with their perception of the world, their way of thinking, their hierarchy of values, their customary and social modes of behavior - see the book *La Mentalité des Russes. Conscience propre aux grands groupes de population en Russie*, Moscow, published by the Institute of Psychology of the Russian Academy of Sciences, 1997, p. 10.
2. K. G. Jung's fundamental analysis of the relationship between analytical psychology and poetic-artistic creation, *in Le Phénomène de l'esprit dans l'art et la science*, Moscow, 1992.

Russian habits, we can only deplore those of arriving late for appointments - including business ones - not respecting work deadlines and obligations, and forgetting to repay loans. But does this mean we shouldn't do business with them?

These are some of the questions every Russian asks himself when he looks around to compare himself to others. It's not a very objective approach. Sometimes, foreigners contaminated by *cultural self-centeredness* appreciate only their own culture and find others "barbaric" or immature. They are unaware of the profound realities of Russian life and cannot understand their "bizarre" and "inconsistent" behavior. Hence the myth of the Russians' "enigmatic and ambiguous character", even their hypocrisy and falsehood, which others repeat out of ignorance, credulity or malice. Each people is unique and has its own share of mystery, and each country has followed a different path from the others. In short, it's not so much a question of *comparing* as of *knowing*.

So we're not so much talking about the "enigmatic soul" as about what makes the Russian character so unique. The model of the fast-moving "rollercoaster", with its ups, downs and unexpected detours, describes it perfectly. The Russian temperament contains traits and qualities found in other peoples of the world. However, for historical, cultural and climatic reasons, the Russians may combine these qualities in a different way. We will try to analyze the particularities of Russians in the general context of the country, without focusing on any one aspect in particular. Our aim is to describe some of their peculiarities and demonstrate that the "enigmatic character of the Russian soul" is a myth that doesn't fit the stereotype: we'll try to dispel it in this book.

This book aims to introduce Russians in successive stages. Part 1 lists the *values shared* by Russians and other peoples, to facilitate mutual understanding. Part 2 (chapters 1 and 2) deals with the *ethno-cultural peculiarities of* the Russians, formed since the earliest times in Russia and almost unchanged since then: their *way of life*, the *rules of* social *behavior, and* so on. Then (chap. 3) we look at their *outlook on life*, in particular their famous collectivism, their sense of justice, their relationship to freedom, property and morality, their tendency to alcoholism, and other curious aspects - in short, everything that makes them so different from other peoples. The mentality of Russians after perestroika will be the subject of Part 3. The last part, on the other hand, deals with what it's useful *for businessmen to* know when they want to work with Russians.

The book is aimed at a wide audience. It will help foreign partners to avoid many mistakes when working with Russians, and to find answers to their questions about what they find objectionable about the Russian character and the Russian people in general. Valuable advice is given at the end of the book.

As for the Russians, it will be interesting for them to see themselves from the outside, to reflect on what brings them closer to and differentiates them from other peoples, and to understand why Pushkin (chap. 3), even two centuries ago, asserted: "We have not changed and the whole world is foreign to us!" Where does this come from? And could it be that nothing has changed since then?

PART ONE - HUMAN VALUES: WHAT UNITES US?

1. First reference points: appearance, language

It's safe to assume that French people preparing to go and work in Africa, South-East Asia or Latin America will adapt more easily in these countries, because they know in advance that they'll be dealing with people who are totally different from them - whether by skin color, eye shape or exotic "get-up".

Being willing to find obvious external differences leads the individual to be more tolerant of them, softens the "culture shock"; "they are different from us anyway, so we should not be surprised by anything. When Westerners visit Africa, everything is done to remind them that they are in Africa and they expect nothing else - whether it is in the restaurant, in the way negotiations are conducted or in the style of local business.

But when it comes to relations between Russians and Europeans, it's precisely their outward "resemblance" that's disconcerting: we're talking about the same white European race, dressed in European style. What's more, Russians are fluent in English, and less so in French or German.

In the days of the USSR, things were simpler: it was easy to tell the Russians from the foreigners. And Russians' faces could be distinguished from the "European" crowd by their overly tense or obviously emotional expressions. And if, in the past, they would not go unnoticed in the streets of European cities because of their ridiculous attire, today it's quite the opposite: they are often well-groomed, wearing expensive clothes in brighter colors than, say, the average Parisian. For Europeans, it's still surprising to see pretty Russian women with well-groomed looks and expensive clothes. Incidentally, it's not just the wives of the "new Russians" (nouveau riche) who strive to look attractive, but also people who, by European standards, are far from wealthy. This attitude among Russian women is a tradition that goes back to ancient times.

A Frenchman visiting Moscow for the first time is likely to discover a rich city with its own unique character, but one that is utterly European. The inhabitants have a European look - and they "relax", thinking that everything here is exactly like home. However, this is not always the case, as the Russians are a different nation, with their own qualities and mentality. Let's not forget the old adage: "Clothes don't make the man". It's not without reason that Russians say, "You meet according to your clothes, but it's the spirit that does the rest."

Language is also an important point of reference when socializing with Russians. The peculiarities of the country's culture, psychology and mentality are reflected in the language spoken, in the use of words, which give a particular flavor to the world. Hence the immense difficulties involved in translating texts from one language to another. We know that professional translators at the United Nations face this kind of problem every day. Certain words are often difficult to translate adequately into another language. It is, for example, very difficult to render in some European languages those notions familiar to every Russian: *space, will, freedom, well-being, bravery, laughter, cordiality, loneliness, spleen, nostalgia* and many others.

In turn, the *way people interact with each other* determines the gestures and stereotyped speech patterns of each nation. It goes without saying that these practices vary from country to country. The Japanese don't shake hands, they bow, and they don't blow their noses in public. The Greeks look you in the eye and nod when they mean "no". The French kiss people they don't know (and vice versa) and clean the sauce off their plates with bread. The British eat peas with a fork and play golf in the rain. All these ways may seem amusing to us, but we can make them our own in order to become accustomed to them. Or to distract ourselves. Even if, deep down, this behavior won't have any impact.

In principle, you can learn about a people's customs, preferences and taboos; you can embrace their religion and study their philosophy. But only the study of the language will enable you to break down barriers and perceive the world as the interlocutor of a different culture. It's very important for businessmen to take this into account.

The important thing is that the representative of each culture has a different way of looking at the world. You may be tolerant and open-minded, but you can't feel and perceive the world like someone from a different culture, because you don't speak its language. Yet every person's speech is strongly determined by the construction of their native language. Generally speaking, you can learn about a people's customs, preferences and taboos; you can even marry them and study their philosophy. But only by learning the language can you extricate yourself from your native tongue and perceive the world as the interlocutor of another culture. It's very important for businessmen to take this into account. In short, if you want to do business successfully with Russians, you need to know Russian.

If we analyse the human values shared by Russians and Europeans, we can cite the following points:
- respect for intellect, science and education;
- Love of country, patriotism;
- pride in the history of his country, its culture and its great men;
- the natural desire to be happy;
- the predominance of tradition, conservatism;
- the desire for justice;
- temperament and sensitivity;
- sense of humor;
- Artistic sense, taste, aptitude for artistic creation ;
- sociability, love of discussion.

As we can see, there are many points that bring us closer together: these same criteria will not, however, suffice for the individual of a different nationality who really wants to "build a bridge" between the two cultures. It's only by mastering a certain knowledge that you'll be able to ask the "right" questions, "get the other person talking", talk to them and listen attentively.

Because the same values mean different things to the French and Russians, and have their own particularities.

Let's take a look at some of them. Here's one, for example, which is universal and also applies to businessmen.

2. Respect for the intellect and intelligent people

In today's world, there's a growing interest in intellect as an important and positive value. And that's normal: it's much more pleasant, simpler and enriching to deal with an intelligent person than with an imbecile. As the Russians say, "With an intelligent person you learn, with a fool you get bored".

However, it's only recently that scholars have begun to ask: but what is an intelligent man and what is an intellectual? What makes a man intelligent (or can he be considered intelligent)? Experience, the ability to learn, the ability to take others into account, or the ability to adapt to any situation and find solutions to difficulties? And do the criteria for determining an intelligent man agree from one country to another?[3]

In the Russian mentality, and even in the Russian language, the notions of "intelligence" and "intellect" are differentiated and delimited.

For the *Russians,* the word "intelligence" necessarily includes a notion of morality and ethics, while intellect corresponds to the equivalent European term, i.e. it includes in itself an element of rationalism. Only the first notion has an indisputable value for Russians.

What do people in different countries have in mind when they talk about an "intelligent man"? This notion varies greatly from country to country.

In South Africa, for example, an intelligent man is one who is willing to work for the family, respect the elders - that is, the notion of *intelligence* has an important social connotation, and attention, speed of assimilation and observation take a back seat.

---

3. Russian psychologist N. L. Smirnova examines these problems *in* "The model of intelligent man: a Russian study", in the book *La Mentalité russe : questions de théorie et de pratique psychologique*, Moscow, published by the Institute of Psychology of the Russian Academy of Sciences, 1997.

Americans use completely different criteria to judge a person's intelligence. Important to them are: 1) pragmatic problem-solving: the person "reasons logically", "considers all aspects of the problem"; 2) elocution: the person "expresses himself well and clearly", is generally "loquacious"; 3) social tolerance: the person knows how to "take others as they are" and "takes an interest in those around him".

The *Japanese* have a completely different idea of intelligence. For them, this quality, especially in women, includes the individual's behavior in society. To be considered intelligent, you need to be able to empathize with others, empathize, listen and be discreet. It's also important to "be a good speaker", "be sociable" and "know how to tell a story with a sense of humor". Last but not least, we find criteria such as "knowing how not to waste time", "knowing how to plan ahead" and "being original". So, as we can see, Japanese intelligence criteria have nothing in common with those of Americans!

The work of *Finnish* scholars on intelligence highlights the following factors: 1) the habit of cooperating in society: "2) the ability to solve problems, to easily understand and study something new; 3) dynamism; 4) "knowing how to defend one's point of view", "being persevering", "easily linking knowledge"; 5) prudence, precision, the ability to plan before acting, achieving objectives in life and at work, and so on... As you can see, the criteria defining intelligence differ greatly depending on whether you're in Finland or Japan, and even more so in Africa...

Among *Russians,* quite different factors are taken into account to define an intelligent person. For them, the *social and ethical factor* is the most important: discretion, honesty, benevolence, kindness, sincerity and the desire to help others (10.5%). In second place is a taste for reflection: erudition, intelligence, a good education, a love of reading, a flexible and creative mind (9.1%). In third place comes the *ability to be organized,* i.e. to disregard one's emotions, to be pragmatic, not to repeat one's mistakes, to find the solution to a complex situation, logic and the ability to focus on the goal. In fourth place come the *relational qualities of the individual;* the art of pleasing, the art of expressing oneself well, the sense of humor, sociability, being a good interlocutor (6.8%). And it's only at the end of the list that qualities such as *experience*, *diversity of interests*, *capacity for work*, *wisdom* and *critical thinking* (5%) are mentioned - in other words, what plays a leading role for, say, the Anglo-Saxons.

If we make a general cross-cultural analysis of American, Finnish, Japanese and Russian mindsets on this question, we come up with a surprising result.[4] Social characteristics and social behavior are what all these countries have in common in their definition of the intelligent man. Of course, depending on the culture, these qualities are more or less important.

On the whole, Americans and Finns have a very similar idea of the intelligent man: for them, the most important thing is the *ability to learn*, i.e. the *cognitive* factor.

The Japanese and Russians, on the other hand, put the *social factor* first, the *ability to adapt to the surrounding environment.*

Perhaps this is due to the difference in mentality between the West and the East, or more precisely, to the rationalist and individualist traditions of Western society versus the collectivist habits and "unscientific" (by European standards) way of thinking of the East.

It's no coincidence that Russians make a radical distinction between concepts such as "intelligence" and "intellect". For them, the "intelligent man" is characterized by spirituality, delicacy, social responsibility, high moral qualities; he is not supposed to be an intellectual, have a higher education diploma and use his mind. And one can be an intellectual while being harsh, rude and ill-mannered, and even foolish in the ordinary sense of the word - in a word, without arousing any particular respect.

However, Russians have, to this day, retained a "European thirst" for spiritual culture. In Russia, a person's level of culture is traditionally judged by the number of books he or she has read. Comparisons in this area between Russians and foreigners are not always to the advantage of the latter. In your dealings with Russians, if you wish to make a good impression on them, bear in mind this Russians' approach, perhaps not necessarily objective, to assessing a person.

---

4. A similar analysis methodology is given in the previously cited article by N. A. Smirnova, p. 123.

Thus, in terms of their *traditions* and *way of thinking*, Russians are *closer to the East than to the West, although this does not* prevent them from *developing the cultural traditions of Europe*. In the Russian mentality, where two principles coexist - Eastern and Western - it is, however, the *Eastern qualities that predominate. And moral and ethical qualities, as* well as *the individual's behavior in society,* play a predominant role. Whereas in the Western perception of the "intelligent" man, the elements of rationalism, logic and eloquence occupy a predominant place.

3. Love of country

"The individual without a homeland is like the nightingale without a song".
(popular Russian proverb).

By all accounts, the French live in a world with France at its center. They are fed up with their history, and tend to think that their country is the origin of models of democracy, justice, state and legal systems, philosophy, science, the culinary arts and the "art de vivre". And it's up to other countries to draw inspiration from them! It's for this reason that the French generally know little about other peoples (due to their school curriculum) and behave towards them with condescension.[5]

Compared to the French, Russians are not as self-confident and haughty in their love for their country. Their patriotism is not rooted in a sense of achievement; it's something more physical, more emotional. This is reflected in Russians' almost physical attachment to the places of their childhood and youth, in their excessive nostalgia when they lose touch with their homeland, and in their almost inability to put down roots abroad.

The specific character of Russian patriotism is also historically linked to the cult of power and the state. In Russian culture, love of one's homeland is inextricably linked with love of one's native land, the natural landscape and - against all logic - the state! In Russian history and culture, the structure of

---

5. R. D. Lewis, *The Civilization of Business in International Trade*, Moscow, ed. Delo, 2001, p. 280; see also Theodore Zeldin, *The French*, Collins Harvill, 1988 (translated into French and Russian; published in Moscow, ed. Progress ("Du Progrès") in 1989).

the state has generally had a special significance. The Russian soldier fought for "his faith, his tsar and his homeland": it goes without saying that these notions were inseparable. From a historical point of view, the Orthodox and State elements occupied a special place in Russian patriotism. But that's not all. The few centuries that have pitted Russia against the Catholic West and the Muslim East have also played a part. Surrounded on all sides by "heretics", the Russian people imagined themselves to be unique, exceptional and different from all others. This feeling has, over the years, given rise to and reinforced messianic ideas about Russia's great predestination in the history of mankind.

All these entanglements made Russian patriotism not only a *cultural phenomenon* involving love of country (attachment to its history, nature, culture, etc.), but also gave rise to an original perception of Russia's *destiny*, its particular relations with the rest of the world, the conception of a "specific path" and, strictly speaking, a feeling of "historical solitude".

There's one more quality that's highly valued around the world and makes us all alike: a sense of humor.

4. A sense of humor

With the development of international communications, business people are meeting more often and getting to know each other better. It's natural to want to forgo an over-serious tone and create a more relaxed atmosphere to forge closer contacts. Exchanging jokes and anecdotes helps, in many situations, to break through the wall of silence and mistrust and win others' goodwill towards you.

Humor is notoriously difficult to cross national borders. Why is that?

Firstly, it's perfectly obvious that the "victim" of your mockery may not see the funny side of your humorous reflections. For example, French anecdotes about Belgians will be appreciated for what they're worth in Brussels. Similarly, we doubt very much that the French will be charmed by anecdotes about, say, the lightness of Parisians.

Secondly, we may well be unable to appreciate a foreign joke or anecdote, not because it's overtly directed against our interlocutor, but quite simply because the latter lacks the knowledge of the cultural context, the precise information about the country that prevents him or her from appreciating the joke at its true value.

Is there such a thing as national humor? Before answering this question, let's recall the existence of international humor, i.e. certain jokes and forms of humor present in all cultures. This is the case, for example, of the *farce*, well known to Russians and French alike. There are also many anecdotes told in many countries, such as the unexpected arrival of the husband while his wife is with her lover, or jokes about restaurants, elephants. But even international humor reveals differences in style from country to country.

Here, for example, is an old anecdote about journalists who used to organize a competition for the best article on elephants. The headlines were:

English: "Elephant hunting in British East Africa."

French: "L'amour chez les éléphants en Afrique équatoriale française" (Love among elephants in French Equatorial Africa).

L'Allemand: "Origine et évolution de l'éléphant indien entre 1200 et 1950" (600 pages.)

The American: "How to transport the biggest and strongest elephant."

The Russian: "How we sent an elephant to the moon."

The Swede: "Elephants and the organized social state."

The Spaniard: "Elephant fighting technique".

The Finn: "What do the Finns think of elephants?"

This joke may have originated in the press conference corridors, but it highlights the various national weaknesses: French sauciness, Russian pride in previous successes in conquering the cosmos, American braggadocio, and the eternal Finnish concern for what others think of them. The Finns generally laugh out loud at this anecdote. But Russians can scowl if they feel their national dignity has been wounded.

Still, it's a good idea to know what Russians like to laugh at if you want to lighten the mood and win their trust.

By the way, here's an example of an anecdote in which (Soviet) Russians laugh at themselves. Question: "How does American AIDS differ from Soviet AIDS?" Answer: "American AIDS is incurable, whereas Soviet AIDS is invincible."

Anecdotes are one of the most popular genres in Russia. The person who possesses the art of telling anecdotes is a welcome guest in any house, he has a special authority at every table - to organize the party as happily as possible. The storytellers are so appreciated that many of them have been encouraged in their career by their mere talent to entertain the public and especially the authorities.

It is no exaggeration to say that the *anecdote* (a short, funny story told in person) developed very quickly and had its heyday in the USSR, precisely under Soviet rule and, what is more, thanks to it. Strict control over private life and no less strict censorship of literature and the media fuelled the development of this new genre. The failings of the system, the outrageous errors and, quite simply, the stupidity of the rulers of the day were plain for all to see. But criticism could only be expressed in conversation, in the form of a short story, without loss of dignity and without particular risk. Incidentally, people were subjected to severe persecution because of "political" anecdotes, and there is no shortage of witnesses to say that these people were condemned to the Gulag or, in the best of cases, had their careers, health and lives shattered.

Every anecdote was constructed from the ironic commentary of a situation, which by itself evoked horror or tears, but in the anecdote it appeared to be comical. The nature of this laughter - light irony or bitter sarcasm - depended on the subject. Long years of training in this genre have developed in Russians a particular relationship to humor; namely, "quality" humor, genuine and subtle, which must necessarily include a note of sadness or, as the writer Nicolas Gogol put it, it must be "laughter through tears".

Other, frankly light-hearted humor with erotic and sexual overtones (i.e., scabrous, "Rabelaisian"), "salacious" humor, may seem crude and primitive to Russians, and therefore no fun. Besides, you'll never find the word "love" in Russian anecdotes. There are plenty of "family" anecdotes, in which spouses may dislike each other, change, regret having married, but divorce is always avoided. A change of spouse will in no way provoke a divorce; it will merely be the pretext for a scandal. For example: "The husband arrives home, his wife is in bed with her lover. Here come the reproaches and suspicions again! 'You believe, as always, in your impudent eyes, but not in your own wife!' shouts the wife, her spirit querulous as she crosses her robe..." But sometimes the deceived husband doesn't notice the change in his wife at all, doesn't pay her any attention, is caught up in another passion: "I arrive home one day. I see that my wife is in bed with a guy. I was immediately suspicious. I run to check the fridge. I was right: no more vodka." Many Russian "family" anecdotes give this idea of the Russian family (not always justified) that, in general, it's the woman with the long arm and the sharp tongue who's in charge, she's the one who wears the pants. With that, the husband deserves it, insofar as he's an imbecile, incapable of earning money, passive in bed, a great lover of drink - in short, a useless being for the family.

In addition to "on the spot" political anecdotes and "family" anecdotes, there were whole series of "national" anecdotes (remember that the USSR was a multi-ethnic country). (Remember that the USSR was a multi-ethnic country.) In these anecdotes, the traits of certain nations were the butt of jokes.

For example, in the days of the USSR, Russians were fond of anecdotes about the Choukes, the Russian equivalent of French jokes about Belgians. The Choukes are a people of the far north. The anecdotes that target them are generally linked to their lack of understanding of real life in Central Russia, their naivety and their good-naturedness. Chukas have their share of misadventures, especially in the big cities, where they get lost like children and can be swindled by anyone. For example: "A Chouke arrives in Moscow and finds himself on Red Square. As if spellbound, he listens for hours to the chimes of the Kremlin tower. Having noticed it, a shrewd Caucasian asks him: 'Do you want to buy this carillon?' The Choukes are known to have a lot of money and no idea how to spend it in the deserted tundra. 'Oh yes, I do!' - 'Very well, give me two thousand dollars and I'll get a ladder.' The Tchouke is still waiting for him. The following year, the story repeats itself, but the elder brother of the previous one, who has already heard of cunning and ill-intentioned people in Moscow, has decided not to trust anyone. And now the same Caucasian approaches him, asking if he doesn't want to buy the Kremlin carillon for two thousand dollars. 'All right,' replies the cautious Chouke. 'Take the money, but I'll get the ladder'."

In the series of anecdotes about *Caucasians*, their national traits are mocked: their impetuosity towards blondes, their overweening pride, their taste for the high life and broad gestures. An example: "In Moscow, a French woman arrives for the first time, speaking not a word of Russian and lost in the big city... Seeing her, an enterprising Caucasian comes to meet her. 'Parlez-vous français?' she asks him shyly. Whereupon, he looks her straight in the eye and replies, 'Of course I do!'" The Caucasian (more often the Georgian) with his quirky accent and confident "macho" demeanor lends a special humorous note to these anecdotes.

In the series of Caucasian anecdotes, the struggle for supremacy between Georgians and Armenians occupied a prominent place. An example: "Armenian radio announces that on Mount Ararat a copper wire has been found two meters deep. This is followed by the comment of Armenian specialists: 'This proves the existence of the telegraph on Armenian territory already two thousand years ago.' In turn, the Georgian radio announced: 'The excavations did not reveal any copper wire on Armenian territory. This proves the use of telegraph and wireless radio in this region already two thousand years ago.'" Anecdotes on this theme are slightly tinged with irony, aggression and sarcasm have no place in it. After receiving their independence, these republics are no longer part of the repertoire of jokes between Russians.

Subsequently, anecdotes about *Ukrainians have* become very popular in recent years. The "peasant" character of Ukrainians is mocked in these anecdotes, in keeping with the stereotypes about them - their open love of bacon, their gluttony, their stinginess. An example: A Ukrainian woman asks, "Apart from bacon, do you eat apples?" - "Yes." - "How many do you eat? A case?" - "Yes." - "Two at once?" - "No problem." - "How about three cases?" - "Three crates maybe not, but I'll bite into every apple." In these anecdotes, Ukrainian speech is pronounced with a lilting accent and a characteristic southern Russian "g", making these anecdotes extremely comical to Russian ears. Why the intonations of the Ukrainian language make Russians laugh so much is not entirely clear. It's quite possible that Ukrainian is not perceived by Russians as an advanced literary language, but rather as a provincial dialect reminiscent of Russian slang.

It should be noted that the country's *cultural context*, and above all the cinema, played their part in the development of numerous series of anecdotes. There were many films, watched over and over again by several gene-rations of people, entire extracts of which were known by heart and taken up by the public, who turned them into proverbial phrases. For example, one of the most varied and beloved series of anecdotes among Russians was the one about Vasily Ivanovich Chapaev, an uneducated Rusty hero of the Civil War. The film *Chapaev,* often watched by the older generation, was the source of this series of anecdotes, every line of which every Russian knows by heart. These short, "stereotyped" phrases are the source of these funny stories. For example: "Vasily Ivanovich has his troops line up and asks: 'Comrade soldiers! Why do birds need money?' - 'They don't need it, Vasily Ivanovich,' the soldiers reply. - 'Quite right, my eagles! Then I did well to drink the one that was supposed to go to you!'"

Following a popular TV series about a high-level Soviet spy who infiltrated the enemy during the Second World War, a series of anecdotes appeared about Chtirlis, the Soviet spy who skilfully got out of any situation and liked to deliver his profound thoughts. For this reason, Chtirlis's anecdotes were as philosophical and ironic as his hero. An example: "Chtirlis goes on a mission and sees an Arab in national costume coming to meet him. "That's Bin Laden," Chtirlis says to himself. "That's Chtirlis," says Bin Laden to himself." They are close to what Russians call "English anecdotes", built on absurdity and wordplay.

Today, there's a whole host of "black humor" anecdotes about the "new Russians", about their stupidity, mispronunciation and inordinate thirst for a "life of luxury". To be precise, it's not so much the "new Russians" as the "new bandits". They are highly sarcastic and reflect the contemptuous attitude of the great mass of Russians towards those who believe that money and how to spend it are the most important things in life. An example: "A new Russian complains that he's tired of buying a new Mercedes every week. His interlo-cutor sympathizes (what a beard, indeed!) and asks him what happened to his last metallic-gray Mercedes-is the car permanently broken down or did it have an accident? - 'Not at all, but the ashtray was full.'"

After perestroika, the political anecdotes so beloved of Russians lost their popularity. Brezhnev used to be laughed at, enjoying his senile slump. An example: "A member of Brezhnev's entourage tells him, 'Christ has risen!'

And Brezhnev replied: 'I'm aware of it; it had been brought to my attention, but I had forgotten it!'" Then it was Gorbachev's turn, who took the brunt of it for his anti-alcohol campaign, chatter and political miscalculations. For Yeltsin, the jokes were rather good-natured, like laughing at a politically clumsy "bear" or rather an "elephant in a china store". But anecdotes about Russia's current president are unpopular.

Nowadays, Russians much prefer patriotic jokes, where in various competitions (including sexual ones), they "don't look bad" against the French, Americans and especially the Ukrainians. Here's an example: "The three Presidents (American, French and Russian) argue over who is the most skilful and can accomplish, for example, something incredible: getting a cat to eat mustard. Bush struggles for a long time, trying to force the mustard into the cat's mouth, but he can't do it: the cat takes revenge by scratching him until he bleeds. Chirac strokes it for a long time, whispers softly, tries to persuade the cat, but, of course, does not succeed in making the cat lick the mustard. Our (Russian) president doesn't think for long and smears mustard under the cat's tail. Tom screams in pain and starts licking the sore spot. And the President proudly adds: 'This is how things are done here - willingly and singing!'"

Incidentally, an inexhaustible topic has recently appeared for the wordsmiths, related to the rise to power of "Petersburgers", that is, people from the city of St. Petersburg. These stories were inspired by real events in the country: the reshuffling of the political elite. If before it was usually Muscovites who "ran the show", they have now been pushed out of the power structures (see also Part 2, Ch. 3, § 6) with the arrival of the new president of the Russian Federation, who is from St. Petersburg. This has happened so openly that it can only fuel the Russians' sense of humor. There was even a time when the television news broadcast the following anecdote: "On every train from St. Petersburg, a member of the presidential administration approaches the passengers; he approaches them in turn and asks them if they don't want to join the government in 'capacity' as 'Petersburgers'." And here's an anecdote recounted by V. Zhirinovsky: "A guy applies for a position of responsibility. The personnel manager asks him, 'Did you work for the KGB?' - 'No.' - 'Were you born in St. Petersburg?' - 'No.' - 'But you do have some relatives in St. Petersburg?' - 'No.' - 'Well, all right. And what's your address in Moscow?' - 'I live on Leningrad Avenue.' - 'Well, you see! We got there in the end.'"

Of course, a little humor during negotiations between businessmen can be obviously of great help: to break the ice, to speed up the time of reflection, to relax the partner and dispose him well towards you, to gain his confidence from man to man. But there's a downside to every medal, and a downside to every risk. What may seem entertaining and funny to a Frenchman or an American may cause the opposite reaction in a Russian and even lead him to look at you with a bad eye!

You have to be careful, especially when it comes to jokes about Russian current affairs. Perhaps this has something to do with Russian (Soviet) patriotism. Russians, as representatives of their country, feel responsible for everything that happens there, even for their President, who is not always up to the job. Russians like to make fun of their government, and frequently do so in the presence of foreigners, but... if it's coming from you, it may seem out of place.

Religious, cultural and other differences mean that not everyone laughs at the same jokes. Ultimately, if all values are relative and conditioned by a given culture, humor, patience and even truth are no exception. It is important to remember that laughter is not only a manifestation of joy, it can sometimes hide embarrassment, contempt or sarcasm, or can be interpreted as such.

And now let's take a universal quality that makes us all the same.

5. The desire to be happy

Everyone wants to be happy and wonders what happiness is. More than one philosopher has attempted to answer this question.

In connection with the subject of this book, we will attempt to study the question of happiness from the angle of Russian culture and the spiritual traditions of the Russian people. All the more so as this aspect is particularly topical today: the country is going through a difficult period in its development, a transition in its usual landmarks and concepts. It is known that the moral problem of happiness appeared in ancient Greece and was actively developed by the philosophers of antiquity (Plato, Seneca, Stoics, etc.). In the consciousness of European peoples, it was particularly linked to the Christian faith. "Blessed are the unfortunate" is one of the leitmotifs of the Gospel according to St. Matthew, happiness is the reward for patience, humility in the struggle against difficulties, honesty and fairness.

Orthodoxy has left a strong imprint on Russian consciousness, especially in their *philosophy of* everyday *happiness.* Paradoxical as it may seem, their idea of happiness is dominated by *suffering.* Foreigners have long since pointed out this peculiarity of the Russian mentality, calling Russians masochists and hypochondriacs. This judgment is crude and superficial.

In fact, Russians do not conceive of *happiness as such*, but as an isolated fact or an aspect of life that one can simply organize, "build", achieve, etc. They conceive of happiness in a *complex way*: in relation to suffering and unhappiness. There is a cause-and-effect relationship between happiness and unhappiness. This idea is reflected, for example, in Russian proverbs: "There is no happiness without unhappiness", "One fears unhappiness, but does not see happiness", "He who does not know need does not know happiness", and so on.

This same idea can be found in Russian folk songs. The great poet Alexander Pushkin paid close attention: he never ceased to be amazed that "unhappiness in family life is a distinctive feature of the character of the Russian people. The usual content of Russian songs is either the lament of a young beauty being married off against her will, or the reproaches of a young husband to his unloving wife."

The same *consideration for misfortune can be* found throughout classical Russian literature of the 19th century. The theme of unhappy human destiny and spiritual suffering predominates. Incidentally, this is not Shakespeare's tragedy, where passions boil and blood flows. No, it's about broken destinies, failed personal lives, the unhappiness of a wounded soul, an unfulfilled life. This is not a tragedy accessible to logic and common sense, but a tragedy at the level of intuition, the feeling of a soul in pain. The evocation of the soul's suffering in Russian literature and folklore leads to the conclusion that: *suffering is the manifestation of the soul,* and therefore of life itself! And the *absence of suffering does* not mean *happiness* in life, but is often a sign of loneliness and coldness of soul, or simply indicates stupidity and an immature personality.

This is precisely how the theme of the "Russian soul" is treated in F. Dostoyevsky's novels. His books persuade the reader that suffering is important because it purifies and sublimates the individual. Suffering is quite simply indispensable to becoming someone. Suffering teaches indulgence, making us more attentive to the lives and suffering of others. "Misfortune teaches wisdom", as the Russians say.

This particular regard for the unhappy aspects of life has, in turn, determined the extremely reserved attitude towards happiness in life. Happiness is a dream, an ideal and, in the best of cases, a brief episode of life never to be experienced again.

Seen in this light, it's worth noting that, in the Russian mindset, the question of the *moral right to be happy*, that of happiness and fault, is of extreme importance. Why is it, for example, that it frequently happens in life that, despite having all the outward attributes of happiness, having achieved all the goals he has set himself, having fulfilled all his possible and unimaginable desires, man, alas, fails to find happiness? Why is this? Man is prevented from doing so by a certain moral sentiment. Let's recall the beginning of Pushkin's drama *Boris Godunov*. He says he has "attained supreme power", but his soul knows no happiness. Neither power nor life brings him joy; he senses misfortune, and nothing, nothing can soothe him except... his conscience.

Thus, to be happy, one must have a "pure conscience", free from any sense of guilt: such is the Russian archetype. Showing off one's happiness, flaunting one's success in life, is perceived by Russians as a sign of "amorality", mediocrity and even stupidity. This is why, when asked "How are you?", a Russian will answer quite differently from a European or an American, and will try to avoid such a direct question or to play down the fact that he or she "isn't happy".

This is what makes Russians so different from Westerners. The exaggeratedly "happy" responses of Europeans, and Americans in particular, are understandable: over there, you have to be happy, always feel "in top form" and smile. Your personal feelings are of no interest to anyone. A well-bred person should not show them. If you do, you risk losing the respect and trust of your colleagues and acquaintances, and your chances of a career and a high position in society. Losers in Western society can't count on indulgence, or even hope that those to whom everything has worked out will show them such sentiment.

Another interesting point to emphasize: lifestyle, happiness or unhappiness, satisfaction or dissatisfaction with life are not always closely linked. For example, according to a public opinion survey, 75% of Russians are dissatisfied with their life and material situation; they complain of living without hope and ideals; they feel stress, irritation, sadness and other negative feelings.

Such a high percentage of unhappy and depressed people is alarming. Recently, sociologist O. Zdravomyslova conducted a similar survey on Russian radio. Russia emerged as the undisputed leader in terms of the number of unhappy people in their personal lives: 42% of Russians declare themselves *unhappy*, compared with 1% of English people and 0% of Americans[6]! How strange! And yet, it would seem that there's no shortage of reasons to feel unhappy in these countries: half of all marriages end in divorce after just one year together, there's no shortage of family conflicts, people are as sick as anywhere else, and children aren't just a source of joy. But no! Despite all their failures and problems, they don't consider themselves unhappy! This attitude to life can only arouse the admiration and envy of Russians!

Material prosperity is not the only reason for this optimistic attitude to life. An international survey conducted by the Hellap Institute in different countries and regions of the world does not establish a strong link between the level of material affluence of these populations and their feeling of happiness. For example, it has long been known that South Americans, who live on the poverty line, are happier than Europeans. Ukrainians are happier than their Russian or Belarusian neighbors, despite the Chernobyl tragedy.

---

6. I. A. Djidarian, article "The Problem of Happiness in Russian Mentality", from the book *Russian Mentality: Psychology of the Individual. Conscience. Représentations sociales*, Moscow, published by the Institute of Psychology of the Russian Academy of Sciences, 1997, p. 44.

The CEC countries would appear to have roughly equivalent economic indicators. But it appears that the Belgians, Danes and Dutch are the happiest in their lives, while the French, English and Italians are the least satisfied[6]. This is why it can be said that, whatever efforts are made to achieve happiness, each people has its own conception of happiness and unhappiness, linked to cultural traditions.

The most interesting feature of Russians seems to be their good heart and their capacity for compassion, kindness and care towards those who are unhappy and need help. Russians perceive the misfortune of others without judgment, without prejudice, and even better: without a sense of superiority. For them, misfortune is not the result of a personal fault, but a twist of fate from which no one is immune. There's a Russian proverb: "You can't escape hunger or prison".

It is interesting to note that the etymology of the Russian and French words for "happiness" is totally different, which in itself reflects the difference between these peoples in the conception of the feeling of happiness. In French, "bonheur" literally means "a good moment", "a pleasant hour" capable of giving rise to a feeling of satisfaction or joy from the simplest things: a good meal, a good cup of coffee, a sunny day, not to mention the more substantial manifestations of happiness. N. A. Berdiayev, in his book *Self-consciousness*, maintains that "the French compared to us Russians know how to enjoy life, to get the maximum pleasure from it, to be satisfied with intellectual and material nourishment."[7]

This relationship to life is not always understandable to a Russian. The French often give Russians the impression that they are much less demanding in what they expect from life. It seems simpler and easier for the French to be happy, and they are not as nervous as Russians.

It's not so easy to feel "Russian happiness"! The Russian word for "happiness", *schast'e*, comes from the ancient Hindi sæ?' ("good") followed by the word *schast'*, meaning "destiny", all of which together form "a happy destiny". Other language historians say that *schast'e* comes from "joint

---

7. N. A. Berdiayev, *Self-Consciousness. Experience of a Philosophical Autobiography*, Moscow, ed. Mysl ("Thought"), 1991, chap. X: "Russia and Western Civilization", p. 255.

participation in something". Russian happiness is not always realized in material terms. A good meal, comfort, a sunny day or even success are not enough to make a Russian happy. It's all about destiny and relationships with other people!

That's why there's no point in criticizing them for not smiling, for being often sad, for complaining unabashedly about life, or for the fact that their songs are also sad and make you feel blue. These are not whims on their part. It's part of their outlook on life, and we have to deal with it tactfully. And while *happiness requires effort on the part* of the individual, there's no point persevering in *unhappiness*: it arrives regardless of actions and efforts.

It's understandable that the Russians' benevolent, compassionate attitude towards misfortune has determined their stereotypical behavior: they don't try to conceal their misfortunes, which may disconcert a Westerner unaccustomed to such outpourings. Westerners shun such an attitude, finding it hard to imagine that it could be disinterested. The Russian, on the other hand, is accustomed to talking about his misfortunes, to recounting his sorrows, without doubting for a second that he will be listened to attentively and that people will try to help and support him afterwards. The feeling of compassion is deeply rooted in the Russian mentality and is still present today. It is the experience of a people who have endured and suffered a great deal, who have been in need and have learned to behave with dignity and without hysteria, even in the face of the greatest misfortune.

However, Russians should not be regarded as morose, as eternally dissatisfied pessimists, as whiners who know only how to complain about their lot. It's just not true. Happiness, "in high demand" for centuries, the complex reality and cold climate trigger a psychic compensation mechanism. This is reflected in the natural need to enjoy life "here and now", without postponing the possibility of experiencing immediate joy, without waiting for a hypothetical "later" - resulting from a planned action. Russians have developed psychological qualities that enable them to experience positive emotions in everyday life, which may seem incomprehensible and miserable to others. For this reason, the most important wisdom is to be able to enjoy life in all circumstances. It's natural, and in fact quite simply essential, to "recharge your batteries", regain vital energy and keep your soul firm. It is this psychic compensation mechanism that enables Russians to "hold out" and cope with difficult living conditions. Otherwise, the only alternative is alcohol, drugs - as any foreigner can see for himself - and, in the most desperate cases, suicide.

In spite of everything, the majority of the Russian population is in good health (both physically and mentally) and knows how to combat the austerity of life. This is expressed in their pronounced and constant taste for all kinds of feasts and celebrations, which can last for more than a day, at dinner tables, where they sing and dance. The Russians' resistance to the gloom of life is expressed in the profusion of festivals, public holidays and non-working days. Winter festivals (Christmas and New Year's Day) and spring festivals (Easter and May) last several weeks. Usually, any "public holiday" in the calendar can turn into a "popular holiday" lasting several days, especially if it falls on a Sunday. So "government-ordered" holidays extend into weekdays. In almost all parts of the country, this interrupts the rhythm of work, which never ceases to amaze foreigners: is the country's situation so miraculous that we can "rest" and celebrate for weeks on end? This tradition has distant roots.

Before the Revolution, popular holidays took up almost half of working hours and encouraged drunkenness. The authorities and the Church did what they could to combat this tradition, and reduced the number of public holidays to 98 (including 52 Sundays), which was still *twice as* many as in Austria-Hungary, for example.

In Soviet times, the number of public holidays was reduced, but largely offset by "professional" holidays. For propaganda purposes, practically every Sunday the government announced a holiday dedicated to a specific professional category. Thus we had "Fishermen's Day", "Militia Day", "Tradesmen's Day", "Railwaymen's Day", "Teachers' Day" and so on. There was hardly a profession that didn't have its own holiday. It's true that these holidays fell on a Sunday. It's also true that only the representatives of these professions were concerned by the holiday in their honor. But what enthusiasm there was for "celebrating", decorating each other with medals and rejoicing wholeheartedly! The impressive media hype and well-stocked buffets depended directly on the professional branch of the national economy. Despite the collapse of the USSR, this tradition has continued to this day. And not just in Russia, but also in the former republics (particularly Ukraine and Belarus). The previous system has collapsed, but the taste for celebrations and festivities is not dead!

The Russians' penchant for the "joys of life" is expressed in the habit of "letting go", of "taking it easy", which in practice corresponds to "being with friends" with strong drinks, in accordance with the popular wisdom saying "Live, don't look at the expense, party with friends". The natural optimism of the Russians is also evident in their love of funny stories and anecdotes, amusing surprises and jokes, and in the way they burst into a thunderous laugh that brings tears to their eyes, expressed by the Russian verb *khokhotat* (difficult to render in other languages). Linguists, incidentally, claim that this verb has no equivalent in any European language other than Portuguese.

Russians have always been so fond of leisure that, almost 300 years ago, they created the typically Russian phenomenon of the "dacha". Europe didn't experience a phenomenon of this kind until the late 19th century. Prior to that, Protestant Europe had a tradition of little rest: Sundays were devoted to church and family, and vacations were rare. Rest was reserved for a small, well-to-do class of idlers. Rest was virtually excluded from the European way of life, and this contributed greatly to the Western economic boom. Thus, "dacha living" in Russia can be seen both as social progress and as a contribution to Russia's economic backwardness. However, while the Russians were "indulging" in the joys of life, the Europeans were relentlessly building their affluent society.

On the whole, when it comes to feelings of "happiness or unhappiness", Russians can be disconcerting: rare are those who, like Russians, can rejoice so cheerfully and exuberantly, but equally rare are those who, like Russians, can fall into despondency and experience *toska'* (an untranslatable word - a kind of Russian-style "spleen"). Perhaps this is the origin of the myth of the "enigmatic Slavic soul", so inconsistent and contradictory.

The Russians' character and taste for festivities can indeed astonish the foreign observer: "They're so cheerful - and there's no reason for it!" Compared to life in Europe, life in Russia may seem austere and uncomfortable to foreigners, but against all logic, it is cheerful, carefree, rich in events and human contacts.

And Russians, of course, appreciate European life for its comfort and tranquility, but find it difficult to tolerate its monotony, which for them is synonymous with boredom due to Europeans' "inability" to enjoy themselves "really", i.e. thoroughly and boisterously.

Conclusion of the first part

We have therefore studied the commonalities between individuals from the most diverse cultures possible, which are *fundamental human values*. They constitute the essence of every being and are present in the consciousness of every individual. They are a great help to those seeking to establish contact with representatives of another civilization, to their mutual understanding and to the sincerity of their relations.

But there are two things we mustn't forget.

Firstly, universal values, despite everything, do exist and can serve as a starting point in human relations. It's precisely these values that you can draw on when building relationships with people from a different culture, and not just with Russians. *Respect for the* other person's *intelligence, love of country*, a *sense of humor* and a *desire to be happy* are all elements around which you can build your first contacts.

Secondly, bear in mind that the same human values formed in two different cultures may have a different content, a different meaning, a different resonance linked to the mentality of each of these peoples. And even if, at first glance, you have the same vision of things, don't forget that this "same perspective" can have a different meaning.

PART TWO - RUSSIAN ETHNO-CULTURAL TRADITIONS: BETWEEN EAST AND WEST

The range of shared fundamental values does not, however, obliterate the differences associated with the peculiarities of *material civilization, lifestyle, stereotypical behavior* and the peculiarities of Russian *social behavior.*

In principle, the Russian *way of life* and *national character are* discussed below. The French philosopher Helvétius spoke of this as early as the 18th century, defining the character of the Russian people as "their particular way of seeing, feeling... and living". Its origins are inextricably linked to the country's geography, climate and history. Added to this is the geopolitical situation. As long as a century ago, Russian philosophers, in their assessment of Russia, observed that Russians are neither a purely European nor an exclusively Asian people, and that the country brings together two worlds, two civilizations.[8]

Russia's *orientalism* is unique, devoid of the exoticism we find, for example, in Indian yoga, Chinese ceremonies or the cosmic secrets of Tibet... We can speak of Russia's "orientalism" if we bear in mind the two components of its culture.

The first is *Byzantine*, borrowed from Byzantium after Christianization according to the Byzantine rite in 988. The Byzantine Empire, formed after the fall of the Roman Empire and from the latter's eastern territories, existed from the 4th to the 15th century (i.e. for 1,200 years!). It was then the leader

---

8. N. A. BERDIAYEV, *The Russian Idea. Problèmes majeurs de la pensée russe du XIXe et du début du XXe siècle,* from *Sur la Russie et la culture philosophique russe: les philosophes de l'étranger de l'après-Octobre 1917,* Moscow, 1990, p. 44.

of European civilization, and was populated by Syrians, Greeks, Armenians, Copts and others. Which means that Russia remains spiritually linked not so much to the East as to the Middle East. Old Russia has inherited certain characteristics from Byzantium: the centralized state apparatus, the taxation system, the absence of social compartmentalization, village communities and urban communes, churches with numerous domes, traditions of iconography and coats of arms with the double-headed eagle.[9]

Byzantium's influence continued even after the fall of the Empire: in the 15th century, the idea of "Moscow - Third Rome" was born in Russia, transferring the worldwide importance of Byzantium to "Rus" (Old Russia). Moscow was seen as the last Orthodox bastion, the symbol of the purity of the faith. This, in turn, engendered *messianic consciousness* in the Russian model - the idea of Russia's specific role in the history of mankind. It's no coincidence that Russia bore the brunt of the Golden Horde invasion of Khan Baty (one of Genghis Khan's successors) in the 13th century. After many wars, it overcame the Ottoman Empire and freed south-eastern Europe from Turkish slavery. Both world wars took their toll. "No one, like the Russians, came to the aid of others. No one, like the Russians, caused their own destruction", says the poet Eugene Evtushenko. These words reflect the dominant "Russian character": actions against oneself in the name of some lofty (and often illusory) goal, contempt for one's own interests. In its most extreme manifestations, this messianism has gone as far as excessive nationalism and even chauvinism. The idea of its exclusivity and its "role as savior of the world" has been cruelly felt to this day, as it has dragged the country into many bloody and ruinous wars; and this idea was not totally abandoned in Soviet times, feeding the propaganda machine that presented Russia as being "at the forefront of progress for mankind". Experience has shown that messianic ideas cost Russia dearly. It is only now that Russians have begun to come to terms with the idea that "every state must have only one 'objective': that of creating the conditions for the well-being and happiness of its citizens".

---

9. *Encyclopedic Dictionary*, Moscow, 2000.

The second eastern component of Russian culture is the fruit of its many contacts with the *Tataro-Mongols* resulting from *Tatar* influence. This is not just a question of Russia's geopolitical situation, but also of its history. Relations between Russia and the Tatars took many forms. It's true that there were many clashes between the two sides. Everyone is familiar with the results of the Tatar-Mongol invasion: the destruction of cities, the massacre of populations, the severing of traditional ties with Western Europe, the truce in the country's cultural development, the general hardening of morals, the appearance of coarse words in the Russian language, and so on.

But this is only partly true. Russians and nomads not only fought each other, they also sympathized and traded with each other. The steppes, populated by nomads, were criss-crossed by transit routes linking Russia to Central Asia and the Near East. The Tatars influenced the development of the Russian state. According to the philosopher S. N. Troubetskoï, "the Moscow state was born thanks to the Tatar yoke". The Russian tsars came into being once the Tatar khan had been overthrown. Moreover, scholars believe that it was precisely the Tatars who gave the conquered Russian lands the foundations of the Russian state: *autonomy*, *centralism* and *serfdom*.

The Tatars have influenced the most diverse aspects of Russian life. According to scholars, it was precisely under the influence of the Turkic component that a particular *ethnic type was formed*, at the origin of the psychology of the Russian man. The Mongols also brought cruelty to criminal law: they introduced lethal punishment, whipping and torture. Many Mongol terms relating to money and taxation have survived to the present day in the Russian language. The Russian Tsars borrowed the etiquette governing diplomatic relations from the Tataro-Mongols. This helped them to establish diplomatic relations with the other states of the Levant, and explains the misunderstandings in their relations with Western countries, as the rules of Western and Eastern etiquette did not correspond.

The Tatar-Mongol invasion has left deep traces in the memory of the Russian people. It was a severe lesson for the Russians, showing them the danger of internal dissension and proving that the establishment of a strong, unified state power is essential to survival. The Russians' victory over the Mongols gave them a sense of their own *strength* and *national pride*, a sense of *patriotism* and a *distrust of foreigners*. These qualities are still present in the Russian archetype.

It is precisely Russia's position at the crossroads of Western and Eastern civilizations that is at the root of its *duality*. With one foot in Europe and the other in Asia, Russia has combined the traits of both Eastern and Western civilizations. But even more important is the appearance in Russia of representations of the world and ideas foreign to the two known cultures. Their very originality makes them foreign to both the West and the East. They have created an atmosphere in Russia that is conducive to diverse, dynamic, tumultuous and, above all, original cultural development. But, on the other hand, it is precisely this originality of Russian civilization that has condemned it to incomprehension by other countries, one might even say, to its own cultural isolationism. Hence the many clichés and preconceived opinions about Russia, including the famous judgment about the "enigmatic Russian soul", incomprehensible and unpredictable insofar as it is impossible to find the "key" to the "secret" of the Russian psyche.

Forget speculations on the "elusive character" of the Russian people, and let's persist in the following opinion: Russia's geopolitical situation has influenced the emergence of a *particular cultural model*, i.e. "the profound orientations of a collective unconscious" (C. G. Jung[10]) that are *immutable, unconscious in individuals and hardly subject to modification*. This means that the same qualities and peculiarities of Russian behavior could be observed during the Christianization of Russia and the reign of Ivan the Terrible, as well as during the Soviet period. This applies to: the way of life, the stereotypical behavior of Russians in everyday life, the peculiarities of the habitat, clothing and food, the public morals and personal ethics of each individual, the orientations of the conscience and conceptions of life and other specificities of the Russian archetype.

---

10. See note 2.

It's a mistake to try to explain the behavior of today's Russians by tracing everything back to the Soviet period and juggling with pejorative clichés (such as "Homo sovieticus" and "sovok" - short for "Soviet"). As for the peculiarities of today's Russian behavior, the appearance of this or that incomprehensible or off-putting detail, let's remember that these date back to ancient times and have hardly changed over the centuries, constituting the very structure of the *Russian archetype.*

I. RUSSIAN MATERIAL CIVILIZATION AND LIFESTYLE

1. The housing problem in Russia

Working with Russians, you'll quickly realize that the housing problem is one of the most topical and acute in Russia. Indeed, from a European perspective, Russia's housing problem is a major one. It dates back to the Soviet era and has remained unsolved for decades.

The most unfortunate thing for Russians is not that this problem remains unsolved, but that the "housing issue" has effectively discredited the Russian cultural model, destroyed the traditional moral order and endangered the lives and psychological health of several generations of individuals.

The root of the problem is that Russians had no access to private property in Soviet times: they were denied this right. They could not buy, sell or inherit property. They could only enjoy it, after a sort of "transaction" with the state, which consisted in obtaining from it a free housing area and a "registration" in the passport confirming the right to enjoy it. It was as if, for the rest of his life, the citizen of the country was "offered" a home by the State. On one condition: loyalty to the state. If not, the State would withdraw the "gift" without a second thought, and the person "without a roof over their head" would be left destitute. For the Soviet state, housing was a means of manipulating the country's citizens. What's more, the causes of the "housing problem" were in no way economic (e.g., the lack of square meters of living space in the country, poverty and so on) but social: they appeared to be the result of a deliberate state policy.

The State had a monopoly on housing. It was responsible for its construction and distribution. Soviet citizens paid a symbolic sum for their homes, which did not exceed 15-20% of communal expenditure. For example, for an average salary of 250 rubles, public services combined (housing, gas, electricity, telephone, etc.) did not exceed 10 rubles (of course, the amount depended on the quality of housing and services).

On the one hand, it made people's lives easier, developing in them a certain carefree attitude, an indifference to money and, in general, to the material aspect of things.

On the other hand, as the country's citizens were not involved in finding the most essential thing for themselves - housing - the shortage in this area was permanent and only got worse. In fact, according to the Soviet constitution, "every citizen of the country has the right to housing". But this right was only proclaimed, and nothing guaranteed it. The "housing question" was particularly critical in the country's main industrial centers. It was very difficult in the two capital cities, even if, according to the statistics, it wasn't so tragic. The party elite, on the other hand, was doing very well. The exact figures for those in need of housing were hidden or falsified. It was only after perestroika that sociological studies were published showing that, in 1990, 45% of the population of the country's cities were in dire need of housing.

The "housing waiting lists" that were drawn up by the district political committee are a significant reminder of this problem. In order to be registered on these lists, individuals (or families) had to deal with bureaucracy and prove the validity of their housing claims. In Moscow, for example, you didn't have to have lived there for less than 10 years (and have the "right of residence" in your passport), your previous living space didn't have to exceed 9 m^2 per person, and so on. If, for example, a family of three had a 28 m^2 room in a communal apartment, they were not entitled to register on these "lists" and had to make do with this space for the rest of their lives.

And if, as luck would have it, the district's political committee took an interest in all your documents and put you "on the waiting list", you would then have to face another no less exhausting ordeal: waiting no less than 10-15 years.

Naturally, trying to get on the waiting list for housing, then speeding up the process of obtaining it and finally getting the opportunity to increase the number of square meters meant that citizens had to resort to various stratagems and trickery with the law. Anything was possible: sham marriages, divorces, registering distant relatives or elderly parents living in the countryside on their living space, pregnancy certificates (and not just fake ones), certain diplomas. The fact is that, at the time, representatives of certain professions (writers, scientists, artists) enjoyed state privileges and were entitled to a larger dwelling. This not only implied the use of documents, attestations, certificates, etc., but also encouraged corruption, bribery, the use of personal connections and other intrigues.

The struggle for square meters of housing, for the right to have it (if possible in a big city) was so fierce that sometimes people forgot all moral principles and did not hesitate to use any means, even the most cowardly. Numerous testimonies show that in the 1930s, at the height of the Stalinist terror, it was common practice to denounce an innocent person to the KGB on the basis of false testimony, in order to be able to get back their apartment. This period, which marked a whole generation of people, did not fail to have repercussions on the psychic health of the nation as well as on the evolution of its mind.

Individual housing in Russia has taken many forms over the years. In the 1920s, immediately after the establishment of Soviet power, a vast experiment was carried out on the Russian people. A new form of housing was introduced: "communal apartments" or *kommounalki.* The name comes from the Latin *communis* ("common") and is closely related to the word "communism". - the main objective proclaimed by the new government.

In the 30s and 50s, *kommounalki were* the main form of housing in the country. This achieved several objectives at once. Firstly, with their creation, the Bolsheviks were fulfilling *their propaganda promises*: to drive the rich out of their apartments and humiliate the socially "harmful" (aristocrats, scientists, doctors, etc.), and to install in their place all the needy, those who had previously lived in poverty, in other words the proletarian and peasant strata of the country. Until 1925, virtually no new housing was built, while the rich and the large apartments were considerably less numerous than the poor. For this reason, the previous owners were pushed into the smallest and most remote rooms, while the remaining rooms were occupied by families - one family per room - or, sometimes, by groups of several people "squeezed together" against their will.

Secondly, the *kommounalki* represented a new type of housing for Russia, with its own *rules* and *particular form of administration.* In each apartment, a "dean" was appointed to hold the reins of power: he drew up "rules" that were prominently displayed: these were the list of those who, in turn, had to clean the apartment thoroughly - from cleaning the toilets to waxing the parquet floor in the central corridor: the "dean" oversaw order, cleanliness, so to speak: each apartment had its own little dictator in terms of everyday life. It doesn't take much imagination to imagine how these little dictators "crossed the line" at their whim...

Thirdly, community apartments reflected a specific way of *living together* and *relating to one another.* They were a way of experimenting with a new way of life, of combating the petty-bourgeois mindset. The traditional Russian family was described as a source of selfishness and individualism, a threat to socialist society. Most people in the Western world can't even imagine what this meant in reality. The "Iron Curtain", the lack of information in the press and literature, the reluctantly told stories of the occupants' humiliating living conditions in communal apartments, meant that this way of life remained ignored by foreigners (even those from former socialist countries). But insofar as this system was lived for decades by millions of Russians, their lives deserve to be described.

It's hard to imagine that for all the occupants of this type of apartment, there was only one kitchen, one bathroom and one toilet. One can only imagine the drama and battles that took place between families to go to the bathroom, for example, or to take a shower, not because it was "one's turn" but because one felt like it! Washing oneself, one's clothes and the dirty children after a walk became a real event, a ritual.

But even more painful was the promiscuity of different people who "didn't get along". Owning a home in the USSR was never the result of choice, since it was centrally allocated according to the will of a district political committee official. For this reason, under the same roof could live "former" peasants and workers, students and pensioners, doctors of science and alcoholics - all were forced to put up with promiscuity, not always pleasant and unhygienic.

Let's not forget that, in the communal apartments, there was one family per room, and as the years went by, this number grew. Family life confined to a narrow room (sometimes housing two or even three generations of people) could not fail to have an impact on the Russians' nervous health. Overcrowding and unnatural promiscuity meant that relations between husband and wife, parents and children, brothers and sisters were seriously deteriorating.

Finally, with communal apartments, a *new aesthetic* was introduced into people's daily lives. Concepts such as "bedroom", "study", "dining room" and so on were dropped. This division became outdated due to the impossibility of realizing it and, later, was even partly forgotten. Here's an anecdote: "A foreigner arrives in Russia and begins to recount his life, savoring the effect: 'This is my bedroom, and here is my study, over here is the children's room...'" The Russian listens patiently, then starts to get fed up and interjects, "Yes, all right, don't bother, we have everything the same, only without partitions."

Generally speaking, it was not so much the *principle of aesthetics* as the *principle of hygiene* that was important in communal apartments. The heavy velvet curtains that collected dust, the couches with cushions, the heavy, cumbersome furniture belonged to the past. They expressed bourgeois and petty-bourgeois art. Nowadays, preference is given to light, neutral furniture that can be easily dusted and cleaned.

The "hygiene mania" was so strongly entrenched, that once a week, all rooms for common use were severely tidied up, cleaned and washed with chlorine - in accordance with the rules laid down by the apartment's "dean". Any attempt to break this obligation was punished.

All in all, communal apartments are one of the most enduring examples of Soviet reality, including the first stable *aspects* (from the 1920s onwards) *of Soviet life*. It's interesting to note that in the Russian language, the designation of an individual dwelling requires some clarification: "private apartment". This means that, in the inner logic of Russians, the concept of communal living in an apartment to be shared with strangers is clearer and more normal. You can only understand "Soviet life" from the inside once you've experienced life in a communal apartment.

And again: communal apartments are interesting because of their *significant contribution to shaping the Russian national character of today.*

On the one hand, between neighbors who didn't choose each other, scandals and hatred prevailed, and the boundaries between private and social life disappeared. At home, it was impossible to let oneself go and "loosen" one's tongue: indiscreet ears were always nearby. In communal apartments, neighbors knew everything about each other: who slept with whom, who ate what, who thought what, reinforcing the impression of total state control. Let's not forget the practice of denouncing the "enemy of the people", when the informer, as a reward for his diligence, received the available accommodation whose previous owner had been sent to the Gulag. Cynical and self-interested people were used for this. The threat of "I'll tell on you" has not been forgotten to this day. It goes without saying that this practice was bound to increase the corruption of moral principles.

On the other hand, it's impossible to feel hatred all one's life, one eventually tires of it... And then the individual resigns himself, learns patience, pity, he pays attention to the misfortune of others... In communal apartments, it's together that one celebrates feasts and funerals, sends future soldiers to the army, brings up children, takes part in the neighbor's worries...

Many Russians (almost the entire post-war generation, the elderly) have been brought up in the cramped confines of communal apartments and can't imagine any other way of life. They are not used to an autonomous and independent private life. They can't stand solitude, and sometimes it's impossible for them to fall asleep without someone else in the room. So don't be surprised to hear someone who spent their youth in a communal apartment say that they have fond memories of it, and that in their new apartment they are often bored and lonely...

Even in today's Russia, communal apartments can still be found, although they appear to be a pure relic of the Soviet regime. That regime collapsed a long time ago, but that doesn't stop the people who were forced into these apartments from being condemned to lead this unnatural life to this day.

It's true that the social composition of tenants has changed: dynamic, enterprising people with higher education or business backgrounds are no longer living there, and are buying a home worthy of the name. But not everyone has money or energy to spare, which explains why in Moscow, for example, communal apartments account for 6% of housing in the city center, whereas in St Petersburg, where the standard of living is lower, the figure is much higher.

In the late '50s, Russia saw the advent of *Khrushchevki* ("Khrushchevian housing") - cheap, prefabricated five-storey apartment blocks built under Khrushchev. In these buildings, which formed uniform gray concrete blocks throughout the cities of the Soviet Union, each family had a small but individual apartment - with a total surface area of 25-30 m². It wasn't a palace, of course, but owning an "independent" home was seen as a mark of prestige and success in life. The fact that private life was no longer subject to the diktat of one's neighbors provoked a kind of revolution in the Russian mind, giving them a taste for autonomy, independence of opinion... even to the point of non-conformism and the creation of a dissident movement. The cultural phenomenon of "Moscow kitchens" in Russia can be traced back to the *Khrushchevki* era. There, in a friendly atmosphere and in the presence of simple *zakouski* (appetizers), the tradition of a free exchange of opinions was born, including criticism of the Soviet regime, independence of spirit... These unfortunate apartments were designed to last 50 years, and now they are being razed to the ground in order, wherever possible, to build skyscrapers in their place.

Today, the situation in Moscow and Russia's major cities has changed considerably. Recent years have seen the emergence of a large number of improved housing units, well-appointed apartments, large housing estates and "cottages". Just ten years ago, *state housing* accounted for almost *half of* all rental apartments in the Russian Federation - now it's just 6%[11].

---

11. *The Regions of Russia*, Collection of Statistics, State Committee on Statistics of the Russian Federation, Volumes 1 and 2, Moscow, 2000, p. 154.

63% of Russians have been given the opportunity to buy (rather than be given "free") an apartment according to their means, desires and interests. Housing construction has taken on colossal proportions in Moscow (based on an estimated 360 m^2 per 1,000 people), even more so in Astrakhan (718), Belgorod (632), Tyumen in Siberia (500) and many other Russian cities, which until then had not been considered important.[12]

Unfortunately, these new homes are only available to the very wealthy in the business world. In Moscow alone, between 2,000 and 8,000 apartments are bought every month. The average price of a square meter is about $1,000. Housing prices in Moscow sometimes exceed those in advanced European countries. Most of the buyers are business executives and senior managers of commercial enterprises.

Despite impressive housing construction, the housing problem has yet to be fully resolved. In 2001, the UN Special Session on the Problems of Urbanization was held in New York, at which the development prospects of the world's largest cities were examined. According to the commission's data, each person in Russia today has 18.9 m^2 of living space. This figure, considered "normal" in Russia, is clearly inadequate by international standards of living. In its final report, the UN commission simply notes that "the population of Russia lives in very cramped conditions".[13]

2. The house, its layout, its decoration

Most buildings in Moscow and other major Russian cities are imposing, with many storeys and entrances. Depending on its status, each building in this category tries, in one way or another, to protect its inhabitants. The most prestigious and expensive residential districts are separated from the others by solid palisades and private guards whose services are not free; in other words, they are out of the reach of the average Russian. The cost of their services is about 2,000 rubles per month (about $70). They patrol not only the building but also the street and the whole surrounding area.

---

12. See note 11.
13. Revue *Rousskii Vestnik*, 2001, n° 9, Paris.

In large cities, the use of concierges and gatekeepers is becoming more and more fashionable. Each apartment pays for these services from 10 to 15 rubles per month, depending on its size. It is often retired grandmothers, powerless to resist threats or aggression, who take on this work (due to its very modest remuneration). Despite this, the tenants of the building feel safer, and acts of vandalism or violence against children are less frequent. It is more difficult to pass unnoticed through an entrance where such a singular "controller" sits.

Cottages are extremely popular among businessmen. Of course, this type of dwelling is not yet accessible to the middle class, but it does exist and is presented as the businessman's calling card, a sign of his financial affluence and business success. What's more, it's an attractive investment in real estate. These "cottages" (often referred to as "palaces") are usually built to form a hamlet of 20-30 houses located not far from the arterial road leading into town. This makes it easier to get to work, organize and protect the houses. You will notice that these cottages are not very popular with many Russians, as they are convinced that these villas cannot have been acquired in an honest way. As a result, the owners of these villas have to live by the adage "my house is my fortress", with security guards, dogs and high fences...

It is only recently that the term "real estate market" has entered the common language, as this concept has existed for only ten years. It is one of the most dynamically developing "markets" in Russia.

In the city, the comfort of apartments can vary, and the interior can also depend on the owners. But what does not vary is the dirtiness of entrances, staircases and elevators. To suggest that Russians are indifferent to cleanliness would be to over-generalize. So how can this be explained? It seems that the acts of vandalism that are perpetuated in Russian building entrances are of the same nature as those taking place in the suburbs of almost all European cities: they are due to the uprooting of the population. The majority of the world's urban population today is made up of individuals who have hastily changed their place of residence and even their citizenship, arriving at their new home from who knows where - village districts, other republics and cities. Thus, before the Revolution, *city dwellers* made up less than 10% of the population in Russia, and now they make up 75%. Where do they come from? From the countryside, of course! Most of Russia's current city dwellers have only been city dwellers for a generation. This may explain the dirty entrances, broken windows, graffiti-covered walls and, generally speaking, the large number of poorly-maintained homes... A transition period is undoubtedly necessary before people can put down roots and learn to care for their homes and surroundings as if they were their own.

In the Russian mind, "home" (*dom*) *is, of course,* the apartment. Good housing conditions are considered to exist in large cities, when there is, for example, one bedroom per person in the apartment.

What criteria should you take into account when choosing a home to rent in Moscow? These are :

1) A large kitchen of at least 10 m².

2) The floor. Traditionally, we try to avoid the first and top floors.

3) The style of the building, the year it was built. For example, buildings from the "Stalinist period" (i.e. from the late 30's to the early 50's) are very popular; they are generally brick-built with high ceilings and large rooms (20-30 m²); or well-designed 17-23 storey buildings built in recent years.

4) Location in a prestigious neighborhood and healthy environment.

5) Proximity to the metro is very important; in big cities, there are "dormitory towns" with no businesses but only apartment buildings.

6) A balcony, or even better: a glass loggia.

7) Parquet is more expensive than linoleum. Tiles are only suitable for kitchens.

8) The presence of a telephone line.

Many wealthy Russians have their apartments renovated in the "European style": a renovation that, in their view, corresponds to European standards. This includes the rearrangement of rooms, the use of the most advanced technologies, contemporary design and so on - in short, a very expensive refurbishment.

Why do we say "European-style"? This can only be explained by the complexes of the "new Russians", for whom anything European is no match for the country's most prestigious standards (including the Kremlin). Only the "European class" can match the level of their pretensions. The term "European" thus corresponds to a specific standard, which is always very

high. Gradually, the qualifier "European" has been added to the denomina-
tion of other objects in buying and selling, particularly on markets. When a
seller speaks of a "European lock" instead of a simple "lock", of a "European
door" instead of an "armored door", of a "European glue" instead of an
ordinary "glue", this means that he wishes to convince the buyer that the
merchandise is of excellent quality and even of the best possible quality.

And yet, the wealthy "New Russians" make up only a small percentage
of Russia's population (no more than 7%-10%); most of them reside in
Moscow, St. Petersburg and other major cities home to industrial giants.

The "middle class" of Russians living in major cities make up 6-8% of the
population. Their monthly income amounts to $320-480 per month per
person.[14] They can afford to eat well, buy nice clothes, common household
appliances, almost everything except a car and an expensive apartment.
A "European renovation" is usually still too expensive for them and they live
in traditional type apartments.

It is more likely that you will not be able to see in detail the interior decoration of the Russian apartments and get some explanations. It is not the
habit of Russians to show you their home, even if it is your first visit. This is
quite different from the hospitality traditions in France, where the owners of
the house show their guests for the first time their home in great detail. So
don't feel offended if you are not given this opportunity in a Russian house.
Perhaps the hosts don't consider their interior worthy of being shown, or
think that there are more interesting things to discuss in their relationship
with you than material matters.

In any case, what can be considered a "typical Russian apartment"? In
most city apartments, there's no clear dividing line between bedroom, living
room and study. It would be ideal if there were, but there aren't enough
rooms. Usually, it's only the children's room that's really separate, especially
if the child is still small. In the largest room - which can be considered the
living room - there is no bed, but the couch usually serves as a bed for one
of the family members at night. During the day, this couch is decorated
with a carpet or embroidered covering. And if, for lack of space, there is no

---

14. *AiF* (Weekly *Argumenty i Fakty)* survey, 2002, table 3.

bedroom, then it's rare for spouses to have twin beds. Traditional beds in a middle-income Russian household are rare. Moreover, there is no bolster under the pillow, and large sheets and blankets are not used to tuck the bed in, as they are in Europe: instead, square, double bed sheets are used, with the blanket slipped over the middle. In fact, during the cold season, it's generally very warm in Russian homes, so there's no need to "save heat" by tucking in a sheet and blanket. This way of sleeping seems uncomfortable to Russians.

The room where family members traditionally gather is the kitchen, especially if it's a large one. Perhaps this tradition dates back to the communal past of almost every Russian. This is where people spend much of their free time, where family members and sometimes guests gather, as well as friends and relatives if they're close. As in the main room, you'll usually find a telephone and a small television set; a picture hangs on the wall, and a host of decorative objects brighten up the room. It's not just cooking that's done here, it's living! But you'll rarely see dishwashers, microwaves or food processors - these are luxury items for the average Russian. Although every working family has its own fridge and washing machine.

Nowadays, it's fashionable for wealthy families to have antique or fashionable foreign furniture in their apartments. In this respect, the apartment of a well-to-do family in Russia is practically no different from a European apartment. But walls are covered, above all, with wallpaper, unlike in Europe where walls are painted. Perhaps because of the cold climate, Russians prefer wallpaper, which creates a warmer, more intimate atmosphere.

Russians traditionally give pride of place to bookshelves and bookcases. Books in a home reflect the family's level of culture, and Russians have always had respect for books. This distinguishes Russian homes from European ones, where material objects are given pride of place. In a Russian home, books are the "hallmark" of the house, and at a glance provide information about the tastes and interests of its occupants: about their profession, their possible interest in art, their "hobbies", their knowledge of foreign languages, and other information... without having to ask questions.

Unlike many other countries, you'll see carpets in Russia, even in the homes of very modest people. Russians are very fond of carpets and cover not only the floor but also the walls, usually next to the sofa or bed. This gives their homes a somewhat oriental feel. Carpets are considered to make the atmosphere warmer and more comfortable.

In the past, in every Russian home, an icon hung on the wall of the main room in the *kras'nii ougol* (the "pretty corner"). Today, it's more a question of sacrificing to fashion: there are few apartments in which you won't see an icon on the wall or on the shelf next to the books, even if the family isn't religious.

What's important in any Russian home is the *ouiou't* ("feeling of well-being") - a word sometimes difficult to translate into European languages - a warm atmosphere, making life pleasant and soothing the spirit, even in a modest dwelling. It may be that this original attachment to well-being at home and to the enhanced individuality of each home is a reaction to the experience of living in communal apartments with their forced asceticism. What's more, it's as if the well-being and warmth experienced in the Russian home were there to protect from the street - with its cold and dangers lurking everywhere. Russian homes exude a much greater sense of well-being than European and American homes, where, according to Russian taste, everything is too "primed", exposed, calculated for external effect and cold (to the extent that heating has to be conserved). Russians, for example, are amazed at how much Europeans, before Christmas, like to decorate their windows with dolls, figurines, garlands and so on. And the effect of these sparkling decorations is not intended for the occupants of the house, but for the street, i.e. they are exposed to the gaze of potential passers-by. For the Russians, it's hard to understand this "hijacking of the idea" for outside effect; it's hardly perceived as stupidity. Indeed, for them, everything that happens behind their windows or door is completely irrelevant.

If you're a guest in a middle-income Russian home, you may be struck by the profusion of knick-knacks: lots of house flowers on windowsills or low tables, all kinds of coverings, elegant napkins and tablecloths, rugs and doilies, curtains, pictures and numerous photographs on the walls, small vases, statuettes and other knick-knacks, not to mention long-lasting senti-mental reminders of events and people.

The apartment of modest Russians is usually clean, but the haphazard profusion of knick-knacks gives an impression of excess, incoherence and real spontaneity. So much for the style of an authentic Russian home.

You will rarely see truly antique objects in a Russian home, where the master of the house can say: "This is from my grandmother", except, of course, among the "nouveau riche" who are crazy about antiques. Almost everything has only been used for one generation, or two at the most. This simple observation speaks volumes about the abrupt changes that virtually every family in Russia has gone through in the course of its existence, when it had to get rid of all the past and start living again. The heritage of the old can only be found in museums, antique stores and the homes of the nouveau riche. Historical events have cut Russians off from the cultural context of the past. Arriving in Europe, Russians are genuinely amazed by the profusion and affordability of antiques to be found in flea markets and in the homes of even the less well-off French.

3. Toilets, bathroom

The "weak point" of Russian houses is the toilet or bathroom, especially in low-income households. Not all of them were able to re-equip their apartments with Western sanitary ware, and what remains from Soviet times is really of very poor quality. So it's hardly surprising that taps leak, flush toilets are old and malfunctioning, and the enamel in cast-iron bathtubs has either worn off or turned black from scouring with corrosive powders.

But this does not mean that the owners are negligent about cleanliness, but rather that they lack the means.

Toilets in the countryside and in dachas make an even sadder impression: without running water, they are dilapidated wooden cabins in the vegetable garden or in the field. In the summer it is still bearable, but in the winter these facilities threaten health. Try "sitting" in one of these cabins when it's freezing outside!

What's more, the primitive appearance of these buildings doesn't mean that the householders are so poor that they can't have a more dignified toilet built, or at least have the old one repaired. No, this is the tradition. In

Moscow, the anecdote goes that the "new Russian" had a castle built in the medieval style, with turrets and a copper roof; the toilets are in the style of the castle, with turrets too, but located independently in the courtyard. In this, he simply followed Russian tradition, according to which the expression "to go to the courtyard" means to go to the toilet (which can also be in the house).

4. Hygiene

One of the most positive aspects of public health in the Soviet era - it ended with the collapse of the USSR in 1991 - was what we might call the "medical campaign to prevent infectious diseases". It often took the form of a cleanliness and hygiene campaign. And since this campaign was carried out by state agencies, it was taken very seriously. In every polyclinic, school, pioneer camp and kindergarten, grocery store, drugstore, canteen and other public gathering place, brightly colored signs were prominently displayed with the slogans: "Wash your hands well!", "Wash your hands before eating", "Cleanliness is the guarantee of good health", and so on.

These slogans were hammered into people's heads for decades from the moment they were born, and stayed with them all their lives. And it wasn't just slogans, there were concrete "actions" too. For example, in primary schools, a special type of "nurse" was chosen: a very careful little girl who checked your hands and ears before letting you into class. Anyone caught (usually a boy) with dirty hands or ears was ostracized and booed out of class to go and wash his hands!

And the word "lice" was only whispered, because their presence in a child was something shameful, almost a "disgrace" for parents in their child's upbringing.

Such a virulent campaign could not fail to permeate the consciousness and habits of Russians. From childhood onwards, everyone has been inculcated with the unconscious reflex to wash their hands as much as possible. Wherever Russians find themselves, whether they've just returned from shopping or taking public transport, they systematically wash their hands before sitting down to eat.

For this reason, Russians won't be at all surprised if, as a guest in their home, you ask before sitting down to dinner: "Where can I wash my hands?" The only thing that could embarrass them is that their bathroom doesn't correspond to "European standards" and isn't in very good condition.

Yet another Russian grooming habit: wash-up, wash-down, shave, wash dishes and even do a little laundry under running water only. Russians are flabbergasted to see, for example, how the English plug up the sink, fill it with water and start, say, shaving or washing themselves or the dishes.

This Russian practice of *letting the water run* differentiated the Slavs from all other neighboring tribes as early as the 4th century[15]! It was a sign that enabled ancient historians never to confuse the Slavs with other tribes. The Varegues, for example, washed before meals in a communal basin. This daily habit of washing, shaving, dishwashing or even laundry by filling the sink and using a stopper, rather than under running water, has continued among many European peoples: the French, the English, the Americans...

But for the Russians, this tradition isn't very healthy and, as a result, they don't like it. And all the arguments in favor of saving water or energy won't be able to counter this habit: they have to let the water run under the tap and, if possible, with a big jet!

Incidentally, this habit, peculiar to "Russian women", irritates foreign husbands in mixed couples to no end, especially when they live not in Russia, but in countries where special meters and measuring devices are used in the daily use of water, making it easier to manage its use.

In Russian homes, sink plugs are only used when you want to take a bath, and afterwards you rinse off thoroughly in the shower. Unlike in other countries, Russia does not try to save water; this practice in the West is a source of annoyance for Russian women, and even provokes their remarks about the "stinginess" of Europeans, who save on everything, even water.

It may be that, in the future, Russians will start to change their habits for ecological and economic reasons. But this is a very long-term process.

Finally, we come to the *Russian baths, a* veritable institution in Russia.

---

15. L. N. Goumiliov, *Ancient Russia and the Great Steppe*, Moscow, Mysl ed., 1993, p. 32.

Do you know how, 250 years ago, the false Dimitri, who claimed to be the Russian Tsar, was unmasked? Simple: he didn't go to the baths. For the Russians, this was the first clue that characterized a "German", a "Pole", a "Latin", a foreigner. A clue which, alas, was not without foundation.

The baths, inherited in Europe from ancient Rome, disappeared twice. Firstly, they disappeared in Europe between the 5th and 11th centuries. The crusaders who descended on the Near East astonished the Arabs with their savagery and filth. The Franks (the Crusaders) appreciated the value of oriental baths and brought the institution back to Europe in the 13th century.

With the Reformation, however, baths were once again and for a long time banned from Europe by religious and secular powers as hotbeds of debauchery and contagion. Indeed, Christopher Columbus's sailors returned from America with tobacco, potatoes and syphilis, against which Europeans had no immunity. Bathing, like the tradition of regular bathing, disappeared. In the Sun King's palace, the ladies of the court were constantly scratching themselves, and not just because of insects. Given their generous forms, these ladies couldn't reach every part of their bodies, so special *lice catchers* and long ivory *scrapers* were invented, which are now on display in museums. Perfumes, a precious European invention, appeared in response to the disappearance of baths.

It wasn't until the 19th century that the baths reappeared for the third time. It is said that the camp baths used by Russian troops on their march on Paris in 1814 were behind this revival. It cannot be said, however, that the revival was very rapid. The first baths, for example, opened in Berlin in 1818, but it wasn't until 1889 that the "German Public Bath Society" was organized, with its motto: "A bath a week for every German." At the start of the First World War, there were just 224 baths in all of Germany.[16] The writer Vladimir Nabokov recalls in his memoirs, *Autres rivages*, that he owed his salvation on his travels through England, Germany and France in the 20s and 30s to a camp bathtub that he took everywhere with him. Bathrooms in Western Europe are, to a large extent, a post-war achievement.

---

16. Extract from A. I. Bogdanov, *Trois siècles de bains pétersbourgeois*, Saint Petersburg, 2000, p. 22.

In the old days, before the development of baths and showers, the only place for ablutions in Russia was the baths. They were heated once a week, and for the whole family it was almost a holiday. Even today, baths are so popular that, often, the deciding factor in building a house, a dacha, a cottage in the countryside, is to have "private baths" built at the same time. In this case, it's a kind of little *isba* (small wooden house) built separately. The baths are a ritual for relaxing in the company of friends and, often, alcoholic beverages.

At present, Russian public baths are not so much a means of washing, massaging or treating oneself as a kind of club for "well-placed" people who often have power or money. It's worth noting that in Moscow, for example, almost half the baths (26 out of 58) were closed under perestroika, and those that remained open were the most expensive, luxuriously decorated and equipped with fountains and pools; they were built before the Revolution. But only the wealthiest have access to them.

Finally, Russian baths are a unique phenomenon, extremely different from Roman "thermes" and Turkish "hammams". They also differ from oriental and European baths. First and foremost, they are made entirely of wood and are devoid of all luxury. In Roman baths, the rooms were made of marble and heated to different temperatures. In Russian baths, heating takes place gradually in a special room. The baths are usually divided into three rooms. The first is the *razdevalka* ("changing room"), which in posh baths can also function as a club with TV, beer bar and other elements for entertainment and relaxation. A gym may be located next door. The second room is the *milnoe otdelenie* ("soap room"), where you can wash yourself in a basin or in the shower with soap and shampoo. It's also here, in the warmth of the room, that you can enjoy a massage. The third room is the *parilka* ("steam bath"): this is a small room with planks on which you can lie down: the higher the plank, the more concentrated the steam and the more you sweat, which is very healthy, as the steam only chases away illnesses. However, to avoid risking your health unnecessarily, you need to be well-prepared for a steam bath.

The most important, of course, is the special massage performed with a *venik* ("broom") made from dried young birch branches. Incidentally, the broom can be made from branches of oak, lime, conifer and, for purists, nettle. In any case, it must be soaked in hot water to soften it before use, and then "whipped", as it were, with the broom. Seen from the outside, this procedure may seem a little cruel: the person being "massaged" in this way can't contain his or her cries and groans caused by the movement of the hot air and the strokes of the broom. But experience has shown that it's precisely this procedure that cures many ailments and restores energy: the onset of a cold, rheumatism, lumbago, fatigue, low blood pressure, and so on.

Naturally, after enduring all these torments, the swimmer dreams of nothing more than cooling off as quickly as possible. That's why he takes particular and acute pleasure in plunging into a pool of cold water, or even better, into the nearby icy river. We can only vaguely imagine the acute sensations the individual experiences during this experiment, and the extent to which it hardens him, making him insensitive to cold and chill.

It's quite possible that you, as a future business partner, will be invited to the "Russian baths" (even if, for snobbery's sake, we call them "saunas"). And it's best to overcome your fears and prejudices and accept. After all, anyone can enjoy a "soft" version of this experience if they're willing and not afraid of the thrills. What's more, this visit, which is extremely beneficial for your health, is an opportunity to get to know each other informally and remove psychological barriers; it can also provide you with personal satisfaction. Last but not least, it may yield more tangible results in terms of "building bridges" and bringing you closer to your future partners than several "Russian-style meals" washed down with vodka.

And above all, can you understand the Russian character without ever having experienced the Russian baths?

5. Pets

"There's no home without a cat, no yard without a dog".
(Russian proverb).

Most Russians, even if they live in the city, have a pet at home: a cat (28%), a dog (20%), a bird - canary or parrot - (8%), fish in an aquarium

(6%), guinea pigs or hamsters (4%). Turtles, rats and other exotic pets are popular with 3% of families.

Pet ownership is most common in families with children. Parents unanimously agree that having an animal in the home has a positive influence on their children: they become calmer, kinder and more attentive to another being, responsible for the animal's life. And older people are happy to buy a pet, especially a cat - peaceful by nature - or a small, affectionate dog. It has been scientifically proven that older people in pet-owning families suffer less from depression, high blood pressure and other psychosomatic illnesses.

One in five Russians has a better opinion of a politician if he or she knows he or she owns a dog, a fact that testifies to their degree of attachment to "our friends the dogs".

Dogs in Russia are usually the subject of a separate chapter. Of course, as in any country, the dog is a symbol of friendship and devotion to its master, which explains why many people are so fond of this animal. However, compared to their European counterparts, dogs have a different function in Russia. Its role is above all to defend its master (or his children) and guard the latter's property, not to serve as a "toy" in the home. And so much the better if he's strong and threatening!

This can be judged by the breeds of dog their owners walk in the park. In France, we see a lot of small poodles, bichons and tiny yorkshires, which you can easily take on a trip in a woman's bag! These dogs are inexpensive to look after, take up little space and consume little. And they're just as affectionate as larger dogs!

In Russia, other kinds of dogs are preferred - hunting dogs, guard dogs and fighting dogs: pit bulls, sheepdogs (especially Asian and Caucasian shepherds, particularly ferocious and trained to fight wolves) and other no less "respectable" breeds.

What's more, you can get a rough idea of the dog owner's standing: the more affluent the master, the more imposing his "faithful companion" will be. Firstly, a sturdy, ferocious dog is able to protect its owner, and secondly, the dog's high price adds to its owner's prestige. And there's good reason for this, given the heavy criminal atmosphere in Russia today. If the police are powerless, you have to defend yourself!

6. Public transport, crosswalks

The inhabitants of Moscow and St. Petersburg and other important cities of Russia are rightly proud of their metro. It is the fastest and most convenient means of urban transportation, capable of carrying 60,000 passengers per hour in one direction. Every day, millions of people use its services.

On the European continent, the Paris metro is one of the oldest, built just a century ago (1900). It is not surprising that the Moscow metro, which appeared thirty years later, appears to this day as more technically modern and spacious. And what is not insignificant is that it strikes foreigners with its beauty and cleanliness. For it was not only engineers and specialists in underground communications, but also the best sculptors, architects and painters of the time, who took part in its construction. Each station has its own architectural and artistic character, and its own decorative theme. It is not for nothing that the metro is called the "people's palace". This was the case at the very beginning of the metro's construction, and the attention paid to decoration is part of a tradition that has been maintained in the design of new stations.

The second largest and most important in Russia is the Leningrad (now St. Petersburg) metro. Due to the war, it was built twenty years later, in 1955. It differs from the Moscow metro by its austere lines and simplicity of decoration. Architectural ideas were expressed differently, subject to the diktat of the new era.

Today, the letter "M" of the metro glows red in the streets of Moscow and St. Petersburg. But the metro also operates in Novosibirsk, Nizhny Novgorod, Samara, Yekaterinburg, Ulyanovsk and all Russia's major cities. Every day, it opens its doors from 6 a.m. to 1 a.m. and trains carry passengers at intervals of 1 to 2 minutes. It really is the most popular and fastest form of urban transport in Russia.

Foreigners are struck by the luxury and beauty of the metro stations, the cleanliness and absence of graffiti on the walls, so common in Europe. As for Muscovites, they never stop sighing: okay, it's beautiful, but so what? But that doesn't stop the trains from being overcrowded and, at rush hour, suffocating! Their eyes have grown accustomed to the beauty, and they don't even notice it - to them, it's just a "normal" metro. But once in Europe, they're shocked to discover walls covered with barbaric inscriptions, austere architecture, dirt and specific smells - not to mention the New York subway!

In large cities, in addition to the metro, a non-underground transport system has been developed: streetcars, trolleybuses and buses. Under Soviet rule, urban transport was precise and punctual. Tickets, meanwhile, were incredibly cheap: citizens had to be guaranteed to get to work on time and without fuss. Most Russians couldn't afford a car.

Today, the situation has changed radically: a car is well within the reach of a family on an average income. Over time, this situation has led to a growing number of traffic jams. If you consider that Moscow's fleet of cars comprises over 800,000 vehicles (buses, trucks, 15,000 cabs, 700,000 private cars, and so on), at rush hour almost 32,000 cars are heading for the city center, creating huge traffic jams on Moscow's arterial roads for hours on end! The average speed can be as low as 10 km/h! For this reason, many people prefer to take the metro: it gives them a better chance of arriving on time! Just like in Europe, people want to make sure that they will not be late for work or appointments.

The number of private cars in Russia's major cities has risen sharply, but the government's urban transport organization is often in crisis: there's a lack of manpower due to low wages for drivers, or there's a shortage of petrol. Some bus lines have been discontinued and the others operate irregularly, causing sterile indignation among citizens. In this type of transport, you'll see mostly elderly people today, since, firstly, pensioners have more free time and are more patient, and secondly, they have the right to free travel in Moscow.

A new type of transport has come to the rescue of public transport: fixed-route cabs, or *marchrout'ki* (*marchrout'* = "route" in Russian). They operate on certain bus lines, doubling them in a way, but their route is much shorter: they are responsible for taking 10-12 people from the metro to a micro-neighborhood. It takes no more than 10 minutes and costs around $0.5 per passenger. For the elderly, this is a not inconsiderable sum, which is why you'll see a completely different public in these cabs: they're usually dynamic people on modest incomes, young or middle-aged: students, teachers, doctors, cleaning ladies laden with bulky bags.

Official cabs are to be found in every city, but they don't have the success of the *levaki* ("moonlighters"), as they are much more expensive. Any car driver (even if it's not his or her own) can become a "moonlighter" in Russia, if he or she wants to make ends meet. Russians, when they're in a hurry, raise their hand and wave to any car driver: very quickly, they always find someone interested in earning a little extra by taking a person on board. This practice is becoming increasingly widespread in Russia as the population's standard of living rises. This tradition of "cab au noir", as the French call it, has distant roots. It dates back to Soviet times, when cabs were scarce and *levaki were* often the private chauffeurs of nomenclature bureaucrats. The word *levak* itself originally meant: one who works "under the table" as part of his job.

There is one Russian phenomenon that is worth mentioning in particular: the antagonism between drivers and pedestrians. What's more, this antagonism is openly expressed in Russia. A car approaching from a side street will not be allowed to pass. Trucks will force their way through, threatening small cars. No driver will brake at a crosswalk if he sees a pedestrian: no woman, old man or child will be allowed to pass: they must wait on the sidewalk until the way is clear. Alas, European politeness is lacking here. A large number of accidents occur on the roads (110 per 100,000 inhabitants) and in 50% of them, pedestrians are knocked down. A great many people are killed in this way.

How can this be explained?

First, drivers may be stressed by poor road conditions that have not been repaired in a long time. Secondly, it's due to the recent driving habits of the majority of motorists: most novices who hold a steering wheel in their hands don't have enough driving experience or the right attitude behind the wheel. Thirdly, it's also a psychological problem of self-assertion: a car, whatever its make, is unconsciously a sign of prestige, of success in life, a "springboard", and those who go on foot are people who haven't done so well, so why "take the gloves off" with them? Fourthly, until recently, due to "unenforced" laws and militia corruption, it was possible to buy any official documents, including a driver's license, in the underground passages. The first generations of "new Russians" did not bother to study traffic regulations and drove "blind".

One can imagine how dangerous these drivers were and the tragic ends they caused. Today, such accidents are rare: even the "new Russians" have begun to change. This does not prevent Russian pedestrians from being extremely careful on the sidewalks of large cities. On the road, and on the sidewalk, a moment of inattention and it is your life that you risk!

7. Automobiles

Until now, for the Russian, the car has been the ultimate dream - a childhood dream, a passion, a fixed idea, a lifelong goal. According to a survey conducted by the newspaper *Argumenty i Fakty (Facts and Arguments)* in March 2002[17], when asked "Do you own a car?", 42% of Russians surveyed answered in the affirmative, and 17% were preparing to buy one. This means that almost half the population of Russia either owns a car or is about to buy one. This figure is close to European standards, whereas only 8 years ago it was 7 times lower.[18] Finally, 16% of the population - those living in big cities, of course - own several cars per family.

Even without paying much attention, anyone can see that on Russia's roads, especially in the provinces where life is more difficult, there are mainly Russian-brand cars on the road, old-fashioned Lada and Moskviths. The dream of every motorist is to acquire a foreign-brand car. To designate these cars, Russians use the word *inomarka*, which means "other brand" (in the sense of "foreign-brand car"), i.e. a car of a much higher class, a prestige car compared to any other, even the Chaika (the "government" car used by all Kremlin pundits before perestroika). Here again, as with the expression "European-style work", Russians make no secret of their respect for the material civilization of the West.

Wealthy Russians readily admit that an *inomarka* is the dream, the lifelong goal of every self-respecting businessman. This dream is so deeply rooted in the scale of values that it has, in turn, created a new scale.

---

17. *AiF* survey, table 1.
18. Revue *Mégapolis*, 1993, n° 1.

Just a few years ago, the word *inomarka* sounded triumphantly in every Russian ear. There was no need to ask, "But which brand exactly?" That wasn't so important, since back then, Russians had no experience in this field. What mattered was that the car was a foreign brand. Nowadays, people have learned to find their way around foreign makes of car, to know which are the most reliable, and so on.

Foreign car sales in Russia have recently achieved some truly astonishing results. In 2000, for example, they rose by 5% on the previous year, and by 100% in 2001. And sales figures for early 2002[19] were already pointing to a 300% increase! This dazzling breakthrough of foreign brands on the Russian market can be explained by the economic boom in Russia's regions. For some manufacturers, the regions account for 30% of sales, and this figure is still rising!

Here, it should be pointed out that in Russia, you don't buy just any brand: it's cheap, economical cars that are in demand, cars that could be described as "workhorses", the important thing being that they're sufficiently comfortable and solid and don't stand out too much! 90% of the total volume of foreign cars in Russia is made up of cars ranging from $7,000 to $15,000, in other words, affordable cars. The best-selling cars are the Daewoo Nexia ($6,900), the Skoda Octavia ($12,000), the Renault Clio Symbol ($8,500) and a few others.[20]

By the admission of these same "new Russians", there is a scale in Russia according to which, regardless of price, model, color, age or condition, the Mercedes comes in first place. This car, whatever its version, is so popular that in recent years, in the Moscow region alone, as many have been sold as in Western Europe in a decade. In terms of prestige, BMW comes next, then Volvo, and only then all the other brands, including French, Japanese and Korean. As we can see, Russians appreciate powerful cars, adapted to bad roads and difficult climatic conditions.

Jeeps (another Russian name: *vnedorojniki*, literally "those that go off the beaten track") are also extremely popular, and not just American-made

---

19. *Finansovie Izvestia*, June 11, 2002, no. 638.
20. Revue *Profil* (in partnership with *Business Week*), 2002, n° 21.

ones... The sheer number of jeeps (Cruiser, Land-Rover, Cherokee and other models) on the roads is obvious. The Russians are so fond of jeeps that their rightful owners run the risk of seeing them "disappear", even with the most stringent protection measures. According to statistics, it's precisely these cars that thieves covet. And businessmen and mobsters prefer to drive around town in jeeps with tinted windows, which is the height of chic!

Of course, this declared love of foreign brands on the part of Russian buyers was bound to lead to the ruin of the domestic automotive industry, which had virtually no chance of recovery. Realizing this, the Russian government stepped up fiscal and protectionist measures to defend the country's production. Since 2002, an additional tax of up to 100% of the purchase price must be paid to bring used foreign cars across the border, which is then paid back to support domestic production. In any case, as we all know, domestic producers are in no position to compete with the world's automotive giants, and this measure is doomed to failure. The additional contributions levied on those who buy a "used" foreign car only serve to irritate the population and increase the wave of discontent with the government.

According to expert opinion, the share of Russian automobiles on the domestic market is bound to decline, despite all the government's lobbying efforts on behalf of its automotive industry.

8. Stores

If you were in Moscow ten years ago, then you cannot help but notice how much the stores have changed since then. Only 8-10 years ago, foreign correspondents would point out in their reports the shockingly empty stalls and endless queues. Today, it's hard to believe that there was a time when every Soviet individual "stocked up" with wartime supply vouchers. Even the Soviet elite couldn't do without them. The Gorbachevs' daughter, Irina Virganskaya, recounts in her interview (weekly *Argumenty i Fakty*, 2003, No. 6) that her family "had supply cards like everyone else, which they used when they went to the stores".

It's easy to imagine, even without a great deal of imagination, the shock felt by Soviet citizens when they first discovered the opulent showcases of foreigners. One can imagine the envy that seized them at the sight, their inferiority complexes, the burning envy that this foreign wealth and abundance aroused, the feeling of humiliation of their own misery and powerlessness... And can it be that these feelings accumulated during all these years and transmitted from generation to generation remained without influencing the Russian archetype? It goes without saying that their impact was not necessarily positive. In fact, the deprivations of the past are still present in the minds of today's Russians: more than others, they are spendthrifts, like to live "on the hoof", stand out from the crowd and show off their personal success through the outward trappings of wealth.

Nowadays, empty store shelves, food on vouchers, the proverbial cheeky saleswoman's phrase: "200 grams of sausage for everyone" - these are all things of the distant past. In the mid-90s, the situation was reversed. Russia was invaded by an avalanche of products from all over the world. But retail trade was poorly organized, and wholesale markets and fairs were more reminiscent of Oriental bazaars in terms of the number of "independent merchants", shabby-looking stand-alone kiosks, "hand-to-mouth" sales, counterfeit goods, production that failed to comply with health laws, and so on. The population's level of well-being was quite low, and people preferred to buy food and basic necessities in open-air markets, where prices were considerably lower than in stores, since merchants did not pay taxes. Today, the situation has changed radically. Nowadays, stores in Russia, especially in big cities, do not differ much from European stores, either in their appearance or in the choice of goods. An essential difference with the Soviet period is the opening hours: they are now open seven days a week, without interruption at lunchtime, and often close much later than stores in Europe.

In recent years, Moscow and Russia's major cities have witnessed a boom in Western chain stores, with hyper and supermarket chains such as *Auchan, Ikea, Le Septième Ciel, Ram Store, Metro Cash and Carry* and others opening for the average consumer. Analysts believe that the opening of other Western store chains in Russia is inevitable in the very short term.

As the signs show, foreign investors are showing great interest in developing their business in Russia. And the Moscow government's policies are favorable to them. The financial strength and reputation of the company give them a significant political influence.

And how does this translate into reality? For example, the representative of a large Western chain can have direct meetings with the mayor and deputy mayor of Moscow and decide any issue to his advantage. This is a privilege unavailable to the majority of Russian companies. And if the mayor or his deputy gives the "green light", then everything is "in the clear" for the entrepreneur.

Unlike in the West, hypermarkets are located not "extra muros" but "intra muros", on the outskirts of cities, in neighborhoods still served by the metro. The builders of these stores understand the specificity of the Russian reality: the standard of living of the country's population is not yet high enough for them to be able to count on the presence of a car in every family. Yet anyone can get to these stores by metro. Even pensioners, for whom public transport is free and who go there out of curiosity, for the novelty, can choose an appropriate object, even if it is modest.

Supermarkets and hypermarkets compete in price with open-air wholesale markets, gradually displacing the latter. They are more substantial sources of taxes, they create jobs, an infrastructure is being put in place, etc. In contrast to the mid-90s, the retail trade is becoming considerably more "civilized": kiosks of the same type are now grouped together under a common roof, the public has access to toilets, guards are on duty, etc., and the whole complex is now called a "shopping mall".

Russia's major cities are witnessing the rapid development of retail trade. Experts at *MAGRAM Market Research* estimate that shopping centers are *doubling* in size every year. However, this still falls far short of what is needed. Moscow, for example, is 7-8 years behind European cities. While London has 275 m^2 of retail space per thousand inhabitants, Paris has 398 m^2 per thousand inhabitants[21], and Moscow has only 20 m^2 to 150 m^2 - depending on the district - per thousand inhabitants, which is very little indeed.

We always mention Moscow first, because it's the gateway to Russia: it's here that the most important life processes are taking shape, and following

---

21. *Profil* magazine, n° 33, 2002.

their impetuous course... As for mentioning Russia's regions, for the majority of them, retail development can only be achieved in the long term. In most cases, their situation can be compared to that of Moscow in the early 90s. In St. Petersburg, for example, the supermarket chain has been very poorly developed. There are open-air markets near metro stations, "old" food stores that have retained the spirit of the Soviet period, and department stores. The few supermarkets are aimed at the well-off. So, in the provinces, there's still a niche for the retail trade.

As well as supermarkets, there are small stores - some expensive, some not - and luxury "boutiques". In the latter, you can find clothes, furs and cosmetics imported from all over the world. Even the most discerning shopper won't be able to resist this profusion of items. The choice, like the price of the goods, is, however, absolutely fantastic. The problem is no longer getting dressed or stocking up in Russia, but knowing where to find the money to do so.

According to Russian sociologists and economists, Moscow is now one of the most expensive cities in Europe. Prices are comparable to those in Paris, and fruit, vegetables, quality clothing and especially wine are much more expensive. It's true that meat and dairy products are cheaper than in Europe. Fish, on the other hand, is overpriced, even if it's not famous - and frozen. Nevertheless, on the whole, it's fair to say that, for Russians, the problem isn't how to spend their money but how to earn it.

Another peculiarity of Russian stores is that they are far from accepting payment by bank card or cheque. The very notions of "bank card" and "checkbook" are relatively new to Russians. Unlike Europeans and Americans, Russians are used to counting in cash. This is why, when you go into a store, ask them if they accept your credit card. Cheques are not widely accepted.

And be careful with your credit card! For their credit card transactions, Russian stores use obsolete devices, comparable to those used in Europe 10-15 years ago! Cards are therefore not protected by a confidential code. If your card is stolen, anyone can use it.

9. The food

Sometimes, a people's culture is better reflected in their cuisine than in the words of their national anthem. The shortest route to understanding a foreign culture (just as it is to a man's heart) is through his stomach. It's safe to say that true Russian cuisine remains unknown in the West. Many of the Russian restaurants fashionable in Western Europe and America are designed, in principle, "à la russe" (with very few exceptions). Here, gypsies, balalaika and a small glass of vodka are the main attraction of the meal, and *pirojki* (small Russian pies) or *pelmenis* (Russian ravioli) are eaten at a premium, of course. These restaurants only serve to convince you that it's easier to simulate Russian cuisine than to understand its secrets and make a success of it. As sarcastic minds say, the West hasn't understood Russian cuisine up to now, because it hasn't had the opportunity to taste authentic Russian cuisine. Hence the lack of respect for all things Russian, prejudice and misunderstanding...

Russian cuisine has a different place in the Russian way of life from that of other peoples. Its importance and interest are different.

French fine cuisine is always, everywhere and by all considered a sign of refined culture. In his study on the French character, the researcher T. Zeldin writes that "French cuisine is more of an art than a science"[22]. Understandably, the French are very picky when it comes to cooking. Of course, they'll happily try *borscht* (beet soup from the Ukraine) and Russian salads, and they'll be enthusiastic about caviar and *pirojki*. But when they return from their trip, the first thing they do is to rush to the restaurant to convince themselves that they are home.

They pay a lot of attention not so much to the subtle preparation of a recipe as to the quality of the resulting product. Russian *kasha* (porridge) made from scratch is something quite inconceivable for a Frenchman. This aspect of French life, however, often annoys Russians. Although in general they like to eat a lot, food is not their favorite subject.

It is important to know that Russian cuisine is not based on an art, but on *traditions* and *customs*. For this reason, it is composed of simpler, more

---

22. Theodore Zeldin, *The French, op. cit.*

rational dishes. This can be seen as a sign of poverty and a lack of culinary imagination. But it can also be seen as a sign of Russian attachment to their customs, as a sign of simplicity in everyday life. Which approach you choose is a matter of taste!

Food is the most important item of expenditure for a Russian family, especially for modest families, the middle class and those who have even less money. According to a study by the Expert Group, the middle class spend 22.7% of their income - almost a quarter - on food. In one month, a family of three buys around $185 worth of products in markets and stores, and spends another $45 in cafés and restaurants during lunch breaks and business meals.[23]

As for the wealthy in today's Russia, the more money they have, the more they spend on food. Not because they prefer to buy the most expensive delicacies and wines, but because, more and more frequently, they no longer eat at home (which would be much cheaper) but in restaurants, where prices are very high.

The best way to familiarize yourself with good Russian cuisine is to be a guest in a Russian home. Today, of course, traditional Russian dishes are rarely served at table. However, it's worth noting that some of them are so popular with Russians that they still form the basis of daily family meals and even restaurant meals.

What makes Russian cuisine so famous is the profusion and diversity of *zakouski* (appetizers) served as starters at the table during a feast. For the Russians, it's very important that the table be abundantly garnished: there must be plenty of everything, so that you're spoilt for choice and your eyes are dazzled by the bright, varied colors and richness of the table. Simply listing the different types of *zakuski* is virtually impossible: they are so diverse! There are different assortments with fish and meat, special salads with spices and a thousand different kinds of salads, just to mention a few starters. There are also the traditional salads that are on the menu of every restaurant and at every home, like, for example, the *olive* salad on New Year's Eve (called "Russian salad" in the West). And every Russian housewife

---

23. *AiF* survey, 2002, table 2.

has her own proud recipe for "home-made" salad, which she keeps secret. It's precisely this extraordinary diversity in *zakuski* and the unprecedented number of soups that make Russian cuisine so rich - as rich as its literature.

One of the oldest dishes in Russian cuisine, *kacha* (porridge) was already known to the Scythians in the 5th century B.C. And today's Russians still appreciate this simple, healthy dish. *Kacha* is made from a wide variety of plant-based ingredients: corn, pumpkin, semolina, rice, buckwheat, millet and more. Depending on taste, it can be prepared with milk, dried fruit or lightly salted butter with plenty of water. It is often eaten for breakfast. As well as being quick and easy to prepare, it's an inexpensive, practical, vegetarian, hearty and healthy dish.

As part of their daily diet, Russians eat a lot of flour-based foods, especially bread. Russian bread, made from wheat and various ingredients, is baked to perfection, and is extraordinarily tasty and fragrant. It's no coincidence that when Russians travel abroad, they bring their compatriots not expensive souvenirs, but their fragrant "black" bread as a "modest souvenir" of their homeland: nowhere else can you find such a thing. Russians traditionally show great respect for this food. Children are taught to eat it at every meal, as "it gives strength", and to be respectful of bread; if they throw away spoiled bread, it is considered a "sin", and they are punished for it.

As proof of the Russians' respect for bread, we'd like to take the liberty of recalling the story of "Borodino" bread, which is a love story. Borodino" bread is Russia's favorite bread. Its appetizing crust is covered with coriander, and it smells spicy and tastes sweet. The recipe for this bread is generally well known, and can even be found on the Internet. But it takes three days for the bread to reach maturity! A minute more or less and it's no longer "Borodino" bread in your hands! The secret of its composition lies with a nun from one of the monasteries on the outskirts of Moscow. In the real world, she was Marguerite Toutchkova, wife of the brilliant young general Alexandre Toutchkov. He was tragically killed in the battle against the French on the Borodino field in late summer, on August 26, 1912. Leo Tolstoy, in his novel *War and Peace*, recalled his heroic behavior during the battle in the person of Andrei Bolkonskij. Marguerite Toutchkova couldn't bear her husband's death, left the world and went into exile in a monastery.

There, after many trials, she devised the recipe for "Borodino" bread. It was a dark bread designed to pay tribute to all Russia's heroes who had died on the battlefield during the Napoleonic Wars.

Russians also have a predilection for *pelmeni*, which resemble Italian ravioli in shape but have a distinctive taste. Of course, real *pelmeni* are traditionally made in winter and are particularly popular with Siberians. Often, the whole family takes part in making this relatively simple dish, "modelling" them by the thousands, then freezing them and storing them in a bag on the windowsill. In modern apartments, they go into the freezer. To eat them, just throw the frozen *pelmenis* in boiling water for three minutes and the meal is ready! It's so simple and so practical! Nowadays, it is not always possible to make "homemade" *pelmenis* in working families. The industry is doing its utmost to fill this "gap": in any store you can choose your favorite *pelmenis* from dozens of others: with meat, mushrooms, chicken... You'll even find sweetened ones with cottage cheese and berries. The last ones on sale in the shops come from Ukraine and are called *vareniki*. They are, of course, much less tasty than the "homemade" ones but they sell well: it is a kind of "fast food" in the Russian way.

And, of course, the traditional dishes of every Russian family include the unmissable *borshch* (beet soup) or Russian *chi* (cabbage soup).

10. Toast

Everyone knows the love of Russians for alcoholic beverages, a real institution in Russia. It's an important aspect of life there, and it's best to be well-informed on the subject if you don't want to risk your reputation, your business, your health and sometimes even your life. Especially since foreigners who observe "Russian customs" from afar often have a preconceived idea on the subject.

Here, for example, is what the American H. Smith tells us in his book *The Russians*: "The West has nothing like vodka, and no one who knows how to drink it like the Russians. Like corruption, vodka is the indispensable lubricant for human relations and the mechanism of escape from reality. The mere mention of it makes a Russian salivate. An uncorked bottle must be emptied. A guest who drinks slowly or sips his glass instead of turning it upside down empty on the table will be told that he is offending the master of the house... A foreigner cannot live long in Russia without risking vodka-induced liver disease... In the three years I spent in Russia, I consumed more alcohol than in the rest of my life."[24]

This view from an American is critical but well-founded. The fact remains, however, that he has made no attempt to understand the phenomenon, or at least to avoid speaking of the Russians in a hurtful tone, calling them all drunken fools. The author generalizes far too much from a concrete experience that happened to him personally. We allow ourselves a few objections. Firstly, not all Russians are drunkards. Among today's Russian businessmen and statesmen, you may well never meet one, especially in recent years. Secondly, a lot depends on you, on the kind of people you surround yourself with. And there's nothing to stop you being more rigorous in choosing the people you deal with.

Incidentally, there is no tradition in Russia of placing your glass "upside down" on the table after emptying it. It is indeed customary to empty your glass in one gulp, but only in the case of a brilliantly delivered and emotionally charged toast that you fully approve of. By emptying your glass after the toast, you are in a way "applauding" it. Europeans are often convinced that after drinking, you should throw your empty glass over your shoulder, "Russian style", which is very amusing for Russians. Russians drink their glass in one gulp, but fill it up once, twice, three times... How many times do you have to replace it?

The traditional hospitality of the Russians can lead the host to "insist on you", with pressures like "out of esteem for me..." and so on. For the Russians, this is a kind of game, as they know perfectly well that you are in no position to compete with them in such a particular "marathon". In such cases, it's better to admit you're "beaten" in advance. If you feel you're not going to make it, you're perfectly entitled not to respond to these provocations by emptying your glass or refusing to drink more than you have to. Just do it tactfully, pretend you have a weak stomach, you're inexperienced,

---

24. H. Smith, *The Russians*, New York, 1976, pp. 161, 163.

don't drink all at once (but don't show it) - in short, be cunning and use your acting skills.

And never spill your glass on the table after you've emptied it to show your host that you're no longer in a position to drink (you're on your tenth glass?...). This was only done by tea merchants in the penultimate century in the "lost holes of Russia" in Siberia. This gesture is bound to trigger a storm of laughter around you. By trying to act "Russian", you'll look like you're trying to ape the Russians. And frankly, is that the desired effect?

Suppose you're invited to a meal where you'll have to drink vodka: vodka is, after all, the national drink, and your hosts will be right to insist that you taste and enjoy it. Luckily for you, Russians don't take aperitifs. Guests are seated at the table where, according to tradition, all the drinks are served simultaneously. A Frenchman will be struck by the wide variety of drinks on offer: vodka (various types), cognac, dry wines (red and white), sweet spirits "for the ladies" such as liqueur or port, as well as mineral water and fruit water. The table must be well stocked and, for practical reasons, everything in the house has been laid out, so as not to have to run unnecessarily to the kitchen for a new bottle, inconveniencing the lady of the house. After all, she's gone to a lot of trouble to prepare the meal, she's tired and she can now sit quietly beside you and enjoy her guests, without losing any of the conversation and even taking an active part in it. After all that effort, she has no desire to run around as European housewives usually do. In a way, she offers you the opportunity to serve yourself at the table. This Russian custom seems very democratic to us.

So, there's a huge variety of bottles on the table. If the meal is linked to a celebration of some kind, the champagne is opened first: Russians are very fond of it. Russian traditions don't really have any rules about which beverage goes with which dish. However, at the beginning of the meal, salty and spicy appetizers are served, which traditionally are best accompanied by vodka.

One thing you should know in advance: Russian "brandy", to which the Russians traditionally give the noble appellation of "cognac", is rather strong and unpalatable; it hardly goes with a dish, so it's better to opt for iced vodka. Especially since, in recent years, it has been imported from the former southern Soviet republics, which is no guarantee of quality. If your health is important to you and you have to choose between two drinks, stick to vodka instead, as it will be less dangerous for your health. As for wines, most of them are also imported from the southern republics, where the secrets of winemaking have been lost and where, for economic reasons, they are not, for the time being, subject to the controls in force. Moldavian wines, produced under French license - which guarantees, if not finesse, at least a quality label - are the only exception.

There's no escaping the tradition of toasts. This tradition was borrowed from Georgia, which became part of the Russian Empire in 1801. It was precisely in this country that the art of pronouncing emphatic toasts, imbued with poetry and philosophical spirit, developed to its apogee. And this art gradually became part of the Russian nobility's customs. During the Soviet era, this tradition spread throughout the population; it was no longer perceived as Georgian in origin and became a rule of table manners, something to be taken for granted. It's a nice tradition: it dramatizes the simple act of eating at the table and follows a precise script.

In Russia, there's usually a host (not necessarily the master of the house) who knows all the guests, and is a friend of the house who stands out for his skill and wit. In Georgian, he's known as a *tamada*; he plays the role of "conductor". He pronounces the toasts and gives the floor to the guests. Incidentally, there is no precise order for the toasts, and everyone is free to raise their glass and express their wishes. Filling a glass yourself and drinking independently (as Europeans do) is not allowed, at least during the first phase of the meal (five to ten toasts are the custom). After that, everyone can drink "at their own pace" without offending the guests. Then everyone helps themselves to hors-d'oeuvres, salads and other dishes at the table (with the exception of the "main course") as soon as the host or hostess suggests the "first" drink.

The master of the house is sure to start by offering a toast to his guest! Once the toast is made, everyone toasts. The one who pronounces it must do it standing. The glasses are filled with wine (to the rim) before each toast. Occasionally, the wine will spill over, and then everyone bursts out laughing: "See how much he thinks of you! At the end of the lunch or dinner, it's appropriate to propose a toast to the health of the hosts, thanking them for their invitation and hospitality, wishing the house prosperity and, of course, praising the culinary talents of the hostess, and so on. It all depends on the audience and the atmosphere at the table.

You will certainly be asked to give a toast at some point, and you should be prepared for this. It can be delivered in the language of your choice (with an interpreter present), and can be brief. You'll win the admiration of the Russians if you try to pronounce the toast in Russian: "to the health (of all present)", "to our meeting", "to mutual understanding", "to our business", etc. Russians have a predilection for toasts to "friendship" or "love". In this way, the table is transformed into a kind of verbal competition, with participants competing to see who can best express what everyone at the table is thinking.

It's assumed that people, in perfect agreement with the speaker's thoughts, will drink in solidarity to mark their assent. And the more successful the toast, the more the assembly tends to drink "bottoms up" in a warm atmosphere. It's this aspect of the Russian table, with its atmosphere of joyful reunion, that is particularly appreciated by Russians. The whole scene may seem somewhat incongruous to a foreign observer: people at the table talk too much, drink a lot and, strangely enough, as if "on command". But if you speak Russian, this scene will have a completely different meaning for you. And if you've ever experienced the pleasure of dining with Russians, the quiet "European" dinners where everyone seems to drink in their own corner will seem very formal and boring!

As for breaking glasses, this is only done at the time of a wedding, to wish the bride and groom happiness, and other (rare) festive occasions.

If Russians do indeed drink their glass in one gulp, it's because they find it a particular pleasure. To convince yourself, try it at home. Prepare a small glass of iced vodka. To do this, put the bottle in the ice compartment of the fridge for a while: the bottle will frost over, the vodka will thicken like a liqueur and lose its strong aroma. Drink a small glass of the vodka in question and immediately afterwards, without wasting a second, eat a spicy *zakouski* or a hot dish. You'll find that you won't get drunk immediately, just a little more cheerful. On the other hand, if you drink vodka the "Western way", which means sipping lukewarm vodka, all you'll remember are the bad sensations:

a rapid intoxication, a heavy head and so on. By the way, Russians can't imagine drinking lukewarm vodka - nothing could be more detestable!

So be curious, observe carefully how Russians behave at the table, and ask them questions. Just like the French, Russians have a unique experience of what's appropriate at the table. Trust them. But it's one thing to understand foreign traditions; it's quite another to follow them blindly, risking your health. Use common sense and be careful!

11. Paradoxes of Russian restaurants

The restaurant situation in Moscow is representative of the country as a whole. First, some figures. In New York, for example, there are 20,000 restaurants, and Paris has no fewer than 17,000. Moscow, on the other hand, has only 3,000 restaurants! This gives the impression that Moscow is not a major megalopolis, but a provincial city whose poor inhabitants, economizing on everything, eat only at home, unable to afford to "go out" to a restaurant. This impression is misleading.

Any foreign guest wishing to dine in Moscow will be struck by the splendor of the capital's restaurants. The entire city center is occupied by extremely expensive restaurants, whose luxury is comparable only to the aristocratic salons of 19th-century Europe or those of Asian tycoons. For example, the *Tsar's Hunting* restaurant on the outskirts of Moscow is in the style of a hunting lodge for the Tsar's court. The prestigious *Pushkin* restaurant boasts antique globes and telescopes, as well as a library of 15,000 antique books. At the *Antiono* restaurant, you can admire a gigantic *perpetuum mobile*, a model of an engine in perpetual motion. Each restaurant has its own image, its own legend based on its cuisine, decoration and entertainment. The cuisine in these restaurants is French, Italian, Japanese, Chinese, Mexican, Scandinavian or whatever you like... It is always first class. Food is usually imported from abroad: mutton, for example, comes from New Zealand, beef from Argentina, truffles and oysters from France, and so on. Usually, the cooks are nationals of the countries of the cuisine on the menu. The recipe for these extremely expensive restaurants lies as much in the "attractions" and entertainment during the meals as in the preparation of delicious food.

In Europe, we go to restaurants in a completely different spirit, with less excitement and pretension than in Russia. One goes there to appease one's hunger in a quiet and relaxed atmosphere or to try some exotic dish without worrying about having to cook. Or simply to get together with friends over a glass of wine and talk about things. The network of restaurants here is so extensive that you're spoilt for choice in terms of service, cost, habits, preferences for this or that world cuisine, and so on. The choice is so wide that it is not difficult to find a restaurant that satisfies the most demanding and modest tastes. In Russia, restaurants have a completely different social function than in Europe. The network of restaurants is not so developed and this sector of activity has only deteriorated since the Soviet era. Russia's pre-revolutionary traditions, monopolism, lack of competition and the growing appetite of its owners have given restaurants a bad reputation.

Let's start with their prices, which are too high. By decorating their restaurants with panache and without skimping on resources, the owners have understood that visiting their restaurants is, for the majority of Russians, an exceptional and memorable event. You won't get away with less than $100 per person - a sum that still exceeds the monthly salary of many Russians. The owners of these restaurants don't target the mass consumer.

For the moment, there are no plans to democratize Russian restaurants, and no one cares about the ordinary citizen, since the chic restaurants have their own clientele. Politicians eat there regularly. For example, the *Pushkin* restaurant has played host to President Putin on several occasions, and the *Czar's Hunting* restaurant is popular with former head of state Yeltsin. Restaurants of this order are often visited by high officials, showbiz stars, prominent economists and lawyers. For them, their appearance in a prestigious restaurant is a sign of their success, of belonging to the "elite".

As for the ordinary customer, he has to "tighten his belt" to go to a "second-rate" restaurant. And this pleasure comes at a very high price, as the prices of these "second-rate" restaurants have the unfortunate tendency to approach those of the fashionable ones. This explains why Russians don't go to restaurants to satisfy their hunger, but rather to celebrate an important birthday, wedding or other unusual and notorious event. This is why, more often than not, one encounters noisy groups rather than quiet individuals concentrating on their food. And since it's customary to "dress up" for a party, you'll find an elegant crowd dressed in expensive clothes. People don't go there to eat so much as to be entertained and "show off". Which explains the inevitable presence of music, variety shows and couples dancing - sometimes wildly! - between the tables. As for the food, you don't go to a restaurant to be picky! At first, people pay attention to the appetizers, but then, in the hubbub of the music, they simply forget what's on their plates; hot dishes get cold, abandoned, while guests dance frenetically around the room.

Of course, there is a very wide range of restaurants in Russia today: from the most chic, European-class restaurants in the city center, to the most modest. The chic restaurants are often found in large hotels such as the *Ukraine*, the *Moskva*, the *Leningrad*, the *Minsk*... named after former Soviet republics and cities. These hotels are generally large Stalinist-style buildings, with huge rooms pompously decorated with marble, paintings, fountains and other trappings of a lavish lifestyle.

However, Moscow has recently seen the opening of several restaurants of modest size but with a warm atmosphere. They are richly decorated and offer good national cuisine. Some restaurants offer Western European cuisine, such as *National* and *Metropole* (located inside the large hotels of the same name); *Berlin* and *Prague* (the latter serving Central European cuisine) are also very popular. But it's the restaurants serving Caucasian, and more specifically Georgian, cuisine that are most popular. This is where Russia's wealthiest individuals spend their time and hold their business meetings. It's also where you can meet the real "bandits" and mafiosi who come to "relax".

As far as the intelligentsia and lower middle class are concerned, an ordinary outing to a restaurant is beyond their means. In the past, doctors, engineers, scientists and professors were perfectly able to afford such outings, although they preferred "intellectual distractions". Nowadays, this type of "evening out" is simply impossible. If they want to eat out, their only alternative is fast food. This term has not yet been fully assimilated by the Russian language: to name these cheap establishments, we use the popular and rather pejorative term *zabegalovka* (from the Russian verb *zabegat,* meaning "to pass, to jump"). The term implies that you enter for five minutes, only to leave again as soon as you've had your fill. These establishments are usually called "Café",

"Buvette", "*Pelmenaya*" (from *pelmeni*, Siberian ravioli), "Café-glacier" and so on. Often, they are also the witnesses and inheritors of "Soviet-style" service. But unlike the *obchepita* (public food) served in the past, the menu has since undergone a few changes. Instead of the usual sausages with peas, *pelmenis* and dumplings with compote, a "European-style" menu is offered: expensive liqueurs and cognacs, microwaved "steaks", ham croissants, *Jaffa* fruit juices, French *Raffaelo* confectionery, *Mars* and *Snickers* sweets. And to make payment easier for businessmen, there may be an ATM nearby, a new phenomenon in Russian life.

In recent years, a number of Western-style restaurant chains have appeared in Russia's major cities, making *McDonald's*, *Grill-Bar* and *Pizza Hut* popular. Prices in all these restaurants are moderate, which explains their success: 54% of Russians surveyed[25] gave them preference. In addition to *McDonald's*, the Russian middle class likes to frequent small restaurants with amusing names such as *Iolki-palki* (only 13%, as it's still expensive), *Rostiks* (6%), *Blini*, *Kartochka* (meaning "potato" in Russian - 5%).

In Moscow, to counteract "Western influence" and demonstrate patriotism in the development of the *obchenita* (public food) system, the city's mayor organized a network of bistros bearing the name *Russian Bistro*. The logo of this type of establishment features the profile of a Russian soldier conquering Paris; this design is even reproduced on the bistro's paper napkins. For the record, the word "bistrot" is Russian. It was imported by the Russian soldiers who had conquered Paris in 1812 and left the ranks of their marching division to have a quick drink and catch up with their fellow soldiers. For this reason, they ordered their drinks by shouting "*bystro*" (meaning "fast"). This is the origin of our famous French "bistrots". These bistros are a good initiative of the mayor of Moscow, although the menu is not varied: *pirojki* (small filled pies) of various shapes and ingredients washed down with traditional Russian drinks such as "walrus" (made with cranberry juice), "kvas" (fermented drink made of apple juice and bread rust), etc. The food is very cheap in these bistros, but only 5% of Russians frequent them and enjoy the menu. They find *McDonald's* meals better and more varied.

____

25. *AiF* survey, table 2.

Of course, there is a very wide range of restaurants in Russia, and the profile and behavior of customers varies according to them. In any case, customers of expensive and less expensive restaurants and cafés have one thing in common: the way they pay. Russians don't check the bill the way the French or Germans do. Likewise, specifying who is inviting and paying for the meal, and carefully checking the change given, is not done in Russia. This behavior, which is normal among foreigners, is still unusual among Russians, who find it unpleasant and humiliating. However hard it is to earn a living, they prefer, out of habit, to spend their money lavishly and without counting the cost. The love of "grand gestures" seems to them a more "dignified" attitude, insofar as it corresponds to their traditions and goes back a long way.

12. Russian leisure and entertainment

Public opinion polls reveal that Russians do not consider *entertainment to* be an essential value, unlike the French, for whom leisure and entertainment occupy a predominant place.[26]

This may be a Russian cultural specificity that was reinforced during the Soviet period when the ideology in place required the individual to live "for the good of society" and not "for himself". During the building of socialism, the Soviets got used to "living for work", they constantly had in mind the motto "Happiness is work". And they often have neither the habit, nor the pronounced taste, nor the European facility for distraction. The absence of a developed leisure industry in Russia compared to other countries is significant in itself.

Judging by opinion polls, Russians regard their leisure time as "rest", as "passive idleness". The middle and low-income classes (with a monthly salary ranging from $100 to $500, which is what half of the Russian population earns) spend the winter in much the same way: in front of the TV set or in the company of friends, or at the Russian baths.

---

26. *La Mentalité des Russes. The Consciousness of Large Population Groups in Russia, op. cit.* p. 114.

Thus, the survey on the question "How do Russians spend their free time?" gave the following results (respondents were given several options to choose from): 74% watch television, 55.8% cultivate their vegetable garden (at the dacha), 54.1% prefer outdoor walks, 54% wash their clothes (!), 38.1% go shopping and 34.5% spend their free time with friends.[27]

On the other hand, it is wrong to speak of the "average" Russian, as society in Russia has always been structured and many parameters must be taken into account to differentiate the most opposed groups.

For example, the so-called "intellectual" professions and people with higher education in big cities used to have a relatively large choice of entertainment: theater, opera, ballet and, of course, cinema. These still exist, but nowadays, educated Russians can't always afford them. There used to be a thriving cinema and film rental industry, now replaced by video rental. Moreover, Russians, tired of daily catastrophes and cataclysms, prefer to watch cheerful films[28]: comedies (38%) or melodramas (20%). Young people, on the other hand, prefer erotic or horror films (one *third of the* population).

Theater has always been and remains very popular in Russia. It is not burlesque or "boulevard" theater, but "serious" theater, with excellent stagings, with many surprises and experimental theatrical effects, performed by famous theater schools. Théâtre de boulevard was virtually unknown and considered to be aimed at an undemanding audience. Chekhov's plays, operas and ballets of the Bolshoi and Marinski (in St. Petersburg), music of Tchaikovsky, Prokofiev, Shostakovich, old Russian romances are familiar to every educated Russian. The "Mecca" of Russian theater remains, of course, Moscow, where the country's best and best-known theaters (including scandalous ones) are concentrated. In the cultural competition between Moscow and St. Petersburg, the roles are assigned: Moscow is, as we have just seen, the center of theater, St. Petersburg, the center of music. The latter has wonderful orchestras, the Philharmonic is the pearl of the musical world and the Marinski (opera and ballet theater) is known all over the world.

---

27. Website monitoring. Ru - *AiF*, n° 37, 2002 - *AiF* survey, table 5.
28. *AiF* survey, table 8.

In Soviet times, *culture was accessible* to all. Anyone could buy a book or a record, go to the theater or cinema, or attend a classical music concert: there were always two or three rubles (less than the price of a vodka) to satisfy that desire.

Of course, the situation is different today, with prices gradually levelling out. Nevertheless, it's true that books and dictionaries in these times of economic transformation are two to three times cheaper than in Europe, and that a seat at the theater (for a play with little impact and performed outside the capital, of course) can cost almost 10 times less than in Europe.

The most popular leisure activities in summer and autumn for all classes are fishing, hunting and berry and mushroom picking in the forest. Before perestroika, many companies (factories, scientific research institutes) chartered special buses to take their employees on "mushroom hunts". Hiking tourism" is widespread, as are canoeing and rafting. In winter, Russians enjoy cross-country skiing in the forest.

It's worth mentioning *sport in its* own right. Soccer, field hockey and skiing are the most popular forms. And, of course, chess: every Russian city has its own meeting place (park, square) for chess players, from the youngest to the oldest. In recent years, the trend among young people has been towards the increasingly popular martial arts: karate, aikido, kung fu and others. Sports reserved for the elite are golf, tennis and sailing. Almost every major city now has its own golf club and tennis courts.

At the same time, we can't say that Russia has a cult of health and sport like, say, the United States. Very few gyms are accessible to people, financially speaking. They used to be free, and playing a sport was a major advantage for admission to higher education establishments. But those days are gone.

Today, according to the Ministry of Health of the Russian Federation, around 10% of Russians regularly take part in some form of sport or physical activity.[29] Incidentally, this derisory figure mainly concerns well-to-do people who can afford to attend paying gyms and own home training equipment. The rest of the Russians cite lack of time or lack of desire. And even if they do feel the desire, they are practically unable to realize it: either

---

29. Website politkom. ru - October 4, 2002.

the sports infrastructure is lacking in their neighborhood (58%), or they can't afford it (33%).[30]

Dachas occupy a special place in people's lives; they are small summer houses - often unheated and modest by European standards - built on a plot of land. Vegetables and fruit are planted here on days off and during the vacations, which sometimes represents a considerable sum of money in the family budget. And it's a place to relax with children, grandchildren and friends. When summer arrives, half of Russia's population stays at home (30% in village communities) or spends it at the dacha (25%), and inevitably goes there whenever there's a day off.

To the question: "How do you plan to spend your next vacation?" Russians answer as follows: "At the dacha, I will dig my vegetable garden and rest at the same time" (25%) or "I will lie down on a couch with a good book" (12%), "I will look for a new love: it will be spring" (10%), "I will visit friends" or "educate children" (5%). But as far as the affluent are concerned, 32% of them currently prefer to go abroad for the summer.[31]

Italy is the "dream country" for 22% of Russians, closely followed by Spain. Finland, closer and less expensive for them, is welcoming and enjoys almost similar climatic conditions. As for trips to Turkey, Greece and Bulgaria, they are even less expensive[32] and offer the opportunity to soak up the sun. As for a trip to France, it's not just a dream for the average Russian, but a symbol of optimal success in life.[33] There are no precise statistics on the number of Russians who have visited France, but we do know that very few Russians are able to go there: it's expensive and, to obtain a visa, you have to go through long and humiliating procedures. Tourists don't stay long and in small groups, apart from the "new Russians" who like to relax on the Côte d'Azur in Nice. The luxurious glossy magazine *Bereg* ("The Coast"), published in Russian, is even aimed at them.

But what do well-to-do people do in cities in winter? In fact, there's no shortage of distractions.

---

30. *AiF* survey, table 9.
31. *AiF* survey, tables 4 and 5.
32. *AiF* survey, table 6.
33. *AiF* survey, table 7.

In recent years, gambling *establishments have* become widespread in Russia's major cities. They offer bowling, dog racing, cock and dog fighting (illegal), roulette, slot machines and more. Psychiatric experts believe that the origin and attraction of gambling stems from the desire to escape reality into an imaginary world (*escapism* is the scientific term). This phenomenon is particularly prevalent among teenagers in their prime. For the time being, this problem has not yet been tackled by legislation, which explains why more and more people are being drawn into gambling. In Moscow and St. Petersburg, like nowhere else in Europe, you'll find an impressive number of *gambling houses* and *casinos.* You can recognize them from afar: their facades are richly and tastelessly decorated with "fake marble", "gilding" or designed in the "style of Egyptian pyramids", medieval castles and so on. In front of the entrance, burly boys, the guards, loom. These establishments are frequented by short-haired, expensively dressed men in long coats and young girls in miniskirts wearing make-up "for combat". A night out can cost up to $1,000.

There are less pretentious *clubs,* without flashy "faux marble" or "faux ebony" interiors. They may offer quite decent cuisine, prepared by a foreign chef (French, Japanese, Chinese, etc.). In one corner, professional musicians play muted music. An evening spent within these walls can cost several hundred dollars ($200-500).

Jazz clubs, art clubs and country clubs can be considered inexpensive. They are either closed (reserved for members only) or open to anyone who can pay $10 to $30 for admission. These clubs are smaller in size, and their interiors are inspired by the "country" theme: bouquets of dried flowers on the tables, hand-crafted tablecloths, trompe-l'oeil painted landscapes on the walls. People like to get together in groups in these clubs.

Dance clubs and *discotheques have been* specially created for the less affluent public. These are usually located in cellars or disused cultural centres. This is where young people gather.

The "good" nightlife can cost from $1,000 in gambling establishments to $200-500 in a good restaurant, and from $100 to $50 in theme clubs! But you can also limit your expenses to 10 roubles at a young person's dance party. All you have to do is make your choice!

II. STEREOTYPICAL RUSSIAN BEHAVIOR AND LIFESTYLE

1. Russian behavior and manners

> "Some love the pope (Orthodox priest),
> others the popadia (his wife), and others his daughter."
> *(Russian proverb).*

Ethno-cultural stereotypes are generalizations made about the stereotypical behavior of a people: they characterize all its representatives and give us an idea of the personality specific to each of them. Thus, we distinguish "German punctuality", "Spanish fiery temper", "French gallantry", "Chinese ceremonial", "Russian superstition", and so on. Observing the behavior of foreigners can sometimes amuse us, and even reassure us of our own "normality" in relation to their "strangeness". Prejudice stems from stereotypes: people accept other stereotypes of behavior from the point of view of their culture, and measure everything "by their yardstick".

When it comes to Russia, one can hear the most varied opinions about its people. All foreigners, however, agree on *the elusive, enigmatic nature of Russia and the "Russian soul"*. Foreigners often quote Winston Churchill, who once said of Russia: "It's one puzzle hiding another." Rather than trying to understand them, it's much easier to give up and claim that Russians have "a grain". Their logic is different from ours, making them difficult to analyze. For Europeans, this also applies to other peoples such as the Chinese and

Japanese. But the exoticism of the latter is more readily accepted, because they are cultures beyond our comprehension. On the other hand, they have a special relationship with everything Russian: it's not exotic enough to be "foreign" to them, yet too different to be "theirs".

You've probably noticed how Russians walk "arm in arm", which makes them recognizable in any city in the world: the horseman advances holding the lady "by the elbow". Two friends can walk arm in arm, regardless of their age. When they meet, Russians embrace and kiss, necessarily *once* or *three times*, and very loudly at that, unlike the French, who pretend to "symbolically" kiss both cheeks. And men pat each other on the back as a sign of affection. These behavioral norms are obvious to foreigners. In scientific literature, this behavior is referred to as "tactile": the person must touch you in order to really feel you, to physically demonstrate their good disposition towards you.

Where do these stereotypes come from? Why do they differ from country to country? Let's not forget that people's behavior is governed by various factors, from the penal code to standards of social conduct. Non-compliance with these norms is subject to specific sanctions and is condemned by public opinion. Most of these standards of behavior are international.

It's more interesting to observe the unwritten norms, the unspoken rules about "how to behave" in a given country. Two representatives of the same culture may well have different opinions on this subject. Breaking these unwritten norms carries no penalty. The *way people behave in society* expresses quite well the feelings and way of life of the representatives of a given culture.

The notions of *tact*, *good manners* and *delicacy* fall into this category. Many of them correspond to the English concept of *privacy* ("non-interference in the life of others") in the broadest sense of the term. For example, many Russians living abroad are astonished when, during a noisy evening at their next-door neighbors', the latter, rather than begging them to be less noisy, prefer to call the police. Russians strongly condemn this attitude, which they consider cowardly, evil and akin to "snitching". It doesn't even occur to them that this attitude is dictated by every individual's right to the inviolability of their physical and psychological territory. No one has the right to infringe this right except the police. This example shows that every culture has its own specific standards of behavior.

Let's turn now to the "not necessarily compulsory" but "desirable" *rules of conduct* for Russians.

The Russians' collective orientation, their constant concern for the "opinion of others", means that their attitude in public places is almost gallant. Men open the door for ladies, offer to help carry a suitcase or a heavy bag, and offer a hand when getting off the bus. Children (especially little boys) are taught to give up their seats in public transport to the elderly, the disabled, pregnant women or women with children in their arms. And if someone, unwilling to give up their seat to a weaker person in the metro, pretends to be asleep or engrossed in a book, you should see the furious looks he or she receives from the other passengers, who make no secret of their indignation! This scene can take place in silence, or it can be the subject of a loud scandal.

Russians don't understand the European habit of "not noting" what is shocking, of not reacting with a look, a word or a gesture. For them, intervening concretely, commenting, "putting things right" is "a matter of honor". For them, passivity in the face of such situations is a sign of cowardice, indifference and egoism; traits usually perceived as the worst faults in Russia. Bear this in mind, as you'll be looked down upon if you don't show yourself to be gallant towards a woman, and so on. You won't be told anything, of course, but you'll be seen as a cad.

Here's another typical case: a queue has formed - it doesn't matter which one - in front of a grocery store cash register or at a ticket office for tickets to a prestigious show. A banal situation in itself, which gives rise to totally different behaviors. Russians, of course, have long experience of queuing, born of total scarcity. Russians are used to queues and have learned to rely on the opinion of all those around them (even if they are potential competitors): they get impatient and angry with those who do not hurry, take their time, delay the others. And if someone dawdles, looks for his wallet or simply chats with the cashier he knows, he can provoke general indignation, an indignation that even manifests itself loudly. And this is not the result of a "lack of education", a character "fit to create scandal" in Russians; it comes rather from the feeling of "being part of the crowd" (and not just being in the middle of it), of "sticking together". The troublemaker acts like an egotist, holding everyone up! Strangers, on the other hand, remain unperturbed in such situations.

Let's try to list other types of conduct that are tacitly condemned by the majority of Russians and arouse their anger.

On public transport, for example, people are particularly annoyed when someone blows their nose noisily, listens to music too loudly, doesn't give way to the elderly or pregnant women, throws garbage on the ground and says rude things (obscene words). Drawing graffiti on walls is considered unacceptable by the whole population (including teenagers). *In public places* (restaurants, stores), avoid using a toothpick, talking loudly or making noise during a film or show.

At home, people don't like to be called between 11 p.m. and 8 a.m., or to have their neighbors' music turned up too loud. *In the company of* colleagues or friends, it is clearly tactless to take an interest in the other person's sex life, to try to teach him or her how to behave, to talk badly about people who are not there, to show a bad mood and to mock national characteristics in the presence of a person of the same nationality!

Russians are particularly irritated by "verbiage", prolix reasoning about something that could be summed up clearly in two words. This is especially true of the French, since their education system is based on the art of eloquence. Russians take a different approach. They are very sociable, like to chat "among themselves" and have difficulty understanding a discourse that is too "formal", "mannered" (in the sense of "not coming from the heart") with complicated turns of phrase. In discussion, for the purposes of argument, a concise and expressive presentation, even if primitive in form, is more likely to convince a Russian than an elaborate and faultless speech.

And the habit Americans - and often Europeans - have of being on first-name terms with people who aren't exactly close to them can shock Russians. They see it as a lack of respect for others, and even as rudeness.

Studies show that men are more accepting of breaking these informal rules of conduct. But women often get angry - especially when they hear sexual anecdotes, rudeness, being approached in the street or being "on first-name terms" for no reason at all. Women don't like to be asked their age, to arrive more than ten minutes late for an appointment, and they can't stand the way men sit on public transport with their legs spread wide apart.

In addition to informal prohibitions, it is interesting to see what is considered "perfectly acceptable conduct". Russians don't mind[34], for example, being invited into a house and asked to look at the family photo album (91.6%), being addressed by first name and surname (90.8%), being asked by neighbors to collect the mail from the mailbox while they're away (86.7%), being asked to take off their shoes in the hallway (85.6%), being talked to while eating (80.6%). On the other hand, they are less appreciative of being asked their age or being called at home with work-related questions.

On the other hand, it would be wrong to assume that all Russians, without exception, are as gallant and well-mannered as English lords. They simply display a different "courtesy". Their behavior on public transport, their gallantry towards women and their efforts to appear as educated as possible (*koultournii'*, as the Russians themselves like to say) are real. But they can also surprise you with their total ignorance of what we in France call "savoir-vivre". Their disregard for the rules of good manners can go as far as a total absence of etiquette and a shamelessness that is shocking to the French. The latter, for example, may be surprised by the incredible mix of extremely varied dishes at the table and the strange logic that governs the service - people eat and drink without any pre-established order - the rather informal way of eating, the lack of knowledge of the proper use of cutlery. Also disconcerting - to mention just a few of their table manners - is the absence of compliments to the hostess or the inability to hold a "worldly" conversation in a cheerful tone, the natural disposition to ask "indiscreet" questions or to display an almost shocking frankness, the way they talk without restraint about politics during the meal... This behavior that does not conform to the French rules of "savoir-vivre" does not mean a total disregard for etiquette. It is just that these rules can be different, original, even when you ignore them and are surprised by them. Incidentally, the absence of etiquette at a Russian table is more than compensated for by spontaneity, simplicity and the obvious interest shown in guests, which should be fully appreciated.

---

34. *La Mentalité des Russes. The Consciousness of Large Population Groups in Russia, op. cit.* p. 199-200.

This is, however, perceived differently by foreigners. They often find Russians too "direct". And according to them, this is not necessarily a quality when a misunderstanding or disagreement suddenly arises. In this case, the French will take great pleasure in palavering to "work out the relationship". Russians, on the other hand, are more impulsive and spontaneous, "sensing the situation" and preferring to act - sometimes in a very "concrete" way, even resorting to the use of their hands. For this reason, when clarifying your relations with Russians, it is advisable, first of all, to be *very careful about the terms used* and to choose them carefully. Russians take words very seriously, literally. For them, your words are not only a summary or an expression of indignant feelings, but the order and even the signal for a concrete action. Take this into account: every word, every intonation you use will be remembered and can trigger an unexpected reaction that can be (physically) very brutal.

Secondly, *one should not expect* superfluous *eloquence* from Russians in this case. For them, their words, like their smiles, have "meaning" and they don't use them for "trifles" such as formalities, etiquette, politeness and so on. This behavior is not the result of a "bad education" or the absence of politeness rules. It comes from the ancestral traditions of the Russian archetype (see the 3rd chapter). French society, for example, for historical reasons, was structured around a complex system of hierarchical relationships (the king, his vassals, their subjects, and so on). And within this system, each social stratum had its own mode of relationship as well as *rules of conduct and a pattern of behavior* established and polished over the centuries. Moreover, each social stratum had its own rules and mode of conduct. In Russia, this hierarchy of relationships was destroyed under the Soviet regime, and this is reflected in the Russian language: there are far fewer polite formulas, less gallant "frills" and fewer innuendoes. Few Russians distinguish "Your Excellency" from "Your Honor" and other formulas. The way in which people are addressed has become simpler, and relationships are expressed more directly and openly; they are also tougher in conflict situations. For this reason, rules of French etiquette that scrupulously respect the rank of the person being addressed and are full of innuendo can go completely unnoticed and seem incomprehensible to a Russian. In return, you shouldn't expect from him what he doesn't have by tradition: neither verbal expressions of attention and gallantry, nor tokens of gratitude in exaggerated form, nor light and superfluous conversation about trifles, etc.

Let's talk about conversation. It has a special meaning for Russians. "Open-hearted conversation" expresses the Russian's idea of a good conversation, as opposed to superficial, mundane verbiage, which can seem tedious and even irritating. A "heart-to-heart conversation" is a long, cordial exchange with old acquaintances or a close friend, without any grandiloquence. And this conversation can go on well past midnight.

What do we talk about? Anything and everything: personal affairs, professional concerns, politics, philosophical questions. The important thing is that the conversation is shared and offers food for thought. There are no taboo subjects, but preference is given to "elevated" themes, such as the meaning of life, new trends in politics, the future of Russia, new literary, theatrical or cinematographic works. Even topics such as financial problems, health and illness - which are avoided in Europe - are addressed. What's more, if you want to share your problems, your Russian interlocutors won't be shocked - quite the opposite, in fact: they'll express their sympathy, start giving you advice and even go so far as to give you practical help. Family matters and children can also be discussed. Children's success is important to Russians, which is why they are proud of them and talk about their children with pleasure; they may, of course, ask you to do the same. These questions should not be taken as mere curiosity, but only as a sign of attention and goodwill towards you.

On the other hand, in a *direct, concrete conversation about money*, Russians don't "feel right", they become embarrassed. They have been brought up to believe that "money is not happiness" and that "poverty is not vice". It's inappropriate to *insist on* this, as it denotes a mercantile spirit, which Russians still condemn today despite the social changes of recent years. In the same way, recounting one's career, talents and individual achievements is interpreted by them as boasting and pride. In this, Russians differ greatly from Americans: they prefer to build relationships not on self-assertion, but by trusting their intuition.

In society, we don't talk about *sex, love* and *intimate relationships*. Men, as well as women, are annoyed by questions about their sex life. The recently published studies in Russia, which found an increase in sexual problems among men, have something to do with this. Of course, it all depends on the level of your relationship with the person you're talking to, but it's safe to say that Russians don't take kindly to crude, indecent jokes and "below the belt" anecdotes in public.

Don't forget that in Russia the French habit of asking questions about the *place of origin of your interlocutor* loses all its meaning. At home, the French can get an idea of the person's character from the answer. Depending on the answer, certain stereotypes will immediately come to mind: "stubborn like a Breton" or envious, superficial like such and such. In Russia, this kind of question is more likely to lead your interlocutor to talk politics or the historical events that led his ancestors to leave their homeland and settle elsewhere. In short, it can lead to sensitive subjects that are best avoided.

Unlike the French, *food is not a topic of conversation* among Russians. And *conversations about the weather*, a favorite topic for the English, are boring and trivial.

Russians often repeat the word *nitchevo* ("nothing" in the sense of "it's nothing") in case of bad luck or failure. By saying this word, Russians try to console themselves for their disappointment or sadness (or that of someone close to them), or to conceal their dismay at a problem that has suddenly arisen. The word consolation *nitchevo* can be equated with a national character trait: acceptance of the vanity of one's plans, resignation in the face of failure. In itself, it expresses the Russian character.

Russian etiquette forbids asking a *direct question about the age of* your interlocutor. Only doctors and officially authorized persons may ask.

Eyewitnesses note that Russians don't thank as often as Europeans, but if you thank them for something, they'll take your gratitude very seriously. There's probably an explanation for this: Russians consider it quite natural to help someone, it's something that doesn't require a formal smile or acknowledgement. Refusing to help someone is seen as rude, showing a lack of education - even if it's accompanied by a kind smile.

Similarly, it's perfectly normal for a Russian to *lend money to relations or friends for an indefinite period* without charging interest. It's a custom that astonishes many Europeans. This type of relationship was established during the Soviet period, when there was no other way of obtaining credit, for example from a bank. You could *borrow* not only money *from friends*, but also their cars if yours broke down. It was normal for your friends to live in your apartment for a while while you were away (while you were at the dacha, on a mission, etc.). Your neighbor, for example, might drop by for a minute in the evening to "borrow" salt, cigarettes, bread or other trifles. Don't be afraid! This in no way means that you'll be besieged on all sides by such requests! Not at all. This type of relationship is only permitted between close friends.

Let's talk about *friendship.* The word "friend" is much more rarely used in Russia; it doesn't have the same meaning as in English or French. For Russians, it doesn't refer to the old classmate, the chess partner, the pal with whom it's pleasant to chat in a restaurant, or the work colleague. The word "friendship" in Russian implies much closer ties between individuals, relationships of trust, a sense of brotherhood and support in life. The Russians say: "It's better to have a hundred friends than a hundred roubles", which is the value they attribute to friendship.

To put an end to "Russian manners", if you've managed to get past the negotiation stage in business relations with your Russian partners, and you're about to sign the contract or have real prospects, then Russians will say "Good luck! And if you really want luck to smile on you, don't just stand there, but say: *"K chertou"* ("To hell with it"). This response may seem a little rude, but it's a guarantee of future success.

Later on, we'll take a closer look at how Russians behave in everyday life and how they live.

2. Russian sociability

Russians are very sociable, enjoying company and lively discussion of both private and professional matters. They can't stand solitude, which they experience as a punishment. Wherever you are, you could be approached at any time - in public transport, on the street, in a café, in a store, etc. - by a stranger. - No matter where you are, you can be approached by a stranger who will engage you in conversation on any subject, without barriers or social prejudices of any kind.

Russians are much more *democratic* than the French in their dealings. They don't hesitate to ask you about anything that interests them, or to ask for or give you advice, whether you want it or not. In their dealings, they take no account of social or professional distance or age difference. An uninformed European may be taken aback by this deliberate familiarity, with unexpected questions or heart-to-heart confidences about "existence". For the average European, only a close, long-standing prior relationship can enable this kind of approach. In this kind of situation, it's best to avoid showing the stranger your embarrassment at starting a conversation, as this could be interpreted as pride. Your reluctance to get acquainted and your apparent lack of openness will make a bad impression and be frowned upon.

And if you have to make a long trip by train or plane, the proximity of a Russian can be an opportunity to hear - even if it means being shocked - an exciting story about his life. In Europe, you can travel to the other side of the country or to a neighboring country in three to four hours, without having to speak. But in Russia, it's a different matter! If you have to make the overnight trip to St. Petersburg, or spend several days on the train to Siberia, you can't cut the conversation short. You may not feel like it, and you may even show it, but you can't escape the "rules of the game". The long journey, the idleness, the monotony of the trip, the small space, the fact that you don't know each other, break down the psychological barriers and make your neighbor particularly open. Russian writers have long noticed this, which is why many Russian novels and stories have been inspired by this setting. Where did Anna Karenina meet her future lover Vronsky? On the train. And where does the mad drama that unfolds in Dostoyevsky's *The Idiot* begin? On the train, once again. It is also on the train that Prince Myshkin and the merchant Rozhogin meet for the first time and the name of the fatal beauty Nastasia Filipovna is spoken. And this is still true today of many novels, short stories and tales. The meeting on the train, the inevitable "heart-to-heart talk" that can turn an entire life upside down, is a recurring theme in Russian literature.

Russia may well be the only country in the world where telephone calls - until now - have been free of charge (only the subscription fee is charged). In the spring of 2002, the Russian state, under pressure from the market, wanted to introduce the principle of paid communications. But the pensioners, who are usually so calm and reserved, then demonstrated and organized lively protest marches where they demanded to keep their last freedom: to talk on the phone without counting the minutes.

In Russia, people take their time to talk on the phone, commenting on the smallest news and important details, gossip, weather, political scandals as well as delicate personal relationships. You can be called at any time, from 11 o'clock in the evening to midnight, even if they have nothing important to tell you, but simply to "show up", to remind you that they are still there and have not forgotten you.

And if the person suddenly stops calling you regularly for no apparent reason, that's a bad sign: it means either that the person in question is ill, or that he or she is "overwhelmed" with problems and needs to be supported or helped quickly, or that your relationship has deteriorated and it's up to you to remedy it quickly, if you want to re-establish it.

3. About the smile

Europeans think Russians take smiling too seriously. Russians don't smile much, and their faces in crowds are concentrated, scowling, as if "closed in on themselves". This can be frightening for those accustomed to smiling easily and freely at the slightest contact, even with a stranger. The French suffer particularly from this, even more than the Spanish, Americans or Germans: it has to do with their standards of behavior and rules of etiquette.

There are reasons why the Russians are so "serious". And it's not just their lives, which for many years did not lend themselves to smiling; no, it's perhaps a trait of their character linked to natural conditions: nature in Russia is much more rigorous and austere than in Italy or California, which is why its inhabitants are more reserved. And if, for the American, it is natural to keep smiling, for the Russian, an unnecessary smile or cheerfulness appears as something suspicious. And in Russian, there's even a proverb on the subject: "Laughter without reason is the first sign of stupidity." In response to a blissful smile, they may even ask you, "Why are you smiling like an idiot?"

The Russian smile has a different function to that which it has in other countries. It must be *meaningful* and the result of an *emotion*, it must necessarily *translate a feeling*: sincerity, confidence, benevolence and, much more rarely, recognition. *The Russian smile has nothing to do with etiquette.* Foreigners perceive Russians' faces according to their cultural norms and their own etiquette, observing only the *form* without trying to understand the *meaning*. Which doesn't always make them indulgent towards Russians.

Russian faces rarely light up with a smile: that's because it's frowned upon to smile at strangers on the street in Russia! If the Russian wishes to express his goodwill, his good disposition towards someone, he uses the expression of the face and eyes, the particular intonations of the voice, the words and expressions... Inspire yourself!

Of course, this model of behavior runs counter to the traditions of many countries, and the Russians themselves understand this. It is said that young Russians are now taught in management classes to "smile the American way" with a broad, open and optimistic smile. Even if some people feel that this teaching is "unnatural", because the "polite" smile is, for them, something artificial and therefore hypocritical. For the time being, the polite smile has not yet become part of Russian customs.

4. Hospitality and cordiality

Russian hospitality is well known to all. The notion of hospitality is so important in Russian culture that three words are needed to express it alone: *radyouchye* ("cordiality") - the roots of this word are *rad douchoi* ("happy in one's soul"), *gostepriimstvo* (literally meaning "welcoming guests", or "hospitality"), *khlebosol'stvo* ("generous welcome"). These words cover similar but nuanced qualities.

Cordiality is not a specifically Russian quality, unlike, for example, the French, for whom a smile and open benevolence are the essential attributes of any well-mannered person, regardless of human relations and personal appreciation of the situation. The master of the house is obliged to offer his guest the best he has to offer, according to the proverb "To a distinguished guest belongs the place of honor". *Cordiality is* more a behavioral trait than a state of mind, and can sometimes be a facade.

The word *gostepriimstvo* ("hospitality") brings to the fore a person's willingness to let a stranger into his or her home, and even to offer him or her lodging. A hospitable person sees his or her home not as a fortress, but as a place where guests are welcome. And for them, guests are a gift of life.

A warm welcome is called *khlebosol'stvo* in Russian and comes from the composition of the words *khleb* ("bread") and *sol* ("salt"), the basic ingredients of our daily lives. It's a more specifically Russian quality; it shows a certain friendliness and a special welcome, marked by generosity towards guests. A hospitable host enjoys treating his guests to the best he has to offer. He has spent a lot of time preparing everything, and his table is abundant and varied.

If you're invited into a Russian home and there's nothing on the table but coffee and cakes, you can perfectly well say that your host is hospitable and cordial (he's even smiled at you!), but not that he's welcoming, which is something the Russians themselves disapprove of.

Russian hospitality is expressed in the fact that they love to be invited as much as to receive. One may invite only one person (to discuss business), but more often than not, the husband is invited along with his wife, even for business meetings. Children of close friends or relatives are only invited to children's birthday parties. Close friends and relatives usually get together for family celebrations (sad or happy). Invitations are usually made orally. Written invitations are only issued for weddings or special celebrations (wedding anniversaries, for example). Lunch invitations are usually issued by 2 - 3 p.m. - and dinner invitations by 6 - 7 p.m.

If you ask the person who's inviting you what to bring, you'll be told: "Nothing at all. Your presence is enough. Don't take these words literally! You can't "order" from a guest, and it seems all the more inappropriate if the guest is a stranger. But if you bring something, they'll be all the more grateful. It's good manners to turn up at the agreed time when invited, but a half-hour delay is perfectly acceptable. In this case, it's normal for the latecomer to find everyone already at the table.

Guests almost always bring flowers for the hostess, and if you don't have flowers, it's best to give an explanation: "I didn't have time" or "I couldn't find it." You can bring a cake, a box of candy or sweets to accompany the tea - and a bottle of wine for the hostess. A bottle of champagne will be very pleasing and, even better, a bottle of cognac, which is expensive in Russia and much appreciated. Vodka and beer are normally provided by close friends. All the food brought by guests is usually placed on the table immediately.

Guests take leave of their hosts at the same time, or each in turn, depending on the journey home. Russians don't stay as long as French people do at their hosts' houses, bearing in mind that the latter are tired, the metro is about to close and cabs are expensive. After tea or coffee, hosts may try to hold you back: "Please stay with us a little longer" or "Are you in such a hurry to leave? This is usually just a polite ritual, a way for hosts to express their unwillingness to part with you.

It is interesting to note that Russians can come to your home without being invited first (even by phone): "dropping by to say hello" has become a common practice in people's daily lives.

Don't let that frighten you! It doesn't mean that you'll be bothered day and night by uninvited guests who will prevent you from living your life. This lack of formality means that you're being treated with great friendship. So you shouldn't be too quick to condemn this kind of relationship if it affects you personally.

When you're invited to a Russian home, there are some things that will surprise you from the start. The so-called "Moscow cuisine" is a typical Russian phenomenon that surprises rather than annoys foreigners and that you may encounter in other big cities. Why the cuisine? Perhaps because of the eternal Russian housing crisis: the main rooms are occupied by children and sleeping parents: the only place where one feels comfortable is the kitchen. It may also be due to the preference of Russians for informal and more intimate meetings around a table. Sitting in a living room with a glass of liquor in hand and "talking about everything" is not part of their customs.

The kitchen is not only the room where guests are received, especially those who have "stopped by to say hello": it's the place where everything in the fridge is collected and where, after the meal, the endless conversations "about life's big questions, politics, the economy..." begin. This spontaneous style of relating is characteristic of all Russian people, not just Muscovites.

And it is precisely these qualities - spontaneity, sincerity, naturalness and cordiality - that are appreciated by Russians in any kind of relationship.

It's not uncommon for a first official reception (at the airport, on the doorstep of a house, etc.) to include a huge loaf of bread on a platter, topped with a salt shaker filled with salt (just a reminder: *khleb* - "bread" - and sol - "salt") gave rise to the Russian word *khlebosol'stvo*, meaning "generous welcome, hospitality"). Strangers are usually confused, not knowing what to make of it all, and try to take the tray, which is usually heavy and cumbersome.

But don't touch the tray! All you're expected to do is take a piece of bread, dip it in salt and pop it in your mouth. Even if it doesn't taste good, think about how you were welcomed "at the highest level", "like a czar" and treated with the utmost consideration. You should know that very few people are granted such an honor!

And remember that when you are invited or receive guests, it is not so much the delicacy of the food and the finesse of the wine, but the special and warm "Russian" atmosphere that is important to Russians. And if you're planning an evening or reception with Russians, you need to focus on this aspect of things - otherwise all your efforts will be in vain! In recent years, Western-style buffets have become increasingly popular in Russia. And although these receptions are more economical for the organizers, and sometimes more effective in promoting business contacts and other meetings, Russians appreciate them much less, feeling more confident and in their element in a traditional atmosphere around a table.

5. Family relationships

Among the *traditional values* most important to the Russian model, the *family* comes first (58% of respondents[35]). *Health* comes second, and only then are values such as *money*, *work*, *home* and other attributes of happiness mentioned.

Warm family and parental relationships are therefore what matter most. 52% of Russians are married, and almost 30% are in the process of

---

35. *AiF* survey, n° 10.

getting married. The divorce rate, however, at around 50%, is as high as in the West.[36]

Although all the families normally found in Europe resemble each other, each family has its own peculiarities, depending on the country. The Russian family is, to some extent, a source of amazement to foreigners.

First of all, people marry much earlier in Russia than in Europe: girls are usually already married by the age of 25, often to a boy their own age, and have a child of their own. They devote themselves first and foremost to raising their children, especially when they are still young (up to the age of 3). At this age in Europe, young people are only concerned with themselves: their education, their entertainment, their careers...

In today's tough economic climate, however, having children is something we're considering for the future. According to statistics, only 15% of students in higher education venture to have children[37]. Just a few years ago, almost *half of* all students chose to have children. The decisive factor in choosing a child is the presence of a grandmother who can look after it. But most students now want to have children once they have a house, a job and the right conditions.

The overwhelming majority marry *for love* (37%)[38], and quite frequently simply because "the time is right" (38%) or "to be like everyone else" (17%). 9% marry because of an unplanned pregnancy they're afraid to terminate. And only 8% of Russians marry out of interest: for *career* or *money*. As we can see, calculation or common sense as arguments for making a "good marriage" play very little part in their considerations.

Secondly, the Russian and the European have a different notion of the family. For the European, it is the family in the strict sense: husband, wife and children. For the Russian, this notion is broader: if you ask your Russian interlocutor about his family, he'll probably tell you about his wife, his children, his grandparents, his brother and sister (if they all live under the same roof). Some Russians may even name their dog, cat or parrot as family members. This extended notion of family can be explained by traditionally

---

36. *Les Régions de l'URSS*, recueil de statistiques, *op. cit.* table 1.

37. *AiF* survey, table 11.

38. *AiF* survey, table 13.

poor housing conditions, forcing all family members to live together in small apartments, with no hope of settling down separately.

Thirdly, the system of couples cohabiting without official registration of the relationship, so widespread in the West, is gradually entering the mainstream, but for the moment is not yet very popular (only 10% of couples). This type of "civil marriage" will only gradually be adopted by the student family. It's as if students are afraid of repeating the painful experience of their peers who married young and got divorced. They want to "get to know each other beforehand".

Here's what American writer H. Smith[39] writes in his book *The Russians* about child-rearing in Russia: "Russians adore their children, spoil them and try to keep them out of trouble. Children continue to live with their parents, even after they have completed their higher education, and often the parents keep them at home and nurture them for many years to come." And it's true! In Soviet times, Russians even heard the anecdote: "I'll look after my child until I retire, and then the state will take over." This joke isn't funny in itself, but it reflects the not-too-distant past when young people in Russia had neither the right nor the opportunity to legally earn even a pittance as pocket money. So it was up to parents to finance the young man's or girl's leisure activities. The economic reality of the time, of course, created this anomalous situation, but children generally accepted wholeheartedly this provision by their parents, which they took for granted. The reality of life has changed, but these relationships are still marked by tradition.

Children are the center of attention, being kissed, tugged, delighted, scolded and "educated" with equal passion. They are dressed in the most beautiful clothes, and fed the best and healthiest food for them, including vitamins. So it's not uncommon for a mother, knowing that black caviar is very good for her child's health, to spend her last pennies on it, not hesitating to dip into the modest family budget and denying herself everything. Such behavior would not even occur to an outsider.

In the Soviet Union, the following slogan appeared and was widely taken up: "All that's best is for children!" And this slogan was not forgotten with

---

39. H. Smith, *The Russians, op. cit.*

the fall of Soviet power; it continues to triumph. Sociological surveys have shown that the success of their children is a priority for Russians.[40] For 20% of them, for example, the main goal in life was to "ensure their children's happiness", followed by "good health" (14%) and "a happy family" (11.6%).

Because they feel like "the center of the universe", children are often capricious, spoiled and behave like little dictators. What's more, Russian families very often have only one child (33%); only 27% of Russians have two. A very small minority of Russians (12%) do not plan to have children. The majority would like to have children, but for various reasons (often economic) can't afford to have more than one, bearing in mind that an only child is more likely to become selfish than one with brothers or sisters.

What is the origin of this long-standing tradition in the attitude towards children? It has several origins. For several centuries now, almost every family in Russia has had to endure tragic events and upheavals. The 20th century was particularly difficult for Russians: the 1917 revolution, the Red Terror, the civil war, the Stalinist terror and an even bloodier war, the post-war ruin, the stagnation, perestroika and the collapse of the existing way of life, and finally the economic crises and other difficulties. The following pattern has become ingrained in the Russian's genetic memory: "My life has been difficult. May my children be spared! May they be happier than I have been!" That is why every parent unconsciously wants to make the life of his children softer, materially easier, more beautiful - at least during their childhood.

Then parents try to protect their children from real-life problems. At any age. While he's away at school, the parents won't stop calling from the office to check whether he's covered up warmly enough for the walk, whether he's done his homework, what marks he's received at school, demanding all the details. And even if the "child" in question is over 30, his parents, who try to take part in every moment of his life, devote an inordinate amount of attention to him: they experience all his problems, try to be helpful and energetically come to his aid. They feel terribly hurt the day the "child" walks away from them without confiding his or her worries to them. This

---

40. *AiF* survey, table 10.

behavior of children (which is normal!) is not well accepted by older parents. They see it as ingratitude, insensitivity, selfishness.

But, like all aspects of life, this *style of family relationship* also has its negative side. The selfishness and insensitivity of spoiled children backfire on the excessive parental love. There is a huge number of immature and irresponsible people in Russian society, unable to adapt to life's difficulties. Many reasons have contributed to this situation, including excessive parental love. This involvement in children's lives exaggerates the role of parental guardianship, "weighs" on children, disempowers them and deprives them of their autonomy and the will to stand on their own two feet. Parents and children alike pay the price.

There are a number of *reasons for* this situation.

First of all, it's the result of traditional Russian social behavior. The *patriarchal mode* (strictly speaking, the *traditional family mode*) is part of the Russian way of life. Secondly, the economic context of the last decades under Soviet rule has largely contributed to the formation of this relationship between parents and children. In times of general poverty and chronic housing crisis, not two, but three generations of the same family lived in one room or shared a cramped apartment.

The habit of living in cramped conditions, the lack of privacy, have, paradoxically, only strengthened family ties in Russia. People have learned to see these constraints not so much as an obstacle to individual freedom, but as a "safeguard" against loneliness, as a way of maintaining the warmth of the home.

6. Father-child and kinship relationships

The relationship between the parents' generation and the children's (already grown-up) generation in Russia differs from that in Europe.[41] As we mentioned earlier, Russians are very attached to their children. And these

---

41. *Russians: Family and Social Life*, Moscow, published by the USSR Academy of Sciences, Nauka ("Science") ed., 1989, p. 6.

ties between parents and children continue, even after the adult child has left the parental home.

For example, even if they live in an independent room or apartment, young people continue to enjoy their "children's rights" for quite some time: they visit their parents for "family lunches", and if their parents live in the country, they bring back produce from the garden (potatoes, fruit, etc.), they try to spend family holidays with their parents and in the company of their childhood friends. As for the parents, they try to take part in all the events of the young household's life.

This differs somewhat from European traditions, where the young couple cannot count on material assistance from their parents - at best, the couple will be indebted to them.

While in the Russian family, it's very important to maintain contact with the new parents (aunt, mother-in-law), relations with the parents-in-law, in the case of an alliance with Europeans, are different: the French parents and the young couple also maintain contact, but somewhat differently. In France, we have lunch on fixed dates with the husband's parents. Conversations with the mother-in-law are relatively superficial: "bothering" her with problems is out of the question. Relations between the new parents are courteous and distant.

In Russia, once a young couple has left the family cocoon and begun their independent lives, they are the focus of special attention from their parents. This is particularly evident among city dwellers whose parents are not too far away. This manifests itself in the form of financial help (at "parties", "wedding anniversaries", "while waiting for pay"), food and homemade dishes. Parents help their children with major expenses: buying an apartment, furniture, a TV set or household appliance, or renting a dacha in summer. With the arrival of the first child, parents turn their attention to the child's education.

The parents help their daughter most when she is off work for her pregnancy, or when the child falls ill. This help is more rarely given to the son. A man needs to be able to solve his own personal problems, and is "less to be pitied" than a woman, who traditionally has a more difficult existence in Russia.

But over time, as the young couple builds their "nest", the situation reverses. It's the children's turn to help their elderly parents, especially when they find themselves alone. The children don't abandon them or send them to retirement homes (as is the case in other countries). Sending your parents away while you're still alive is morally unacceptable. They often invite them to come and live with them. Both generations (children and parents) sometimes move to live together. But more often than not, the elderly refuse to move, making it difficult for the children to care for them. Parents are afraid of "boring" their children, of embarrassing them, or of losing their independence. Often, they spend the winter with their children (in the big cities) and return to their country home in the summer, taking their grandchildren with them.

Older people, even if they have lost some of their unquestioned authority, remain the pole of attraction for younger people. Relationships between siblings and their respective families are not as close as between parents and children. For this reason, the older generation has the role of *holding the whole family together*, linking its members to previous generations, passing on family traditions, bringing all members together in one big family. When the elders die, the ties between close relatives can be broken.

Respect for elders is part of the Russian way of life. And if any tensions arise between parents and children, it's usually the children who are at the root of them. What's more, the new generation is more educated and cultured than its predecessor, and asserts its independence both in its behavior and in its opinions, including political ones.

Of course, it's a shame that Russian old people, after a hard life, can't live as they please and rest as millions of elderly people in other countries do. Their physical appearance and health are far worse than that of their counterparts abroad. This does not prevent them from continuing to help their children and grandchildren. We can only sympathize with their difficult old age. But we can also envy them for making themselves useful to their children and grandchildren right up to the end.

Russians over 70 fought in the Second World War, they've been through the hard school of life, and they're courageous, dignified and patient. In the 1990s, during the economic crisis, many demoralized Russians became marginalized and began begging on the metro, city streets and pedestrian underpasses. Many of these marginalized people were elderly, willing to work to the point of exhaustion. Not just to "survive", but also to help their adult children "get a start in life".

7. Husband and wife: social roles

Traditional Russian family and husband-wife relationships still appear original to foreigners. In their most widespread form, they are characterized by Russians' attachment to *traditional values* and *a more patriarchal organization of the family* than in other European countries.

Since the 16th century, family relationships have been governed by *Domostroy*. *Domostroy* is equivalent to a "domestic charter" in French; the Russian word is composed of *dom* ("house") and *stroit* ("to construct, to build"). It is a set of rules of life and precepts that defends the principles of the patriarchal way of life and the absolute authority of the head of the family - the man, the father of the family. Nowadays, this term is used with a note of irony by the Russians themselves to refer to a family where the omnipotent husband imposes order on all other members. In their extreme form, these rules date back to the distant past, even if they have not completely disappeared.

You can wax ironic on the subject all you like. But anyone, even the most "progressive" man, can fully understand how the supremacy of *Domostroy* could not, in the space of 400 years, have disappeared without a trace, and how it still influences Russian family organization today.

Our description of the contemporary Russian family concerns the *urban family* (90% of Russia's population). The traditional family today consists of a mother, a father and *a child* (33% of families).

Let's say he's off to school. It's usually the wife who gets up first and prepares breakfast for the whole family. She usually gets up at 7 a.m.: school starts at 8:30 a.m. and businesses in town open at 9. Parents come home after 7 p.m.: it all depends on work and their commute home. In big cities, it takes no less than 40 minutes on average to get from home to work.

Typically, the child comes home from school at lunchtime (1 - 2 p.m.), heats up the meal prepared by his mother the day before, does his homework and plays in the playground. When the parents return in the evening, homework is done and the whole family sits down to dinner - at around 8 pm.

Then everyone goes about their business: the husband and children usually sit down in front of the TV. But the wife continues her "day's work": laundry - laundry, tidying up, preparing the next day's meal, washing up, checking notes, not to mention many other tasks - all fall within her domain. Like a bee in its hive, she's always busy, worrying about every member of the family. She's the *mother*, and that's saying a lot...

It's also in keeping with ancient Russian traditions. Since pagan times, the heroine of Russian folk tales has been Vassilissa "the Very Wise", who, at her husband's request, carries out the most difficult tasks: she weaves a carpet of indescribable beauty, she creates a lake with swans, she builds a princely palace while the husband "rests". And in the morning, the husband has to answer for his work. But we don't talk about her, because she's the "Very Wise One", meaning she's very sensible. Her delicacy helps her to stand with dignity in her husband's shadow. And this model of feminine behavior is an integral part of the Russian archetype.

Russian men consider it normal to *physically* help their wives with certain tasks, such as going to the store, laundry or dry cleaner's in the evening after work (especially with heavy or bulky items). Husbands sometimes help their wives with the housework (on Saturdays), for example, by vacuuming or playing with the children. But it's out of the question for him to wash the dishes, prepare the meal or do the laundry! Even though almost every home is equipped with a washing machine these days... It's not a "man's job", and the husband does everything he can "to get out of it".

It's usually frowned upon for a man to have overtly "unmanly" occupations (household chores), to obey his wife willingly, to be excessively soft-tempered or lacking in any masculine "roughness". While we may be sympathetic to this type of man, he'll be described as "spineless" and, more explicitly, "his wife wears the pants". He will even be called a "sissy". A real man is a *moujik* (not in the sense of "peasant"). By *moujik*, we mean a man of authority who knows how to make himself respected!

Finally, another particularity of the Russian family is the *crumbling of its social barriers*. For example, a well-educated wife may well have a husband who is a factory worker or chauffeur, a lower social position by European standards. It's true that, in this case, he often earns two or three times more than his "educated" wife. And even if the educated wife's salary is much higher than her husband's, this doesn't change the division of roles in the home.

Family problems, on the whole, rest on the mother's shoulders. This often jeopardizes the young mother's career, even though Russian law stipulates the same rights and obligations and shared responsibility for the child. This shows how men are favored. However talented and educated a woman may be, she relegates her career opportunities to the back burner. That's the way Russian traditions are, although over time these are also changing.

Today's Russian family, especially in the big cities, is changing dramatically: more and more women are starting to work, control from the previous generation is loosening, women are becoming economically independent, and premarital sexual experiences are becoming more widespread. All this is gradually affecting traditional family relationships, making them more democratic and egalitarian between men and women.

Russians are increasingly resorting to "free unions". It's not true that "European traditions" have yet become the norm in Russia. This can be seen, for example, in the popular TV program "Vivre sa vie", a televised debate on typical family issues. Recently, the debate focused on a completely new family model for Russia: one in which the businesswoman works 16 hours a day, earns a lot of money and supports her student husband. Alongside his studies, the husband performs the traditionally "feminine" tasks at home: preparing meals, washing clothes and so on. All the participants in this televised debate agreed that this was an "American" family model, and that the husband should complete his university studies and then have a good job. But everyone also felt that it was essential for the family to swap social roles if it was to retain its unity and develop in the future. The question of how to share these roles was not addressed.

So for the Russians, it's always the husband who has to look after his family and be its main pivot. We can almost certainly say that the traditional role of the man in the Russian family is that of *head of the family*, *protector*, *source of income*, and *helper with hard physical labor.*

As for the woman, she is obliged to procreate, look after the health and education of her children, create an atmosphere of love within the family, and maintain and protect her home.

Love and *sex* are clearly differentiated in Russian culture. Love is interpreted, in the broadest sense, as a "relationship" between people, while sex is merely a (physical) "intercourse". The one is not related to the other, although for today's youth the notion of sex is often more topical. The notion of "love" for Russians often covers the renunciation of one's "individual self" for the other(s). It is expressed in devotion to a person, in self-sacrifice. True love "à la russe" means becoming one with the beloved: remember Chekhov's famous "Dushchka"! A multitude of love stories in Russian literature (and in real life, too!) begin precisely with a woman's compassion for the *man who* is so alone, so unhappy, so misunderstood... And that's where the trap closes, because afterwards, the man and woman conform to the traditional patriarchal mode, and *the man* dominates.

For Russians, *love* is rarely associated with the material side of life. Russian women are brought up with proverbs such as "With the beloved, happiness is in the hut", "Happiness can't be bought", and so on. This folk wisdom is not always convincing, it is even questionable. However, there are no "practical" truths in the Russian language such as "Love does a lot, but money does everything", as there are in the French language. The statement that "Love and poverty are a bad combination" seems to be self-evident to the French.

Finally, for Russians, there is a very marked differentiation of love between "that which one feels" and "that of which one is the object". It's as if a *single* manifestation (love) had *two components* in their consciousness. According to psychologists, this differentiation is quite specific to Russians[42]. This phenomenon cannot be observed anywhere else in literature or in scientific works. Many Russians prefer to *feel* love rather than *be its object*.

You can get into a Russian woman's good graces if you behave like a gentleman, a protector and an advocate. If you're courting a girl, you must

---

42. *La Mentalité des Russes. The Consciousness of Large Population Groups in Russia, op. cit.* p. 112 and 276.

be prepared to offer her coffee, a restaurant, cinema, theater and so on. In Russia, this is considered by the "weaker" sex to be part of a ritual, something to be taken for granted.

It's precisely in situations like these that foreigners often blunder, not realizing that if they only pay their share, they'll be seen as "stingy", which is bound to lower their "popularity rating". Russian women are used to this kind of attention, they take it kindly or as a due, and don't feel offended like American or German women, for example. They even like it when men behave towards them in a polite and chivalrous manner. The man who pays for them proves that he can be counted on and that he knows how to be gallant.

There's also a glaring discrepancy in the *financial relations* between men and women, due to the traditional gallantry of men. This is because women who accept payment for their services make no commitment whatsoever: there's no exchange for, say, sexual intercourse or flirtatious "womanly beha- vior" and so on. Today's Russian women claim gender equality, defend their right to choose and take the initiative. The same demands from American women are balanced by the fact that they are materially independent. But in Russia, women want to be independent, but prefer to be paid for it. This position is unique in that it differs from the accepted norms of behavior in the West, as well as from the traditional "feminine behavior" of the East.

Financial relations within the household vary from family to family, but it's usually the woman who holds the portfolio of "finance minister" in Russia: closer to the realities of day-to-day life, she's in a better position to manage the day-to-day running of the household. It is also for this reason that she is responsible for running the household. But the husband must remain the main source of income, the breadwinner in the family.

Would you like to know what criteria are decisive for men when choosing a wife? To the question: "What's the most important thing to you in a woman?", today's Russian men answer[43]: intelligence (27%) and sexuality (26%), goodness is also very important (24%), physical appearance less so (11%). With this in mind, 66% of men prefer slim women to strong ones.

---

43. *AiF* survey, tables 14 and 15.

Knowing how to cook and *manage the home* are only important for 9% of men, which may, at first glance, seem somewhat surprising.

In addition, the answer of men who give the first criterion of *intelligence* in choosing a woman should not perplex you. Although we have already discussed this topic, intelligence has a different meaning in Russia and in Europe. And "female intelligence" in no way refers to intellect or intellectual activity, but rather to everyday wisdom, the art of understanding others, of being tolerant and so on. In other words, it's about a person's *socio-ethical characteristics*, their ability to adapt to a community of people and, in this case, to the family.

As this public opinion poll shows, only 11% of men appreciate ambitious, materially independent businesswomen. These are generally employees of private companies, affluent people, but there are also men in the cultural field and even blue-collar workers. Only 10% of men (usually wealthy employees of private firms, casino regulars, young people under 35) prefer efficient women with powerful sexual energy, who know and like how to live life on the big foot, and above all enjoy pleasures and parties. Military men and scientists don't like these women at all, but journalists love them. And most men are extremely suspicious of these "superwomen".

The overwhelming majority of men prefer the "traditional woman". She's not only a good housewife, but also "a friend in life".

The model of the ideal wife for the ordinary Russian is that of "Dushchka", the heroine of a Chekhov story; married several times, she renounces her own life and personal interests with each union, living only for those of her husband. Let's venture to say that, from the bottom of his heart, the Russian man would like to continue to have supremacy in family relations, and to have by his side a discreet and submissive companion, capable of sacrificing his own interests and living exclusively for his family.

It is often difficult for women to oppose these traditional constraints. They try to conform, repeating the destiny of their mothers and grandmothers, limiting themselves in advance to a secondary role in the family.

The women of the "new Russians" often have an unenviable destiny. As life itself shows, many of those who became rich very quickly (businessmen, financiers, but also members of the State Duma and directors of major factories) not only changed their lifestyle with higher social status, but also their wives: they often married young, leggy beauties. On the one hand, one might think that these young girls are extraordinarily lucky: they have rich husbands, luxurious homes, youth and beauty. However, if you take a closer look, you will see that these young women are often very lonely: they usually married too quickly and did not have time to finish their studies; they then abandoned them under the pressure of the husband. They have no friends and languish in solitude and boredom day after day. The husband, after an extremely stressful day, may take out his bad temper on his wife and even beat her. She does not dare to complain to anyone, as she dreads, more than anything, the divorce and more precisely to be thrown on the street with the child without any means of support, without a job, while she is used to a life of luxury. It's very difficult to voluntarily destroy the life you've been used to, even if it's not a rosy one. Some of these women, unable to bear what they've been through, plunge into alcoholism, drug addiction or suicide.

Thus, in Russia, women are the *guardians of the home*, as well as *mothers* (if there is a child) and comforters of men who are going through difficult times. For many centuries, Russian women have selflessly offered their unceasing care and touching attention to their husbands, fathers and children.

The most paradoxical aspect of this situation is that, unlike Spanish, there is no equivalent to the word "macho" in the Russian language. The word *moujik* (a real man) is always pronounced by Russians with a note of appreciation, if not admiration. Which goes to show that traditional social roles in the family are not viewed critically by Russians.

Times change and society is shaken by crises and upheavals, the organization of life changes and it is normal that social roles also change. But in Russia, this evolution is taking place slowly and with difficulty.

8. The position of women in Russian society

As you saw in the previous chapter, the position of women in contemporary society is ambiguous.

On the one hand, there are still signs of chivalrous behavior towards Russian women, who traditionally accept this gallant attitude of men towards her.

In fact, history shows that women in Russia enjoyed more extensive economic and political rights than their counterparts in the West. In *Domostroy* (16th century), husbands who failed to respect their wives were severely reprimanded. And there was no precept of the nobility, as in Poland in the Middle Ages, that a man should "educate" his wife by beating her and, after tying her up, hanging her over the fireplace like a ham. Similarly, Russia never experienced the infamous Western "droit de cuissage". But women had the right to dispose of their own dowry, to conduct business and to withdraw money from bank accounts without legal authorization from their husbands.

This "autonomy" of Russian women in the past may explain, in large part, the lack of success in Russia of the aggressive forms of feminism prevalent in Europe and America, where women have for decades fought for what in Russia was taken for granted.

Soviet power played a considerable role in raising the social status of women: they gained the right to vote (30 years before their counterparts in France), the right to work and to equal pay, the right to education, a developed system of crèches and kindergartens to free up time for private life, and so on... And March 8 - Women's Day - became an official holiday in the USSR in recognition of the important role played by women. As in the past, March 8 is celebrated like nowhere else across the whole country.

However, according to *Domostroy*, the Russian woman's place is essentially in the home. Her vocation is to be a mother and to sacrifice herself for her husband and children. We don't make the same demands of the man (the father): he is, of course, responsible for the children in the long term. But if he wants to get away from the family, for example, drop his wife and children and remarry a young girl, society doesn't judge him in the same way as it would a woman who does the same. Statistics show that only 12% of fathers pay child support after their departure, the rest trying to avoid this obligation.

Russian women must conform to the traditional family model, in which it is *essentially the man, not the woman, who maintains the family*. As a result, women's *rights* are regularly *violated* from childhood onwards. The little boy can behave as he pleases, while the little girl must be calm, discreet and obedient: she must give in to everything - including boys her own age - in preparation for her future role as wife and mother.

In Russia, little girls have little preparation for social success. What more do you need? The most important thing is that you find yourself a husband. The choice in a woman's life comes down to marriage, because to find yourself alone, without a husband, is terrible. An unmarried woman is considered "abnormal" by many Russians, and must be "remedied" by any means possible.

This *ambiguous* position of the Russian woman has led to her *greatly underestimating herself*, compared to the Western woman. Russian women are proud of their education, but few openly acknowledge that the vast majority of women complete their studies at university or institute with the sole aim of getting married and finding a worthy fiancé. There are even "bridal faculties" such as the Faculty of Philology, the Pedagogical Institutes and the Foreign Language Institutes, which are still the most prestigious "breeding grounds" for brides.

Even in Soviet times, men and women had different views on the rights and obligations of the sexes. For example, men are more likely to believe that *men have a greater right to flirt and be unfaithful* than women, and that *men should take the initiative in choosing a partner.* They are shocked if it's the woman who takes the initiative in this area. They don't agree that women should choose their lifestyle without asking anyone else's opinion. Men often consider their obligations towards "weaker" women to be unjustified; the latter, in fact, do not show weakness, and moreover claim equality even where, objectively, there can be none.

The situation of women in today's Russia is particularly difficult. Studies on changes in attitudes over the last ten years reveal particularly damning changes within the family: a sharp rise in the number of divorces (585 divorces per 1,000 unions), a huge number of single-parent families and single mothers, a *doubling in the* number of alcoholic husbands... Perestroika and the financial crises, the development of complexes by men (following job loss) and cheap vodka have all contributed to this dramatic situation. Of Russia's 33 million children, 14 million (almost *half!*) are orphans, growing up without a father. And according to tradition, it's up to women to take responsibility for all this!

The situation would be much worse without them. The men, beset by problems, often "crack". The women, on the other hand, weep and grieve, but then grit their teeth and carry huge bags and packages filled with leather jackets made in Turkey and cheap consumer goods from China; this is how they became *tchelnoki* ("shuttles"[44]). Without the efforts of these women, this abundance of goods would never have seen the light of day in Russia. At their own risk, they borrow money from acquaintances, sign up for a tourist trip abroad (to China, Turkey), buy cheap goods (usually clothes) on the spot, take them home and resell them themselves in Russia at kiosks or markets. Of course, this semi-legal "shadow" trade with its criminal characteristics is not without danger for the "weaker sex". But it's precisely up to women, in times of trouble, to bring home everyday items from China or Turkey. And it's the same when it comes to bringing home the drunkard husband or the children. Someone has to keep life going!

As far as young women are concerned, a new trend is emerging in Russia that is developing very rapidly: *female emancipation*. This is not at all the aggressive feminism that has reached America and some European countries, but rather a *change in priorities*. Until 5 years ago, the main goal of Russian girls was to make a good marriage. They felt compassion for single women, whatever their achievements. Today, girls "don't rush headlong into marriage": 64% of Russians consider that the most important thing for a young girl today is to have a good job, and only 27% support the traditional view (to have a good marriage). In reality, the question resolves itself, and is posed as follows in social and political articles: in a changing society, is it right for women to follow their "natural vocation", i.e. to procreate and bring up children, to maintain the home? Or should she be primarily concerned with earning a living? It seems that not all women are able to reconcile the two at the moment.

---

44. "Shuttles": a new profession in post-Soviet Russia - in the field of "economic tourism", so to speak. The overwhelming majority of today's "commuters" are middle-aged women who used to be engineers, teachers and scientific workers. After the disintegration of the USSR, they found themselves out of work, and commuting enabled them to earn a decent wage and feed their families.

Let's not speculate about women "in general", but rather try to draw a psychological and social portrait of the different categories of women[45] who have appeared in Russia over the last ten years.

A completely new type of woman is the *female entrepreneur*. Her average age is around 36, and she's married with children. Curiously, women with traditional families are more successful in business than single women. More often than not, they set up small and medium-sized businesses. They are better educated and constantly strive to improve their skills. They generally have degrees in economics or the humanities. In most cases, they own their own business or run a firm. They are socially mobile, full of new ideas and entrepreneurial. They are overworked, with 62-hour weeks (they even work on days off). They live and breathe their profession. They are not afraid of autonomy, responsibility and risk. These women are managers, and their leadership style is collegial. Because of the permanent work overload, they feel guilty about not being able to devote more time and attention to their families. This does not prevent them from being generally satisfied with their work. Their income (on average $1,150 a month) enables them to play the role of head of the family. Their elegant grooming and decisive demeanor make them stand out in a crowd.

Another category of women, more traditional in Russia, is the *female performer*[45]. Their average age is 31.7. These women usually marry and have children. The family often lives with elderly parents. They don't earn much (less than half the family budget), so they don't play much of an economic role in the family. Most of them have a higher technical education (60%). Without exception, they are all employees of state-owned enterprises and work hard. Their low incomes are their main source of dissatisfaction at work, which they see as an obstacle to fulfilling their family duties and private life. In their professional relationships, they prefer a "soft", "feminine" style, free from conflict.

Another very common type of woman in Russia is the *female executive*. These are specialists who have made a career of it. Their average age is 32.2.

---

45. Social-psychological analysis of different categories of working women in *Social Psychology of Economic Behavior*, edited by the Institute of Psychology of the Russian Academy of Sciences, Moscow, Nauka ("Science"), 1999, p. 183.

They often marry, but the percentage of women with families is lower than in other categories: they are often single or divorced. They rarely have children. Their income represents little more than half the family budget, giving them a degree of economic independence when it comes to deciding family matters. They have a high level of education (higher education, science degrees with additional training - often in the humanities) and are constantly striving to improve it by obtaining a second degree, internships, taking specialized courses, etc. Female executives are usually salaried employees in management positions. They are very busy with their work and live for it. In business relationships, they opt for a rigid, "manly" style. Their psychology is similar to that of female company directors.

These are the "new types" of women who have emerged in Russia in recent years. These women have considerably altered the social and demographic structure of society. In practice, they have demonstrated the radical change in the way Russians have thought about the happiness and fulfillment of a young woman for many years. The last ten years have seen the emergence of a significant number of "new type" Russian women who have "made it". They often work in private mixed companies, earn high salaries, are economically and morally independent, drive, dress in expensive "boutiques" and wear expensive jewelry. They also master several foreign languages, are determined and have a strong opinion on everything. They have nothing in common with the traditional "Dushchka" who let herself die for love, not being loved in return and suffering from the husband's selfishness...

Studies show that the more power women have, the more "hardened" their professional relationship style becomes, and the less attracted they are to collegial-style leadership.

Thus, the traditional social roles of men and women are increasingly being questioned in Russia. However, almost 70% of Russians consider that it is still much easier for men to pursue a career than for women, even though the percentage of women with higher education qualifications is much higher than that of men. 55% of qualified specialists in Russia are women.

Despite the equal rights of men and women guaranteed by the Russian Constitution, almost *half of* Russians believe that men have more opportunities to realize them than women, and only 35% consider both sexes to have equal rights.

9. Marriages with foreigners

Sometimes the Russian tradition of putting everything on a woman's shoulders makes her want to leave everything behind, marry a foreigner and leave Russia. Statistics show that the number of marriages contracted with citizens of other countries continues to rise. One in four marriages, however, is to people from the former republics of the USSR: these have been dubbed "nearby foreign territories". And an overwhelming number of mixed marriages are with foreigners from "distant countries".

There are many cases of young men from developing countries such as Syria, Vietnam, etc., marrying women much older than themselves. But it's easy to guess what people are looking for in these marriages: permission to stay in Russia, which opens up new opportunities for their business. These are "marriages of interest". However, these cases are the exception rather than the rule. For our part, we're interested in "regular" unions, those that drive Russian men and women to seek their happiness abroad. And this is no longer an uncommon phenomenon: marriage agencies in Moscow and St. Petersburg are springing up like mushrooms, and it's become a thriving business. Last year in Moscow alone, there were 41 marriages with English nationals, 31 with French nationals, 47 with Germans and 23 with Italians.[46]

It's mainly women, not men, who marry foreigners. There are a few explanations for this.

Firstly, men are more conservative, making it harder for them to adapt to new living conditions. Compared to women, they have a higher opinion of themselves. The factors of solidity and stability, as well as the assurance of retaining the "leading role" in their married lives, are important to them.

Secondly - and not least - a man plagued by alcoholism considerably diminishes the attractiveness and chances of a man seeking a happy home. Yet alcoholism is taking its toll on men in Russia. Whereas Russian women,

---

46. Palais des mariages data published in *AiF*, 1997.

as the study shows, are in high demand on the "marriage market". For a start, they have European looks - and there's no shortage of beautiful women in Russia. And no matter how slender and seductive movie actresses and supermodels may be abroad, for an overwhelming majority of Russian men (73%) there are no more beautiful women in the world than Russians.

Thirdly, Russian women are not only pretty, they are also better educated and more cultured than the average European woman. 55% of urban women have higher education qualifications, and they are by far the majority in the fields of education and public instruction, health and science. They love to read, keep abreast of the latest in art and literature, and are quick to learn anything new, including foreign languages. They'll always be "on the ball" and never stand out at a social gathering. Their kindness, hard work and longing for a home are also major assets in the eyes of foreigners. Among their great qualities are their compassion, their highly-developed intuition (see Chapter 1), and their willingness to share in difficult times.

Fourthly, European and American men, somewhat "overtaken" by triumphant feminism, easily get Russian women to play a "background" role. They don't make demands, they support their husbands in life's difficult moments, and they have no pretensions if they've been "properly" educated. In short, these natural dispositions of Russian women partly explain the success of their marriages to Europeans and Americans. More often than not, sincere, reciprocal love and romantic passion are at the root of these unions. However, once the marriage is finalized, it's time to get on with life. And that's when, very often, these mixed marriages run into serious problems. What are the reasons for this?

Firstly, these marriages run into difficulties, if only because the government gets involved. It's not popular to talk about it, but everyone knows: ex-Russian wives living in England and France have spoken out in interviews published in women's magazines.[47] These women are trying to pinpoint the origin of their problems. After his marriage to a Russian woman, the atmosphere in the husband's office changed imperceptibly but radically: without

---

47. Most of the stories relating to this theme appear in *Iabloko'* magazine (March 2002), as well as in *Cosmopolitan* magazine.

any explanation, he was no longer given interesting assignments abroad, and his professional career was put on hold. Then his circle of friends and acquaintances shrinks, and so on. In recent years, Russia's relations with certain countries have become strained, and "espionage" does not always use the most orthodox methods.

Secondly, in addition to the *objective* reasons - state interference in family relationships - there are also *subjective* reasons. The Russian woman's disappointment with her husband is not the least of these. And the failure of any marriage is usually the result of this disillusionment. During the decades of the "Iron Curtain", Russians imagined that Europe was a paradise where, supposedly, everyone lived like Hollywood superstars in a permanent atmosphere of festivity and luxury. At the sight of modest-sized Parisian apartments, numerous immigrant neighbors and small-displacement cars, the Russian woman falls head over heels. High hopes go up in smoke.

And the disenchantment doesn't stop there. The model of the French man as a spirited, gallant, light-hearted and generous lover is also a myth invented by writers, local songwriters and boastful tourists. Only the novels of a bygone era can give us an idea of what French gallantry and the refined art of seduction were like. But today, it's perfectly normal for a couple in love to ask for separate bills when leaving a café. And spouses, when making a major joint purchase or paying their expenses, each "contributes" from their individual accounts. This is the gloomy record of Western feminism. It may be that French women themselves are now complaining from the bottom of their hearts that men have lost all sense of gallantry, even to the point of being rude in public... But the French are exemplary in their firmness, and in no way allow themselves to demean women by giving a pregnant woman a seat on the metro or helping her onto the bus!

Life shows that, for the most part, the French are quite pragmatic. To cite an example, this anecdote about them is their own: "If the light shines at night in a Frenchman's house, foreigners imagine he is making love. But they're wrong: he's just counting his money." This joke is only half true. The mercantile spirit is a widespread trait in French men. And since the French have a sense of humor, they often scoff at this trait of theirs - as if jokingly demanding that their wives save on lights, water and other utilities, chat less on the phone, only shop sales, etc. Russian women are generally not ready for this change of situation. *Being thrifty is* not perceived by her as a positive character trait, but rather as avarice, in its most absurd form. She'll be struck, for example, by the fact that "he" doesn't cut corners when it comes to eating out, but when it comes to heating the apartment in winter... even the well-off French maintain a temperature that barely keeps them from freezing to death! Or, to add insult to injury, the way he washes his dishes under hot running water without clogging the sink "makes him hysterical"! Water expenses and telephone conversations are a constant bone of contention between French husbands and Russian wives, regardless of the household's income level.

When it comes to love, the traditional image of the average Frenchman as an incomparable lover is somewhat exaggerated. Once married, French men set themselves a precise standard (once a week, once a month, several times a day). And to go beyond the limits of this framework, special "training" is required: a domestic dispute with tears, or better still, a refined dinner, a little sweetness, an exception to the usual diet, or something similar...

Hence the gloomy statistics - recorded by many experts - on destroyed Franco-Russian marriages and the resulting single-parent families. What's more, the Russian wife in these couples will always be the party who suffers most: firstly, the husband can, if he wishes, deprive her of any rights over her child, and secondly, she won't necessarily receive any alimony for the rest of her life. The alimony she receives is so modest that it's not enough for her to live with dignity, and she'll be reduced to looking for work.

Disappointments are usually shared. The husband can't help but be annoyed by some of his wife's "too Russian" traits, such as the fact that she can't stand solitude and needs constant company, that she spends hours on the phone, that semi-unknown people often invade the house - and not just to eat, but often to sing loudly after the meal! - That the meal is not at 12:00 noon or 8:00 p.m. in the evening, but at a time that suits her. The usual order and rhythm are totally disrupted, which is extremely unpleasant for her. And last but not least, *she* loves to spend and spends money without thinking, without thinking about tomorrow, without trying to save money, she doesn't wait for the next sales season but prefers to buy what she likes straight away.

But for the Russians, these are not flaws but signs of a "generous tempe-rament", which rather arouses their sympathy. For the French, on the other hand, they are vices to be fought, a lack of practicality and even plain stupidity - in short, a serious cause for divorce.

Let's assume that mutual disappointments are a necessary part of every union. In the end, love passes and we discover what we had not noticed in the heat of passion. And it is only mutual understanding and agreement that will solve the problems in the family. In our view, the difficulty of understanding each other is not due to the "stupidity" of one or the "stubbornness" of the other, but to the *absence of a common language, cultural differences*, different standards of behavior and ways of thinking, and different horizons.

Many linguists share Benjamin Worth's theory that the language we speak not only expresses our *thoughts* but also significantly *determines* their course. In short, the Russian sees the world differently from the French insofar as he speaks Russian and not French. And vice versa. For this reason, the Frenchman cannot apprehend and feel the world as the Russian, not having the *linguistic means* for that. Only by studying the language of his interlocutor can he step back from his mother tongue and apprehend reality differently (see Chapter 1).

As the Russian writer B. Dovlatov, "language is 90% of a person's personality" and one can only agree with this statement. The alternative of one spouse learning the other's language is not the best either. After all, both spouses need to familiarize themselves with each other's language and culture, regardless of which country they live in. Each needs to make an effort to reach out to the other, with a view to mutual understanding. Without this, it will be difficult for them to overcome their cultural differences and find out what is important to each other. For example, notions such as *intuition, destiny, sin, conscience, soul, anguish* and emotional exaggerations will not be perceived by the French, and the frequent use of these words will only annoy them. And *reserve, pragmatism*, a *sense of economy*, the *rules of good manners*, knowledge of a hundred kinds of wine or cheese will be of little importance to the Russian woman.

Added to this are different lifestyles, both culturally and in terms of hygiene, for example. Russian women often complain that life in France,

128

for example, is boring and lacking in events. They find it unbearable, for example, that their husbands don't read anything except their bills, and above all "that we can't talk about anything with him". This situation, particularly distressing for Russian women, is often the first cause of a definitive break-up. "If you can't talk to him about anything, then sooner or later everything else loses its meaning" There may be some truth in this, if we take into account the traditional "Russian appetite for culture". But this should have been considered before the wedding. It seems that both parties have their share of responsibility for the mutual misunderstanding.

All this does not rule out successful marriages between citizens of foreign countries. But to achieve this happiness, spouses must strive to get to know each other. And for this, there is no other way than to study the language and culture of their spouse, to understand his or her feelings and aspirations, and to broaden, with his or her help, their personal horizons and cultural experience.

10. The neighbors

Neighborhood relations are very important in Russia[48], and their particular character reflects, to a large extent, the problem of housing in the USSR (see Part 2, chap. 1, § 1). In the 1930s, living in *communal apartments* or barracks often fostered friendly relations between whole families. After thirty years, many of our neighbors went their separate ways, having obtained their own apartments, but the friendships forged in childhood continued for a long time to come. Many Russians can tell you about this experience.

The isolation of urban life in Russia today means that neighbors may well never cross paths, they don't know each other, and when they do, they don't even bother to say hello. Neighborly ties, however, play an extremely important, almost familial role in the daily lives of Russians.

Even in today's Russia, neighbors have a special role to play that shouldn't be overlooked; it's important to make the most of them, and to do so in your own best interests. For example, when looking to rent an apartment,

---

48. *Russians: family and social life, op. cit.* p. 75.

it's important not only to know its layout and comfort, but also to take an interest in your nearest neighbors. Living together in a defined space, taking care of the cleanliness or the flowers on your doorstep, certain decisions shared by the building's residents (installing an intercom, choosing a janitor, etc.), the layout of the courtyard - all this contributes to bringing neighbors closer together and establishing initial contacts.

Neighbors are appreciated for their mutual help in everyday life and in extreme situations, when you don't have relatives nearby and you need to call the ambulance, for example, as well as in many other situations. In times of need, for example, it's common practice to leave the keys to your apartment with your neighbors - so that they can water the flowers, feed the fish or the house cat. In Europe, it's the concierge who is paid for these functions. In Russia, we're not quite used to concierges yet, and they're considered "outsiders", not completely reliable. Anyone can apply for a job as a concierge, but it's a stranger you can't necessarily trust, unlike a good neighbor to whom you can not only entrust your keys, but also ask to welcome your child back from school to help you out, and so on.

We generally do each other favors. That's how strong relationships of mutual help develop between neighbors. Ongoing contact between good neighbors can strengthen ties. This takes the form of exchanging information and important advice, and organizing leisure activities together - depending on age and affinity. Women, for example, often exchange recipes and fashion information. You can borrow money from your neighbor before you get paid, or "get" cigarettes or bread from him or her at odd hours. You can consult your neighbor about the care and education of your child. Or spend the evening together in front of the TV set or having a cup of tea, commenting on the news.

It's nothing like inviting someone out, even your closest friends. For a start, you've got to get there - on foot or by public transport, dress accordingly, buy flowers or something, etc. - and you've got to be ready to go. Whereas at your neighbors', you can pop in at any time in your home clothes for "five minutes" and be held up for several hours.

But you can appreciate your neighbors, not only because they are useful in everyday life and can help you solve many problems. In Russia, they have another important function: to *enforce, in their own way, the rules of social conduct.* Most often, it's the little old ladies who exercise this control. Any guest who arrives near a Russian house will be able to see for themselves. Already, as you approach the building, you can see the stalls in the distance and the little old ladies on their feet, following with their eyes all those who enter and commenting animatedly among themselves. You can make fun of them, and young people often do: look at those grandmothers, dying of boredom and distracting themselves with gossip!

But on the other hand, they're also useful. They observe children, their behavior on the street or in the courtyards of city buildings, the "correctness" of young people, strangers on their "territory". They make remarks to the children, and can report their misbehavior to the parents, if, for example, they have broken the courtyard gate, don't greet the neighbors, are insolent, etc. If the parents are intelligent, they can help them. If parents are smart, they can't help but be grateful to those who point out what's wrong with their child. In short, these grandmothers willingly exercise the ancient social control that dates back to the earliest communal societies.[49]

In short, you need to know how to appreciate your neighbors and be considerate towards them, even if they are sometimes a source of annoyance because of their noisy behavior, their exaggerated sociability, when they pull you away from your occupations... Good relations with them can only be useful: you'll avoid certain problems and, what's more, you'll have every chance of finding in your neighbor a good comrade if not a true friend.

11. Body language[50]

It is estimated that 80% of the information we communicate to others is gestural. This gesture also varies from country to country.

A typical Russian gesture is to give oneself several flicks on the glottis with the middle finger, which means "drink vodka". It's the origin of the

---

49. *Ibid.*
50. V. Volovik, *The Secrets of Gesture*, Moscow, ed. Astrel-Ast, 2001.

expression: "to throw some behind the collar", "to throw some behind the tie", i.e. to drink alcohol.

This can also be expressed by repeatedly rubbing the bent index finger against the neck next to the collar. This gesture makes it clear that the person has drunk alcohol, is drunk and generally has a penchant for drinking. And as for the origin of this gesture... The story goes that Peter the Great wanted to reward a talented master-at-arms for special services, and asked him how he wished to be rewarded. He asked the tsar for the privilege of drinking for free in any tavern (the state had a monopoly on vodka at that time). At the request of the master, a special imprint was made on the side of his cheek, which confirmed his right to drink for free. This "document" is the precursor of this particular gesture.

Russians don't count on their fingers like the French. Whereas the French unfold their fingers starting with the thumb, the Russians fold them starting with the little finger to make a fist.

The French and the Russians don't use the same gesture - a gesture that is in itself universal - to mean that there's nothing to be done and that we have to accept the situation: the French throw their hand back as if they were throwing the problem behind them, while the Russians throw their hand forward as if they were taking the problem head-on to get rid of the burden.

To tell someone that they're not quite right in the head, that they don't understand much, that they have "a brainless head", all you have to do is lightly tap the temple with your index finger. But if someone turns his or her index finger energetically on the temple, he or she is either "deranged", has done something crazy, or is behaving out of the ordinary.

If you have a problem with transportation and are in a hurry to get somewhere, you will, of course, hail a car. Given the economic situation, hailing any private car on the road will be much cheaper than a cab. How do you sign for this? The Frenchman waves with the palm of his hand downwards as if to indicate to the driver of the car to stop where he is. The Russian, on the other hand, is hitching a ride by raising his hand (as if he were "voting") and waving to the driver. Russians do exactly the same gesture in school class or during meetings when they want to draw attention to themselves and be able to express themselves.

When Russians want to emphasize their sincerity, they put their hand over their heart, in accordance with the proverbial "hand over the heart". When a Russian raises both hands in the air, he's jokingly showing that he's "surrendering", that he accepts your proposals, that he has no further objections or arguments to put to you to continue the discussion.

Placing the little finger on the seam of the pants signifies total submission and obedience, like a soldier before a general. This gesture appeared after the reforms of Peter I, when the army was reorganized and the tradition of "standing at attention" was introduced. The gesture symbolizes blind submission. But don't rely too much on it, as it can conceal the sarcastic behavior or irony of someone simulating total submission.

If you're shown the thumb and forefinger together with a closed fist, it means "a little, a tiny bit". It can be used in a concrete sense, for example, when you ask that your glass of vodka not be filled to the brim. But the gesture can also be used in an abstract sense, for example, when you want to say that someone lacks ideas or dynamism or fantasy, etc.

During a discussion, you may suddenly see your Russian interlocutor's index finger curved ostentatiously in front of his face. By doing so, he's letting you know that he doesn't believe you, that he remains absolutely skeptical of what you've told him. This gesture comes from the idiomatic verb "to lie flagrantly". - i.e. to lie openly, to say something incredible, to exaggerate strongly - and it can be downright offensive.

A very vulgar gesture that expresses a categorical refusal is that of the "fig" with the thumb passed between the index and middle fingers and the fist clenched. This configuration of three fingers evokes mating, with the thumb as a substitute for the male member. If someone makes this gesture to you, you'll have every reason to take offense; however, it doesn't express contempt so much as a threat. Significantly, this gesture was widely used in propaganda posters in the early years of Soviet rule. It represented a workers' and peasants' "fig" directed against the capitalists and bourgeoisie.

Russia is a multinational country, with a predominantly Russian population. Multinational relations between different nationalities have traditionally been characterized by the borrowing of gestures from other peoples. Thus, a threatening gesture well known to Russians as *sekir-bachka* (axe for the noggin) comes from the Caucasus: it consists, when defying death, in vigorously passing the thumb along the throat. Today, this gesture is used jokingly to signify that "this is an ultimatum" ("If you don't do it, I'll cut your throat!"). It's important not to confuse it with the same gesture meaning "fed up". In this case, you press your hand, palm down, against your throat or chin.

It should be noted that in today's Russia more and more gestures of foreign, especially American origin (including improper gestures) are taken over by the youth from movies or TV shows (such as "Victoria" and others). The French should bear in mind that the gesture they use to mean "se défiler, se tirer" (the French "bras d'honneur") is very similar to a totally indecent Russian gesture, especially if you close your fist while giving small blows on the forearm or the bend of the elbow.

In Russia, it's bad manners to lick one's fingers and pick one's teeth in public - which is accepted in other countries. Unnecessary gesticulation and shifting from one place to another during conversation - characteristic, for example, of Italians - annoy Russians. This prevents them from concentrating and understanding their interlocutor, leading an Italian to conclude that Russians "understand with difficulty".

The gestures used in France to express fear ("les boules"), distrust ("mon œil!") or irritation at repetition ("la barbe!") are incomprehensible to a Russian. They have no gestural equivalent in Russia.

12. Omens, superstitions and prejudices

For a European, knowledge of this subject may not have as much practical value. But if business takes you to Russia, knowledge of this particular aspect of Russian culture will enable you to "penetrate" Russian life more easily, and avoid asking superfluous or even tactless questions.

It has to be said that the Russians are very superstitious, and have probably inherited this trait from their pagan ancestors. The habits and mentality of the pagans were so enduring that, even today, they have resisted the authority of millennia-old Christianity. As the philosophers say, "In Russia, natural scents have not been permanently dissipated by civilization... In Russian nature, in its homes, in its people, one often feels a mystery, absent in Western Europe where natural scents are denatured by civilization.[51]"

Why did this happen? Where does this strange peculiarity in the collective consciousness of an entire people come from? By the way, it doesn't depend on a person's level of education. Let's recall the peculiarities of nature, the austere climate, the history of the country, the Byzantine penchant of the Russians for the mystical. This is largely due to people's belief in dark forces, in diablery that can destroy their plans and intervene in the normal course of life. People may or may not believe in omens, but to this day, they're given a great deal of importance, which adds spice to life in Russia.

If you're a guest in a Russian home, for example, and they open the door for you, you hold out your hand in greeting, but they'll smile and say, "No, no, not on the doorstep" and let you into the apartment. Only then will they shake your hand. If for the French, *the most dreaded day* is Friday the 13th, for the Russians, it's Monday, all the more so if it falls on the 13th. There's a physiological reason for this. After the rest and relaxation of the weekend, the body has trouble getting back into the rhythm of work. For this reason, Russians try not to undertake anything important on Monday. They "drag things out" on this day: surgeons try to avoid complicated operations, captains try not to go out to sea, businessmen try to postpone signing contracts until the following day. We try not to lend money on this day, and not to undertake anything new.

Even today, many Russians fear *dournovo glaza* ("evil eye") - hence the verb *cglazit* ("to cast a curse"). To ward it off, Russians (especially women) wear crosses or pins in the seams of their clothes. Russians are often afraid of upsetting their destiny, dreading the envy of others, and so on. If a Russian suddenly starts telling you about grandiose plans for the future or his unexpected good fortune, or tells you that "he has no problems", he will immediately, out of fear and to "ward off" fate, bang his fist on the wood or spit three times over his left shoulder. He'll also spit three times if he's

---

51. N. A. Berdiayev, *Self-Consciousness. Experience of a Philosophical Autobiography, op. cit.* chapter "Russia and the Western World", ed. DEM, 1990, p. 236.

inadvertently spilled salt, as this is a sign of a coming quarrel and he'll try to make up for his mistake.

And if you forget something at home, you're not afraid to go back for it, are you? The Russian, on the other hand, avoids returning, otherwise "the road will be blocked". If he does have to return, he immediately looks in the mirror and knocks on wood. While laughing at himself, he can't help thinking: "You can't swear to anything.

It's the same unconscious fear that drives him to walk around a black cat, if possible, spitting three times over his left shoulder. This, it is said, can only "help". You'll often see this custom of spitting three times so that nothing untoward happens, to "ward off fate".

Many omens are linked to the *right* or *left side*. For Russians, the left side is the lucky side, the right the unlucky side. Remember that to ward off bad luck, you have to spit three times over your left shoulder. If your left eye itches, it's a good sign; if your right eye itches, it's a bad sign. If your left hand itches, it's a sign that you're about to receive money; if it's the right, you'll owe some. If you stumble with your left foot, good luck awaits you; if with your right, failure.

There are also many prejudices associated with *numbers*. As in many other countries, the number 13 (*tchertova dioujina*, literally "the devil's dozen") is supposed to bring bad luck in Russia, but it's not as obscured as it is in the West: there are houses, apartments, car registrations, air flights, etc., bearing this number.

The number 7 is a special one, and in Old Russian, the word *sedmitsa*, derived from *sem* ("seven"), referred to the week. There are sayings linked to this number, such as "seven gathered will not wait for one", which means that if a guest is late, we won't wait for him to sit down at the table. To express that there's no point in doing things hastily, but that it's better to act with circumspection, the Russian will say: "One measures seven times, one cuts once" (the French equivalent is "on retourne sept fois sa langue dans sa bouche avant de parler").

A number with special significance is 3. An explanation is sought in the trinity of phenomena such as: length, width, height; past, present, future; the trinity in the Christian religion. Many Russian sayings refer to this number:

"to get lost between three fir trees" (used to describe a person embarrassed by the simplest questions) - "to hunt by the three necks" (used to describe a person fired from his job or brutally driven out of his home).

It's funny that educated people, even if they don't believe in these "old wives' tales", know them perfectly well. They laugh at themselves or at others, which does not prevent them from spitting three times over their left shoulder "just in case" and touching wood.

Success awaits anyone who, at the dinner table or in any other situation, finds themselves between two people with the same first name - it's a guarantee of success and wish fulfillment. This situation is often the butt of jokes when you're in company. No matter how good you are at music, try *not to whistle* in a house (even your own), at the office or in a car in the presence of a Russian: he'll be convinced that a financial catastrophe is waiting for you, because your whistling means: "You won't have any money."

And why do Russians throw their cups over their shoulders after drinking their vodka? This "hussar" habit (barbaric for sober people) is even parodied when people want to make fun of Russians. Do you know that this is not due to an overproduction of glass in Russia? It's simply due to the fact that Russians believe in omens: when dishes break, you're luckier the more broken pieces you have. That is why people break dishes at weddings and other celebrations to wish "happiness".

And keeping chipped crockery brings bad luck and poverty.

And if you spilled a glass at the party, don't be distressed by the stained tablecloth. It's a sign that you'll soon be invited back to a party.

If you find yourself with a toddler on your lap who, by surprise, has committed "a little childish mischief", don't grieve: it's a guarantee of a very long life, as this sign indicates that you'll have fun at the child's wedding.

Lately, Russians have discovered a passion for the oriental calendar. Even the most sensible people (regardless of their faith) get excited and deliberate, in the run-up to the New Year, about the Chinese New Year: will it be that of the rooster, the monkey or the horse? This is taken into account in the dress worn on New Year's Day, as well as in many other details that may influence (who knows how?) everyone's private life next year.

Superstition, prejudice, belief in omens and other diableries are part of a country's psychology, itself closely linked to its folklore, history and culture. For this reason, it is worthy of interest and attention.

General conclusion to Chapters 1 and 2

We have discussed some peculiarities connected with the *lifestyle* and *stereotypical behavior* of Russians in their everyday life. They are proof that many aspects of material and social life in Russia are highly original; they hardly date back to time immemorial, and they have hardly changed since. From a superficial point of view, they may seem very strange and incomprehensible to a European, which has, in part, created the myth of the "enigmatic Slavic soul".

But many of the things listed are logical in reality and can be explained by historical, climatic and other conditions: they are well-founded and can even arouse esteem. We must not judge the ethnic and cultural peculiarities of people living in these conditions according to our own scale of values, the one we are familiar with and which will make us say that this is "civilized" (insofar as we can understand it) or is not completely so.

Many details of Russian life may escape us, but there's nothing to stop us borrowing these "manners" to get used to them or to amuse ourselves. Attitudes are easy to imitate.

But it's quite a different matter when it comes to imitating *thoughts* and *reactions to* this or that event. You can't see them, you can't hear them, and they are delivered to the stranger with obvious ill will or affected sincerity. Long years of contact, observation and revision of one's own mistakes are sometimes necessary to penetrate the mysteries of a foreign *mentality*.

The problem in intercultural relations is not that you cannot, for example, drink vodka as confidently as a Russian, endure overheated "Russian baths" as easily, use typical Russian gestures, hold your friend "under the arm", kiss three times or tell "Russian" anecdotes and so on. These are just superficial, outward signs of a certain "Russification". And they don't help mutual understanding with Russians.

No, the problem with intercultural contact comes from elsewhere. It comes from the fact that, along with mother's milk, you've been accustomed to relying on *certain notions and values*. It's hard for you to shake them off, to see the world through "other eyes" and understand the logic of a "Russian brain", to grasp the Russian relationship to reality and the unexpected reactions that follow.

III. TRADITIONAL RUSSIAN MENTALITY AND SOCIAL BEHAVIOR

1. Psychological characteristics of the Russian archetype

According to C. G. Jung, "the archetype is the collective unconscious, the social (norms, representations, prejudices, myths) that marks the consciousness of each individual". With this word, we allude to the "key" to "deciphering" the national character. In fact, the Russians are predominantly what the psychologist C. G. Jung called the "intuitive-sensual psychological type" or, as he also called it, the "intuitive-ethical introvert".

C. G. Jung himself defines what characterizes this type of individual: "a special disposition for presentiment, developed intuition and a particularly sensual perception of life". The inner life (moral and spiritual) is important to him.

It's no coincidence that the notions of "soul" (there are many sayings in the Russian language using this word), "truth" (*pravda* in Russian) and the like are fundamental to Russians.

The first condition of happiness for Russians is to have a *clear conscience*, and for that, our conscience must not feel guilty about a fault towards someone, because that can undermine you.

The Russians' *sensual perception of life* explains why they are more imbued with Eastern irrationalism than Western rationalism, hence their passionate nature. Emotions always take precedence over reason, and passions over

141

material interests. Faced with a difficult problem, Russians are more likely to let themselves be guided by the "voice of the heart" than by reason. Objectivity, cold logic and a serene approach to the matter are very difficult to demand of them.

For the Russian, it's "all or nothing", which expresses their extreme nature.

This tendency towards *extremism* in the Russian archetype explains why Russian history has seen so many excesses, why it has given rise to such inordinate projects. We have in mind, for example, the work of Peter the Great who, in the space of a few years, built a capital on swampland and transformed a backward country into a frontline power. Another example is the blind approval and propagation of Marxist ideas; the naive enthusiasm and espionage under Stalin and, now, the unscrupulous flaunting of their wealth by the "new Russians", and so on.

The Russians' sensual perception of life is expressed in their need for close contact and mutual understanding, and their emotional dependence on those around them. In Russia, people don't withdraw into their private and family lives, but "stick together"; they're used to everyone knowing what's going on, and to feeling that they're among "their own kind".

A *keen sense of other people's moods* is also a characteristic of the Russian people. This quality - attention to the other person's personal life - is rein-forced by another observation: the English, Americans and French don't understand their interlocutor's speech at the slightest mispronunciation, because their attention is focused on the way the speech is constructed, on the words. This is in contrast to the Russian, who usually understands his interlocutor even when he has a very bad pronunciation: his attention is focused on the meaning of the speech, which he intuitively grasps. That's why learning Russian in Russia is so stimulating: no one will reproach you for your mistakes, those around you will even try to understand what you can't express but are implying, and they'll even try to approve of you.

Many people mention that Russians, in their relations with others, are, in a way, childlike *confident*, immediately recognizing the positive sides of anything new - new ideas, new forms - and trying to make everything new their own, easily submitting to the authority of a stronger, more resolute person.

Westerners are characterized by their *verbal, logical thinking,* while Russians are characterized by their *intuitive, original thinking.* Westerners act according to their own will and reasoning, and do not establish a truly "reciprocal" relationship with their interlocutor: they only hear what has been said, without trying to *make assumptions based on* what they have heard.

The Russian relies first on imagination and intuition, and only then on willpower and intelligence. The Russian has more resources: his highly-developed intuition enables him to guess the undertones in what has been said, the mood of his interlocutor, his secret thoughts and so on. This enables him to anticipate future trends and changes. From this stems the widespread idea that Westerners are simpler, more "direct" and open than Russians, because they reason logically and only express what they think. What's more, the Russians are sometimes even referred to as "insincere" and "untruthful". It has to be said that "openness" and "frankness" are interpreted quite differently by Russians.

The highly intuitive Russian guesses beneath the surface of what's going on, the mood and relationship of his interlocutor, and *senses* trends and changes to come. However, transforming his hunches into concrete action is a real problem for him! He thinks long and hard about the serious issues of life. And these long reflections don't necessarily lead to decisions or radical changes in his life. His ability to mobilize for concrete action is atrophied. In critical situations where he needs to muster his willpower and demonstrate independence of mind, he's more inclined to turn to "elders", to a "perceptive person", to the leader, to the state. For this reason, he generally wishes for a "strong state" to protect his interests or, at the very least, help him take charge of his own life.

It's this Russian character trait, for example, that is highlighted in Chekhov's plays. The French, for example, often complain about their difficulty in understanding the meaning of these plays. For them, the heroes of the play spend a few hours suffering incredibly, trying to find a way out of an unpleasant situation, culminating in the inevitable scandal. In the end, the hero is on the verge of hysteria, and the audience expects the denouement at that point. But, alas, no! In the end, everything remains as it was and will continue to be.

The characters in N. Mikhalkov's famous film, *Unfinished Score for a Player Piano*, behave in almost the same way. By the end of the film, it's clear to everyone that the hero can't continue to lead a double life of lies and deceit, that he doesn't have the strength to overcome the humiliation and is ready to end his life... The protagonist misses his suicide, calms down and resigns himself, powerless: "You can't change anything in this life, it's not even worth trying."

Many people in Russia live according to this pattern. In complex situations, the Russian is impulsive: he reaches the point of despair, is on the verge of hysteria. But it's hard for them to make a final decision. Under the threat of conflict, he prefers not to fight but to give in. It is infinitely more important for him to maintain "normal" relations with those around him than to enter into conflict with them, even to the detriment of justice, however important it may be to him.

But the Russian is not just the "intuitive-ethical introvert" described by C. G. Jung. There's another quality that's generally attributed to him. By this we mean his *contradictory* character. Many Russian philosophers and historians have focused on this trait, citing firstly Russia's "position between East and West". Secondly, the fact that *Christianity* and vestiges of *animist* perception of the world are united in the Russian soul. The third reason is Russian history itself, with its *eternal conflict* between the power of the state and the freedom-loving spirit of the people.

And further on, we have to make a harsh but justified assumption: the gradual *destruction of the traditional Russian archetype is clear to* see. The Soviet regime has, in fact, reinforced this apparent contradiction in Russians and contributed to this destruction. Earlier, we referred to the brutal transformations undergone by the Russian archetype with the "housing problem" (see part 2, chap. 1, § 1). And this is just one aspect of the reality - there have been many others.

The Soviet way of life was extremely destructive to the Russian archetype. As A. Solzhenitsyn, in his book *Russia Under the Avalanche,* "the Soviet regime always contributed to the rise and success of the worst individuals" and, we might add, to the destruction of the best. For example, traditional moral principles were replaced by ideological

144

postulates that told people: "He who is not with us is against us", "Give your life in the name of communism", etc., with the appalling result that "the best people in the world are the worst". The appalling result was that, in the 1920s, a young pioneer named Pavel Morozov in a Siberian village denounced his father for hiding bread at the kolkhoz. The young traitor's family was left without bread, and the unfortunate boy was killed in retaliation. Propaganda made him a national hero: pioneer detachments, ships, streets, etc. were named after him. Few at the time gave much thought to the morality of the affair...

The *social structure* of Soviet society also dealt a serious blow to the Russian archetype. The new postulate of the *priority of the working class in* particular contributed to this, with the peasantry (less ideologically important) coming second. And the intelligentsia in history found itself like the *prosloïki* (middle layer of jam) in a cake with a very modest place.

The interests of the intellectual class were neglected, with wages and living conditions lower than those of the working class. Proletarians proudly claimed to belong to the working class. In everyday life, intellectual individuals were treated with condescension, while their heirs were looked down upon with contempt.

This *humiliating situation* inevitably pushed them to conformism, complacency and resourcefulness, to manifest their own loyalty, which in time became a personal conviction. This explains why, at one time, writers went to war against A. Solzhenitsyn, not only for his work, but also for his life. Solzhenitsyn, unable to forgive his inner freedom of spirit and "seeking favors" from the authorities.

The existence of a "nomenklatura" had a devastating effect on society's moral principles. This nomenklatura possessed a distribution system within a narrow circle of "corrupt" chiefs who held each other's elbows and formed a network of "solidary sureties". Worse still, this privileged group allied itself with criminal elements (organized in clans) whose principles they adopted: they were *above the law*. The principle of "joint and several liability" was taken up by the masses and put into practice in everyday life. This gave rise to *prispiki* (falsified figures in reports), theft - when everyone "brought in" (i.e. stole from work) everything that could be useful at home. All this became commonplace in Russian daily life. This reinforced their taste for secrecy, their distrust of all forms of power, and their cynicism.

A unique experiment, with disastrous consequences for the moral health of Russians, was the mass internment of citizens in camps (gulags). The destinies (as well as the mental health) of a great many people were destroyed, and this ordeal accustomed them to the inescapable habit of lying and simulation. Entire generations were gripped by a literally "genetic" fear. And this, in turn, led logically to a pattern of behavior in which it was better to do nothing: "The less you do, the better off you'll be."

Young people, who became the new leaders after the collapse of the Soviet Union, were referred to by older citizens as the first "generation of those who did not experience the Soviet knout". Not having lived through that era, they are afraid of nothing, which explains their dynamism and success in any undertaking.

It seems that, more than anything else, it was *the double standards and hypocrisy* of Soviet life that distorted the Russian archetype. Responsible for this were the disproportionate gulf between the ruling elite and the people, brutal state interference in private life and open arbitrariness. Also contributing were the state's relentless propaganda in the face of the people's total indifference to politics, the omnipresent state atheism in the face of hidden religiosity, official megalomania in the face of the pitiful daily lives of the poor people in the queues, survival through the search for "black" income, the "piston" and petty skulduggery of the "porters" who brought home from work whatever they could use...

But the duplicity of Soviet life manifested itself mainly in the instinctive desire of the ordinary citizen to separate his private life from his public life. This explains the Russians' habitual scowl, lack of friendliness, busyness, suspicion and indifference in public places. They also pretend to show their loyalty, their enthusiasm at work... But in close circles among "their own kind", the Russian is unrecognizable: smiling, cordial, sentimental, open-minded, critical of everything that goes on. This "facade behavior" in public only reinforces the contradictory nature of Russians.

Foreigners don't bother to probe Russian life, to understand the reasons for this inconsistency in the behavior of this or that person in different situations. They have clichés in mind, such as the "duality", the "dichotomy", the enigmatic character and even the hypocrisy and falseness of Russians.[52]

It's not surprising that the example of the fast-moving "rollercoaster", with its flights, falls and sudden reversals, is so well suited to describing the Russian character. For you can find practically everything in a Russian: a tendency towards nationalism and an openness to all cultures and new ideas; brutality and extraordinary compassion; the power to do harm and the power to feel deeply the pain of others; the habit of self-blame, respect for authority and love of freedom, bravery to the point of anarchism. The ability to invest oneself in work to the point of self-sacrifice, forgetting everything else on earth, and the softening, passivity, laziness, desire for contemplation, to take a "cigarette break", to have company and, during work, to pour out their hearts to each other...

All these character traits can be found in Europeans, but they are "retracted" and stifled by the corset of civilization and the rules of etiquette; in Russians, they manifest themselves more fully and openly.

According to the results of ethno-psychological studies, contradictory orientations and stereotyped behaviors clash in the consciousness of Russians today. A questionnaire sent out to 305 people by scientists in a number of major Russian cities revealed the main behavioral trends[53]:

1) with regard to *collectivism* (hospitality, mutual aid, generosity, trust);

2) *moral values* (justice, conscience, righteousness, etc.);

3) vis-à-vis *power* (worship, idol-making, administration, etc.);

4) towards a *better future* (hope in "luck", irresponsibility, carelessness, lack of pragmatism, lack of self-confidence, etc.);

5) towards *quick resolution of vital problems* (the habit of stirring, bravery, high work capacity, heroism, and so on).

Let's take a closer look at the orientations inscribed in Russian consciousness.

---

52. H. Smith, *The Russians, op. cit.*, pp. 5-7; R. Kaiser, *Russia: the People and the Power*, New York, 1976, pp. 390-393.
53. L. G. Potchebut, *Introduction to Ethnic Psychology*, St. Petersburg, 1995, pp. 105-106.

2. Russian consciousness

The scientific literature distinguishes three types of social behaviour[54]:
1) "to be like everyone else", "to be together";
2) "to be a personality";
3) "to be different, to stand out from the crowd".
Each of these orientations determines the individual's behavior and values in life.

The first, the desire to "be like everyone else", to "be with everyone else", is expressed in reasoning such as: "We are a people. The maintenance of cultural traditions and mutual understanding between people is its strength. We find it in traditional societies, where an individual's behavior depends less on his or her personality than on traditions, accepted standards of behavior, religious precepts or ideological slogans.

The "being a personality" orientation manifests itself in the person who wishes to realize himself as an individual, to feel his unique "individuality", his own value, to be a free person. It appeared in Europe, where the Renaissance spread the idea that each individual was unique. This orientation taken to its extreme turns the world into a huge house where neighbors are isolated from each other and no one cares about each other.

The orientation of "not being like the others" is expressed in the wish to live one's own personality; to be original and brilliant, to have a rich and varied life. It is often characteristic of youth, outsiders and artists.

In any society, the three tendencies coexist in each individual and they can resurface according to the circumstances of life and the temperament of the person. However, only one dominates to a greater or lesser extent in the cultural model of each ethnic group.

Russians have mainly as a model of conduct the "need to be like others", to "act together". Russia did not experience the Renaissance and Russian culture did not pay much attention to the idea of uniqueness of each individual. The aspiration to "live like everyone else", to "not stand out from the crowd" is much more common among Russians. And it's no coincidence

---

54. A. Karmin, *Civilization Studies*, St. Petersburg, ed. Lang', 2001: *Civilization Studies: Questions and Answers*, Moscow, ed. Gardariki, 2000, p. 250.

that, when asked: "What's most important to you in life?", Russians answer: "equal opportunities for every individual" (72.3%), and that it's much better to "live like everyone else than to stand out from the crowd" (64.7%). Only 31.9% of Russians[55] want to become an outstanding personality, "not to be like everyone else".

These answers may seem encouraging, as an expression of the Russians' *unconscious democratism.* And, time and again, we have been able to convince ourselves of this quality of the Russians by observing their lifestyle and behavior in everyday life (see § 1 of this chapter). However, we must admit that this orientation often prevents Russians from developing their "personality". It's as if the cohesion of the group somehow deprives him of personal initiative and a sense of responsibility. Of course, these qualities are stifled in Russians from childhood by "collectivist education": several generations of Russians have been "trained" at school by pioneer organizations and "komsomols" (Communist Youth), with their iron discipline and emphasis on social values. From childhood, individual initiative was "stifled" by the cohesion of the group.

On the one hand, the disintegration of the personality within the group gives rise to a "feeling of solidarity" and moral comfort for the individual. It is comforting to "not be alone" in misfortune. But on the other hand, it also breeds irresponsibility in one's behavior, choices and participation in everything. In practice, this often leads to an aggressive attitude on the part of the community towards those who have too strong a personality, who differ from the others in appearance, conduct or way of thinking. The whole group can "jump up and down" against such people.

Life in Russia today favors the energetic and enterprising - those who operated in the "shadow economy" of the former Soviet Union's planned economy and were outside the law. These businessmen now provoke a deafening hostility from the people as a whole, especially the older generation. With this in mind, the average Russian understands perfectly well that to succeed today, you have to know how to take risks, adapt and get rid of old

---

55. N. Tikhonova, "The general state of society and the values of Russians" (results of a public opinion poll on the theme of "the orientations favored by Russians"), in the newspaper *Izvestia*, 1997.

stereotypes and habits. But this is far from being within the reach of every Russian, and, as we now understand, not at all out of laziness. Renouncing one's national archetype is perhaps the hardest thing to do in life.

The desire to "be like everyone else" and "fit in" leads to a preference for traditional rather than innovative professional settings. What's more, in this type of society, people often resort to the *usual extensive economy* and develop the *conservative syndrome*. This is reflected, for example, in Russians' reluctance to destroy their habitual way of life: changing workplace, divorcing the hated wife, doing major work on the apartment or moving house becomes a big deal! And changing their place of residence is so painful for them that they say, not without reason, that "two moves are like one fire". It's easier for them to put up with a few inconveniences than to radically change something and gradually get used to the change.

This trend, set against a backdrop of falling demographics and rising unemployment, is particularly depressing in today's Russia. Political and economic instability should stimulate the individual, make him react, look for any job to survive. The loss of a job is responsible for stress, lack of self-confidence, illness, personality disintegration, family disintegration and other misfortunes. Sociological studies, however, show that unemployed Russians (especially men) often refuse to learn a new trade even when there are no corresponding vacancies on the job market, condemning themselves and their families to hard times.

And it's not stupidity, laziness or the legendary *oblomovshchina* ("let-go" - a word derived from Oblomov, a character in Goncharov's novel), but the famous *conservative syndrome*, generally inherent in the Russian archetype and further reinforced during the Soviet period.

First of all, from childhood, Russians were taught to *choose a job for life*, even if it didn't suit their temperament and aptitudes. The individual was afraid to change jobs, fearing that elsewhere it would be even worse.

Secondly, the idea that the state had invested enormous resources in "free" education and vocational training became engraved in everyone's consciousness. For this reason, everyone felt indebted to the state. This enabled the state to combat executive mobility, and *further bound the law-abiding citizen to the workplace.*

Thirdly, the Soviet state guaranteed its citizens jobs. However, this was primarily in the interests of the state, not the individual. The plan provided for the development of this or that branch, the creation of jobs, the number of specialists in this or that field, and so on. The individual became a cog in a totalitarian state with its paternalistic system. And this suited the majority of the population insofar as it gave them the illusion of stability and confidence in the future. It suited the Russian conservative archetype perfectly.

Since childhood, people had become accustomed to being taken care of and to thinking that the state was obliged to help them. They had unlearned to believe in themselves, their strengths and their abilities. The conservative syndrome only aggravated the already difficult situation of many Russians.

What does this syndrome lead to in practice? The Russian's constant desire to "be like everyone else" can lead to spiritual demands and *moral imperatives* influencing *external standards of conduct* or ideological orientations. Public opinion ("But what will people say?") becomes more important to the individual than self-control and a sense of personal responsibility.

It's logical that, under these conditions, people prefer to blame their actions on fate - on someone else. Close friends, family members and relatives may be responsible for an individual's bad fortune. And it's even more convenient to blame society for one's misfortunes. The easiest way, of course, is to blame the state for one's misfortunes and then ask it for help and compensation for the damage suffered.

Of course, in this context, people become indifferent and irresponsible. This explains why there are so many infantile men and children left to fend for themselves in Russia. In everyday life, this has led to traditional anti-Semitism and, now, to the "anti-Caucasian" syndrome.

Indeed, in recent years in Russia, we have seen the rise of nationalist, racist and even fascist movements, particularly among young people, who did not grow up with ideas such as "international friendship" and others inoculated during the Soviet Union.

During the Soviet era, most of the small-scale fruit and vegetable vendors in the markets of Russia's major cities came from the Caucasus and Central Asia. In the collective consciousness, the image of the "Caucasian" (in everyday life) was already linked to the ability to trick and even bamboozle the confident Russian. The disintegration of the USSR saw the arrival of large numbers of refugees from the southern republics in Russia's major cities, the expansion of the criminal network to include more and more representatives from the Caucasus region, the persecution of Russians in the newly independent republics, the military operations in Chechnya... All these factors contributed, to a large extent, to the rise of Russian nationalism.

In the language, the word *Tchiornie* ("Blacks"), for today's Russian, in no way refers to Africans, but to people from the Caucasus (Chechens, Azerbaijanis, Georgians, Dagestanis and others). The coarse word *Tchourki* refers, with the same contemptuous intonation, to people from the former republics of Central Asia (Uzbeks, Kazakhs, Mongols, Kirghiz and others). It's curious that we don't find this hostility towards the Tatars, to whom Russia's history is closely linked, despite their presence in Russia's major cities. And it is striking that the most "Muslim" city in Russia is Moscow (10% of the population) and that the Tatars are respected there and left in peace.

The ancestral Russian habit of always wanting to "find someone to blame" is very worrying. The Russians' own aspiration to "be like everyone else", to "be together" is not, in practice, without its own problems. On the other hand, this disintegration of the Russian into society is not without a certain warmth and appeal. It generates in the individual a feeling of community with others, a feeling of security, stability and confidence in people, of "brotherhood" and especially of moral well-being, happiness and even euphoria. Subconsciously, this translates into the reasoning: "I'm not alone. So I'm not lost, there will always be someone to help me. Among 'my own kind', I'm not afraid of loneliness and other misfortunes."

It's not without reason that everyone notes how difficult it is for a Russian to adapt in the West, regardless of his or her material living conditions. This is where he differs from the citizens of other nations. Having fallen out of the cozy cocoon of "collective" life, the Russian abroad feels like a child who has lost his mother in the crowd. That's where Russian nostalgia comes from! It's not just nostalgia for birch trees, samovars and other clichés. It is the dejection following a feeling of loneliness never felt before, the impression of being lost in a huge and unknown world, the feeling of having been torn away from a big family.

The general desire to "be like everyone else" is linked to a representation of the world that perceives the *individual* not as an *important entity in himself* (so it is with Europeans) but as *part of a whole - society in this case*. This orientation of the Russian archetype excludes individualism, loneliness, self-absorption, and condemns the egoism and self-indulgence so characteristic of Western society.

At the behavioral level, the wish to "be like everyone else" often boils down to "not be worse than everyone else". This logic can lead the individual to perfectly innocent actions such as, for example, the vain aspiration not to be "dressed worse than others", even if this implies a serious breach in the family budget. Hence the Russian saying: "We meet according to clothes, we accompany according to spirit." This explains why Russians attach so much importance to clothes and the trappings of success (watches, jewelry, cars, etc.). And they are very surprised that in France, for example, it is fashionable not to show off one's wealth and that wealthy people prefer to dress discreetly and in neutral tones. It is considered "bad taste" to show off; this is why the French prefer to drive around in small, discreet cars rather than in a Mercedes.

French proverbs such as: "Pour vivre heureux, vivons cachés" (Florian), "Le plus grand secret du bonheur, c'est d'être bien avec soi" (Fontenelle) remain incomprehensible to a Russian mind, if not absurd. For a Russian, such advice, rather than hinting at discretion, is a reminder of French individualism, which will get them nowhere.

However, this principle of "not being dressed worse than others" is not really so innocent, as it arouses envy and hostility towards "the one who has stepped out of line", who has become richer and "climbed the ladder". This turn of events can poison relationships, even between old friends. Russian folklore abounds in scornful sayings about those who have achieved dazzling success, such as: "Out of the mud, he became a prince", "Once rich, he forgot what brotherhood was all about", and so on. But you won't find any endorsements!

On the other hand, this state of mind also has its positive sides: the ease with which they empathize, the desire to help someone who has fallen "lower" and is experiencing a difficult situation. Living among Russians, you'll be moved to tears to observe the sincerity and energy with which they help someone who has suddenly fallen seriously ill or is going through a period of stress. This help comes not only from close relatives and friends - which is only natural - but also from work colleagues and neighbors who, until now, had never paid any attention to them.

A Russian proverb characterizes the generous individual: "He is ready to give his last shirt". Not necessarily to just anyone, but preferably to those who have suffered misfortune. In this case, the desire to "be like everyone else" prompts him to act, to spontaneously help the person in pain - to raise him to the level of everyone else. It's fair to say that it's precisely in extreme situations, in misfortune, that Russians show their best side.

Thus, we have seen how, in line with the traditional model, the wish to "be like everyone else" is realized in Russia. Over the last 10-15 years, the collapse of the Soviet system has been accompanied by a disaffection with social relations in Russian society, a crisis of state power and ideology, and a bankruptcy of the ideas that once made society a unified whole.

Moral values, standards and lifestyles have changed. It's clear that, in the context of *post-Soviet* society, it's much more difficult for Russians to put into practice the propensity to "be like everyone else". This leads to malaise and depression or, on the contrary, to an increase in destructive activity.

Let's look at other psychological characteristics of Russians.

3. Fatalism

When describing the characteristics of the Russian archetype, we can't fail to mention their *fatalism*, their passive-contemplative relationship with the world. Before undertaking anything, the Russian must think it through.

In the West, the motto is: "Don't put off until tomorrow what you can do today." It speaks to people's practical spirit, their efforts to achieve a result as quickly as possible. But in Russia, we say the opposite with the saying: "Tomorrow is wiser than the day before", in other words: "There's no need to rush before making a decision. Who knows how things will turn out tomorrow?" Russian *caution* stems from negative life experience.

The fatalism of the Russians is linked to the fact that, for them, the notion of "destiny" is very important. This notion also exists in French, but it's not as essential. Ask the average Frenchman if he believes in his destiny, if striving to change it according to his desire is, generally speaking, worth it. Often, the person brought up in European traditions will answer with the utmost assurance: yes, of course, in life, it is possible to achieve - and one must - the goal one has set for oneself.

The Russian will simply smile sadly at this naive assurance. The experience of several generations of ancestors has convinced him that many things are predetermined in this life and that many of them happen independently of his will or desire, no matter what he does. Hence his hope in a miracle and his belief in "great coups de théâtre" (when all problems solve themselves), his trust in strong people (leaders) who can change events. It's also the source of the resignation and humility that Russians show when faced with unexpected blows in life. "It's nothing", "Well, it's fate", the Russian says to himself, and accepts the blow of fate.

The harsh climate, economic difficulties and hardships, the trials of war and history do not prevent the Russians from persevering in their chosen path and coming out on top thanks to their endurance. What is striking about the Russians - and what has long astonished foreigners - is their humility and resilience. This is manifested in their ability to acclimatize without faltering, to resist little by little, in short, everything that has always saved the Russian where someone else would not have "held".

Life in Russia has never been easy, and it's no easier these days. To survive in difficult conditions, to cheat fate, not to lose courage, one must always be careful, patient, believe more in a miracle than in oneself, try to save one's strength. This is how the *stereotypical behavior* of the Russian was gradually created - to *be reasonably hardworking*: after all, you never know when and how the fruits of labor will be taken from you! All it takes is a thunderclap, a war, a crisis, or whatever... and the results of all your efforts go up in smoke!

It may be that the habit of saving one's strength and the reluctance to acquire wealth explain, among many Russians, the indifference and even contempt towards the bourgeois attachment to property and material goods.

For them, devoting one's life to hoarding is an aberration: you take nothing with you to the grave! You have to *live for the moment on earth.*

As for the extreme circumspection of the Russians (the result of their negative experience), it is compensated by other qualities: *audacity*, the *absence of prejudice* and the *taste for risk.* These qualities are the flip side of fatalism, when the individual blindly trusts his destiny, his lucky star. This character trait is reflected in sayings such as "Nothing ventured, nothing gained" and "If you're afraid of the wolf, don't go to the woods". And everyone here has heard of the famous "Russian roulette" game, where you play with death at the rate of a single cartridge per revolver. "Putting the nerves on edge" is considered one of the Russians' favorite occupations. In fact, this inclination to defy fate and take chances is known as "chance" or "Russian luck".

Blind hope in luck makes nonsense of energetic action, which also makes the individual careless, indifferent to the results of his work. He may work "over his head" or remain passive in a critical situation - until the crucial moment when he's forced to "get a move on" in order to survive and avoid unpleasantness.

Of course, "Russian chance" simplifies life, although it's debatable: God only knows how many times this habit of thinking has been successful, led to luck, to "everything running smoothly" where a single mistake has led to technological disasters... In the Russian press, the euphemism "human factor" is often used instead of "Russian chance" when tragedies and disasters resulting from mistakes, lack of professionalism and simply childish irresponsibility are mentioned.

4. The relationship to freedom

An important component of the Russian archetype is the *love of freedom* and its highest expression: *inner freedom, freedom of spirit.*

This reality is often called into question: the liberal press (abroad and in Russia itself) assumes the opposite - that Russians are submissive, passive and even servile. As far back as the Middle Ages, early travelers and ethnologists spoke of the slave-like condition, silent submission and passive stupefaction of the disenfranchised Russians. As, for example, Gerberstein and Olearii in the 16th century, the Marquis de Custine in the 19th and the first Russian "democrat" Radichev. During the perestroika years, the Russian press was inundated with articles on the mass consciousness of Russians, which had remained totalitarian: they were said to accept state arbitrariness, and what's more, they approved of it.

The extension of empire in Russian history refutes the idea that Russians were slavishly subservient. In social life, the Russians' love of freedom was expressed in their rejection of the state. When the Russian peasant realized that state policy would not change ("You might as well bang your head against the wall"), he left to seek happiness elsewhere, moving east and north, settling along countless rivers where he burned and cleared new land in the forest. Historically, the Cossacks are the heirs of these bold, enterprising individuals fleeing the state. The settlement of northern Russia and Siberia was made possible by these *freedom-seeking* individuals, far from state power. They fled and settled new lands. Sooner or later, the state caught up with them. So as not to destroy the insubordinate villages, the *voivodships* (provincial governors) imposed additional sizes (taxes) and let them live on the land. Further afield, the same scenario was repeated. This is how the Russian Empire gradually expanded. If the Russian people had really been submissive and patient, Russia would have been limited to the borders of the Muscovite kingdom; it might then have developed not extensively but intensively, as in European countries. But it was not to be.

Interestingly, the contrasting view of the Russians - as a people capable of rebellion, "cruel and absurd" according to Pushkin - has been reinforced in a totally paradoxical way. Indeed, it may well be that the Russians are the world's best when it comes to popular uprisings, peasant wars and city rebellions. Injustice and impatience have been at the root of the social conflicts of the last three centuries. These confrontations have sometimes taken on proportions and forms that are simply frightening. We need only recall the resistance of *millions of* old believers who, *for three centuries,* opposed the transition to official religion to the point of immolation, not wishing to change the attributes of their faith.

Despite the Russians' fatalism and infinite patience, they are reluctant to accept what they hate, to find *consensus,* to approve what goes against their principles. To give you a very simple example, remember how Russians cross the street at red lights! This totally shocks the Germans... So the widespread idea that Russians are anarchic souls, that they are "insubordinate", is well-founded. That's why we shouldn't put too much faith in the so-called "submission" of the "oppressed" and "eternally suffering" Russian people, or in their innate anarchism.

One of the paradoxes of Russian life is that freedom in the *political regime* has generally not been able to coexist with the *individual lifestyle of* Russians. *Politically,* Russia does not fit the European model of democracy: for almost 400 years, it was an absolute monarchy, then a totalitarian state led by the Bolsheviks.

At the same time, for centuries, *relations between individuals in everyday life were democratic.* Russians, to give an example, dislike conventions, the subtleties of etiquette, polite smiles (which they perceive as false). They are hostile to formal apostrophes by title and position - preferring those by name and patronymic.

Earlier, we mentioned the virtual disappearance of social barriers between Russian families, which in itself reflects the absence of caste prejudice (chap. 2, §7) and the *existence of democratic mores.*

This democratic behavior on the part of Russians extends beyond the family; everywhere, depending on the context, social barriers break down. Friendships can be formed between people from different social classes and even different standards of living, provided they have common passions or interests, or shared memories of childhood and adolescence. These relationships are far more important to them than class membership.

What dominates in the Russian: the tendency towards anarchism or submission? The debate is not over. It would seem that the opposing points of view depend on one's interpretation of a given fact. Unconditional compliance with the law can be seen as "an innate taste for order", but also as "slave-like docility"; lawlessness, on the other hand, can be seen as "the aspiration to live freely, for oneself", as well as a manifestation of "anarchy" and "Russian insubordination". The line between disorder and love of freedom in this sense is quite blurred, which brings us back, in spite of ourselves, to the contradictory and not always consistent character of Russians - to the "rollercoaster" model.

5. The traditions of Russian collectivism

It is generally accepted that *collectivism is the* most outstanding feature of the *Russian archetype.* Practically all the books on the Russian mentality (see Bibliography) refer to it. This "feeling of solidarity" of Russians sometimes arouses envy and admiration of Europeans. This was shown, for example, by the poet R. M. Rilke, who loved Russia and its culture.[56]

The origins of collectivism go back to the pagan times: it is at that time that the primitive character of the Russian archetype was formed. Over time, however, this character trait changed.

Historically, *collectivism* developed as a cultural norm: the thoughts, will and actions of the individual had to conform to the demands of society. The aspiration to community, to the "collective", already existed among the ancestors of the Russians in pagan times. Unlike Christians, public behavior, the general interest and the *primacy of the collective over the individual* were always more important to pagans.

This is why, when making important decisions, the Russian, like the impulsive pagan, will act unconsciously, not only in his own interests, but also taking into account the opinions of those around him.

Thus, *collectivism*, a legacy from the earliest times, was bequeathed with the traditions of paganism. Earlier, we mentioned Russian patriotism, attention to the public interest, the aspiration to unity and community, and other qualities stemming from the mass feeling of wanting, by tradition, "to be like everyone else" and "to be in concert with everyone else". Even today, *collectivism is* considered an inherent Russian quality.

But what is it really?

Joint action by a group of individuals does not necessarily mean the presence of a collective. True collectivism isn't just about solidarity and mutual aid: it's also about acting for the recognition of the collective as a whole and of each of its members. It's a *state of mind that* makes each individual feel like an active member of the collective, with his or her private life serving the common good.

---

56. R. M. Rilke, *Vorpsvede. Auguste Rodin. Letters*, Moscow, ed. Iskusstvo, 1994.

Numerous popular sayings such as "L'union fait la force", "Malheur partagé n'est malheur qu'à moitié", "Il est doux de mourir parmi les siens" and others have expressed this collectivist spirit in Russian behavior. However, rather than an apology for collectivism, these sayings *deny the feeling of solitude* and express the need, for every individual, to have by his side a kindred spirit, a close person with whom to "share his sorrow".

But isn't the negation of solitude the same thing as collectivism?

The 20s and 30s, the years of "building a new society", were imbued with a collectivist spirit. And the acts of heroism during the Second World War are an even better illustration of this state of mind. The history of this period is rich in unprecedented sacrifices in the name of victory over fascism. Then, by tradition, this same spirit manifested itself in the work emulation of the 60s and 70s, and continued until what is now known as the period of "stagnation". Almost all official Soviet literature is based on real events, when people spared neither their strength nor their health, and performed - sometimes at the cost of their lives - feats of hard work for the "good of the fatherland". And it cannot be said that these actions were not spontaneous, that individuals felt threatened and obliged to act at the price of sacrifice. People's behavior back then was sincere and impulsive, especially in times of war.

As far as emulation at work is concerned, it's sometimes hard to argue with people's desire to stand out, to "not be like everyone else", the desire for glory, social recognition and esteem as self-affirmation, a source of personal ambition bringing benefits: decorations, money, a springboard in the professional career...

Today, the assertion that "collectivism" is the Russians' main trait seems open to question. More often than not, researchers *confuse collectivism with the Russians' taste for getting together*, their sense of "sticking together", their desire not to stand out from the crowd by showing originality, their constant concern for "what people will say", their love of public festivals and popular fairs, their tradition of hospitality, etc. - in short, anything that might reflect their behavior in society.

But that's not the essence of collectivism at all! True collectivism can only be said to exist if the individual is aware that he or she is only "a precious cog" in the whole machine, and that the machine could not function without him or her, and would grind to a halt. And the Japanese, so devoted to the interests of their "native" company and their homeland, are probably the only people with this mindset!

Unfortunately, we have to admit that *this state of mind is not entirely characteristic of the Russians*, even if their behavior is still marked by a genuine collectivist spirit inherited from the past.

We tend to agree with the philosopher I. Ilyine, for whom the Russian is the opposite, with his taste for *individualization*[57], his innate individualism, his tendency to be "himself", to defend his ideas, to have his opinion on everything. According to Ilyine, Russia's great plains facilitated people's isolation; there was no need to "live in harmony" with one another, to put up with one's neighbor at all times. The density of a cramped population, so characteristic of the West, accustomed people to organizing themselves to get along. But for the Russians, it was easier to run away somewhere else than to adapt to someone or cooperate. The age-old influence of Asian nomadism (Tatars) dispersed people even further; it destroyed the spirit of collectivism.

And under Soviet rule, the spirit of collectivism was perverted, life accustomed everyone to separating their public (state) life from their private life, to opposing state interference in their private lives in every possible way, and to despising those who served the state in this unjust task. Collective enthusiasm existed only on the screen and in the pages of official art, and expressing personal enthusiasm within the community was merely a means of boosting one's career, a way of obtaining material goods and recognition from one's entourage. With the collapse of the Soviet Union and the destruction of state structures (including free education and medicine), every Russian was left to fend for himself.

So the claim that all Russians are great collectivists (especially in today's Russia) is highly debatable.

---

57. I. Ilyin, *On Future Russia*: Selected Articles, edited by N. P. Poltoratskii, Moscow, Voenizdat ed., 1993, pp. 118-120.

6. The clan system in contemporary Russian society

In the first paragraph of this chapter (on the Russian archetype), we already mentioned the *destructive effects* of joint and several liability *on the Russian archetype.*

At the end of the Soviet regime, as ideological propaganda became less pervasive, the *traditional aspects* of Russian collectivism were perverted and took on a different meaning, even if they remained the same in appearance. Thus, in the 1970s, the *clan system was* introduced. *Clans* were particularly powerful in the cultural sphere - cinema, theater, painting and literature, television, prestigious university chairs, journalism. Each creative profession had its own narrow circle of "chosen ones". A clan was characterized by its attentiveness to "its own" (as well as to its wife, husband and children) and its coldness (and even annoyance) towards those who sought to "break in" to this circle.

Entry into a clan was only possible through "one's own", through relatives, friends or classmates, after having proved one's loyalty and attachment to the clan's common interests. This system of clan formation exists in all areas of Russian life. This defense, and more precisely the circle's *solidary guarantee*, gives rise to anomalies: the children of singers become singers, even if they have no voice; the children of popular actors become mediocre directors; those of university professors inevitably teach alongside their parents; as for the children of diplomats, they inevitably make their careers in the Ministry of Foreign Affairs, and so on. As if there were no other path for them.

And what's even more astonishing is that this trend is so deeply rooted in society's traditions that not even the fall of the Soviet Empire was able to put an end to it. On the contrary, in recent years it has developed into absurd forms that are obvious to anyone. Whatever sphere of activity you're in in Russia, you'll encounter multiple, ramified clans everywhere, made up not only of relatives but also of friends, classmates, neighbors - depending on the prestige of the sphere of activity. In Russian, this is known as "having the plunger", and it's the best way to ensure that all doors open to you.

Each clan generally forms horizontally, and is made up of people of roughly the same age. They are usually not so much relatives and friends (as in other countries) as classmates, faculty classmates, i.e. people united by common interests and the same profession. At present, for example, the Russian economy and the country's political elite are made up of 3-4 classes of economists and lawyers who have graduated from the prestigious universities of St. Petersburg and who act "hand in hand". Previously, this niche was occupied by physicists and mathematicians from Moscow's elite institutions. Over the past two years, the succession of elites has relegated "Muscovites" to working outside the country's borders, mainly in industrialized countries such as Europe and the USA.

It is practically impossible to break the system of clan solidarity. And not only because it corresponds to an old tradition. The consolidation of a society without laws or justice is necessary, one way or another, to enable work in production and, even more so, in the economy.

And *clans play a stabilizing role in* relation to this. For while laws cannot maintain order, it can be established on the basis of moral criteria: trust and the personal relationships associated with professionalism. In any sphere of activity, personal trust in the individual is paramount. This is how a clan is formed.

On the one hand, this is not bad in itself, as clans at least help to maintain a certain stability and line of continuity in society.

On the other hand, it prevents talented outsiders from entering any sphere of activity. And it makes any attempt of an active person outside the clan useless. It also reinforces conservative stereotypes in any activity, prevents opposition and encourages the repetition of mistakes. Ultimately, true professionalism and clanism are incompatible. They are mutually exclusive.

The Russians' highly developed conformism creates a group *cohesion* that, from the outside, resembles collectivism. In practice, this leads to a silent solidarity between all members of society. The consequences of this joint guarantee can only be negative for the evolution of society, its economy, corruption and so on. This system hampers tax collection, the fight against the black economy and, in general, makes it impossible to trust anyone.

This conformity also has, however, positive aspects. It increases the possibilities for each individual to adapt within society.

In a difficult situation, Russians follow this pattern: they pick up the phone and call everyone they know. This old-fashioned reflex of obtaining something "through an acquaintance", "by piston", is part of the Russian way of life.

Group cohesion and surety act primarily on the behavior of people working in companies and public administrations, i.e. where it's possible to cheat on taxes, hide additional income from the tax inspectorate and so on. And in these companies, the authoritative figure is generally not the director or head of the establishment, but a simple accountant with economic training, capable of presenting a financial report "in the best light" and concealing his boss's embezzlement for a bribe. He himself remains in the shadows, "not standing out from the crowd". This is how the joint guarantee is reinforced. Putting an end to it from within is virtually impossible; only strong pressure from above could do it, and even then, success is not guaranteed.

In situations where people are not bound by common interests, when they are forced against their will to act autonomously and take responsibility for their actions, when economic stimuli are redoubled, this group cohesion quickly disappears. It is, for example, less and less present in private companies and businesses, especially after the 1998 crisis and when many shell companies with non-professional staff (made up of relatives, childhood friends, etc.) disintegrated and were reduced to nothing.

7. Relationship with the State

An important feature of the Russian archetype is the *sense of nationhood*, the feeling that state policy has a bearing on the fate of the individual, a matter of personal interest to the Russian. In this sense, the Russians are an *extremely politicized* people: regardless of their level of education or profession, every Russian today closely follows the press and what's going on in the "antechamber of power", as if his or her personal life and well-being depended on it.

At the same time, the Russian archetype is characterized by an innate fear of, and voluntary submission to, the state. From the earliest times, the state has been perceived by Russians - just like the tsar and God - as the supreme judge and, at the same time, as a defender and protector.

Where does it come from?

It is claimed that the Russians have never been a simple nation: they have always been a "super-nation", a "super-ethnic group", the "weft of a fabric embroidered by other nations"[58], a very rare ethnic event. The ethnic roots of the Russians are interwoven with those of the Slavs, the Finns, the Turks and God knows what other tribes. This means that the Russian state has never been exclusively national. There have always been many foreigners among the Russian tsars and in the Russian state apparatus. And maintaining the unity and integrity of such a vast country could only be ensured by a heterogeneous state. So the Russians are the *result*, not the beginning, of *a process. From* the outset, they have been more concerned with the *political* idea than the national one; historically, they have developed a political consciousness. For example, even in the not-too-distant Soviet era, 80% of Russians perceived and referred to themselves as "Soviets", i.e. not in terms of their nationality, but in terms of their political system. It's hardly surprising that, in Russian culture, the power of the state has become the object of a special cult.

Many people ask: "Why and how did such a powerful state come into being in Russia? Why is it so powerful in the face of the individual?" To answer this question, we need to analyze the historical facts.

For a long period in its history, Russia was a fortress under siege. According to the calculations of the historian S. Soloviev, Russia was attacked every four years between 800 and 1237. From 1240 to 1462, 200 (!) enemy incursions were recorded. From 1368 to 1893 (in the space of 525 years), there were 329 years of war! In all, Russia has experienced *one year of peace for every two years of war*[59]! Few countries have had this experience: Russia has constantly had to defend its independence and sovereignty. As the philosopher Ivan Ilyine (1882-1954) put it: "Over the centuries, our concern was not for better housing or a better life, but simply to eat better, hold out, avoid immediate misfortune, overcome daily dangers; it was not so much a question of obtaining justice and happiness as of defeating the enemy or misfortune...".

---

58. A. I. Solzhenitsyn, *Russia Under the Avalanche*, Moscow, Russkiy Put' ed., 2001, p. 114.
59. See N. Losskiï, *Le Caractère du peuple russe*, books 1 and 2, ed. Posev, 1957, book 1, p. 49.

Russia's particular history reflects *the development of its political awareness: mobilization and defense of its external borders* have been considerably stepped up. This was a gradual process. In ancient Russia, princes were not autocrats, and their social relations were highly democratic. The prince of yesteryear *had no absolute power*, and this power was delegated to him under certain conditions. "The prince was the first among equals and, like a father, had to be severe and just."

This is why, since ancient times, the Russian people have maintained *a* strict but fair *ideal of power*. And if the prince broke these rules, he was reprimanded and dismissed. Prince Andrei Bogolioubskii, for example, wanted to rule "despotically" in the 11th century, but was assassinated following a plot by the "boïards" (or "boyars", as the nobles were called in Slavic countries). To assert that "autocracy has always been inherent in the Russian people" is an untruth that should not be propagated. The idea of a supreme power gradually appeared and asserted itself in Rus under the influence of the Tataro-Mongols. Mongol khans ruled Russia for several centuries, and Russian princes retained their power and freedom of action within the country. But the grand prince was no longer elected, but *appointed by the khan.* And the Russian prince had to pay homage to the khan under conditions that were humiliating for the Russians. The power of the khans was unlimited and absolutely despotic. It was from this period onwards (13th-14th century) that princely power began to acquire monarchical features, and the principle of equality between the prince and his *drujina* disappeared. Even the term *droujina* disappeared from common usage, to be replaced by "court" as in Europe. The prince's way of governing was undoubtedly influenced by his Asian conquerors.

Over time, this form of government gradually penetrated the political consciousness of the Russians. Subjects began to depend entirely on the will and whims of the prince; it became a habit, then a tradition. And the relationship between master and servant was gradually transformed along these lines.

Thus was born in the Moscow state a power that could *exist outside and above the law.* This power gradually acquired a sacred character. As the religious philosopher P. Florenskii noted, "in the consciousness of the Russian people, absolute power is neither a right nor a formality, but the will of God". Thus, the power of the tsar was perceived not as a concept of law but as a religious idea.

With the fall of Byzantium in the 15th century, the Muscovite princes took on the title of "tsar" (from the Latin *Caesar*, "Caesar") and, in 1547, Ivan the Terrible was crowned tsar. The title "tsar" became official, it was not a title but rather a divine appellation with a mystical meaning. "The Tsar's will is God's will", he was "God's administrator on earth", and his power was unlimited, allowing for total arbitrariness, as in the reign of Ivan the Terrible. And from 1649, the *person of the tsar* was directly identified with the state in the code of the Holy Synod. The sacralization of the monarch (and at the same time that of the state) was further strengthened under Peter the Great. During his reign, the monarch definitively assumed the functions of a patriarch. From the 18th century onwards, all events in the life of the emperor and his family were celebrated by the people as religious festivals, with the active support of the Orthodox Church.

The historical context of the time thus contributed to the emergence of autocracy in Russia, which gradually became identified with the state in the minds of citizens. And the state power consolidated over the centuries became an essential component of Russian culture. It was perceived by the people as the only defense against enemies, the guarantor of order and security in society. Relations between power and population were traditionally patriarchal and familial: the tsar was the "little father", the head of the "Russian line", and the "sovereign's children" (the people) were obliged to carry out all his orders, at the risk of seeing the line perish. The tsar, although severe, was just, and this belief was firmly anchored in the popular consciousness. All the misfortunes of the people came from the officials who deceived the sovereign and distorted his will.

For centuries, such dependence accustomed Russians to the idea that the life of the individual depended not on the law, but on the "will of the tsar", and that it was "by bowing to the tsar" that one "found the truth". But more often than not, they convinced themselves that they had to endure, because "God is in heaven and the tsar is far away". Traditionally, power in Russia is maintained through fear. The common people fear the town sergeant (the

167

policeman), who in turn fears the town governor, who in turn fears his department head, and so on up to the Tsar. In the popular consciousness, power has always been associated with the "master" (the lord): we can only protect ourselves from misfortune and find justice in a concrete person, invested with power, and not by resorting to the law.

In our opinion, this relationship to power did not change in the Soviet era, which put into practice the old principle: "It's not the law but concrete people who govern." In Soviet times, "decisions of the Communist Party and the State" and "decrees of the Central Committee of the Communist Party of the Soviet Union" carried more weight than laws or the constitution.

This practice, handed down from one generation to the next, encouraged people to bypass the law when deciding on the most vital issues. And the traditional fear of any representative of power reached its apogee in the Soviet era.

Today's Russians have not changed their attitude towards law and power. As in the past, people fear the town sergeant, and today's Russian citizen does not trust the police and is afraid of them. The relationship between the individual and the state in today's Russia differs from that in the West. In the West, the state acts as a *guarantor of the individual* in his or her relationship with society, whereas in Russia, society - not the individual - is at the heart of the relationship between the state and the individual. *In this respect, Russia is closer to Eastern than to Western civilization.*

These observations do not, however, lead us to conclude that Russians are predisposed to a totalitarian society. For them, the ideal state is one that looks after the interests of "the people" and not just those of the state apparatus. In addition to maintaining order and security, it would also have a social function, organizing life at the individual level.

The patriarchal type of society (which has been rooted in the Russian archetype for centuries) means that people fear the state, but are also *entitled to make demands of it in* the same way as a son makes demands of his father: they can demand *justice, assistance, compensation for what has been lost,* without giving anything in return. *It is* precisely in this state of mind that we are witnessing waves of discontent in Russia: people are demanding their salaries, maintaining order, fighting crime, repairing the heating system, protesting against the closure of mines or a popular TV channel, etc., waving flags in front of public administrations in Moscow. Political naïveté and demands on the state prevent them from understanding that justice must be sought elsewhere, and that it is better to call to account the actual people behind this illegality rather than the weakened state. But it's still too early to abandon the cultural tradition forged by history.

According to analysts[60], the pyramid is the model that best represents today's society for the majority of Russians (55.6%). At its base are the majority of the country's population; at the top, the country's political and economic elite, crowned by its "patriarch", the Tsar, the General Secretary of the Communist Party or the President. From an early age, Russians have been imbued with this model of society.

But it's interesting to note that younger people, who make up a third of today's population, see today's society as two groups with virtually no communication between them: the smaller vase represents the "new rich", and the larger, the rest of the country's population. It goes without saying that this construction lacks stability and solidity.

8. The Russian sense of justice

A sense of justice means respecting the law, freely fulfilling one's public duties and private commitments, and organizing one's life without committing a crime. A sense of justice is based on self-respect, inner discipline, mutual respect and trust between citizens and each other, and between citizens and the State. And this is in line with the profound observation of the philosopher Ivan Ilyine: "The more firmly and deeply rooted the sense of justice is in the people, the easier it is to govern them, and the less dangerous a weak power will prove to be[61]."

The Russians' sense of justice has a heavy historical legacy: the apanage discord and Tatar yoke of the Middle Ages, the influence of nomadism and brigandage in the southeast, the countless popular uprisings, revolts and

---

60. *Les Citoyens de Russie: leur sentiment de bien-être et la société dans lequel ils aimeraient vivre*, analysis commissioned by the Moscow office of the Ebert Foundation, Moscow, 1998, p. 20.
61. I. Ilyine, *On Future Russia, op. cit.* p. 278-279.

incessant palace revolutions of the 16th and 18th centuries, the revolutionary movement of the 19th century, the Soviet regime of the 20th century... "All this only developed those temperamental traits that can be characterized as *lack of discipline*, Slavic *individualism*, Slavic *taste for anarchy*, natural *ardor*" (I. A. Ilyine).

Little by little, a sense of justice has taken root in the Russian people, which only a strong power can withstand ("stern leadership"). Weak power has only ever given rise - and will do so for a long time to come - to a feeling of total permissiveness, corruption and general decadence.[62]

The principle "God is in the sky and the tsar is far away" expresses the people's relationship with the established order (the state, the law, the rules). And this relationship could be defined as follows: there's no point in seeking justice, there's no point in hoping for it... For this reason, everyone is free to do as they please (hence the despotism of rigor and peasant deceit). People rarely have any admiration for an individual's uprightness or obedience to the law. Instead, Russian folklore abounds in popular "wisdoms" such as: "He went straight ahead and fell into the trap"; "It's not by going straight ahead but by taking circuitous routes that you'll succeed", and there's even the saying: "If you're not caught, it's because you're not a thief." The ruse is generally approved. The logic here is quite simple: since life is such that "God is in the sky and the tsar is far away", you can only rely on yourself. That's why you can afford more than the law allows. There's no need to be afraid of breaking the law, of changing "your destiny". It can't get any worse anyway. Patience has its limits, and discipline is only acceptable within certain limits. Russia is a vast, flat territory, and you can always flee and seek "freedom" further afield.

In Russia, it's *not so much the laws as the people who enforce them that are important*. The saying "The law is the reins of the horse that you hold and drive forward with the spur" expresses the traditional relationship of the people to justice, where, "without an individual approach", the case will drag on and on, before finally disappearing into the red tape of the bureaucratic machine. To win a case (regardless of whether you're right or wrong), you

---

62. *Ibid.*

have to be able to "put your hand in the purse", i.e. give a bribe. This reflects the depravity and impotence of the legal system.

A century ago, peasants made up the overwhelming majority of the country, and serfdom, which had kept them in a state of slavery, was not abolished until 1861. The landowners, enemies of emancipation, decided the fate of the serfs themselves. This is the origin of the expression about the master who "arrives to judge". And in Soviet times, this little phrase was transformed into the axiom "The boss is always right". The notion of the boss in this case was interpreted in the broadest sense: for the employee, it meant the manager; for the manager, his hierarchy; for the hierarchy, the "decisions of the party and the state" in the context of five-year plans, decrees to combat... alcoholism, non-conformism and so on.

Before perestroika, the overwhelming majority of lawyers specialized in criminal law (on the prosecution side). Very few specialized in civil law (and even fewer in economic law). In the USSR, legislation prohibited intervention in the economy. It was, so to speak, the Communist Party that had appropriated the role of court. It discredited justice, transforming it into a repressive body. The party had its "justice and police organs" (*the party committee*, extremely feared by all) - in every company, every administration, every organization. Officially, legislation existed, but according to tradition, it was *not the law* but its *interpretation* that counted. And it was not professional jurists who processed and handed down judgments, but specialists in "socialist morality" - party careerists.

So, disenfranchised people and impotent courts in Russia do not date from today or from the Soviet era, but go back much further. Today the economic situation has deteriorated to the maximum and it is more crucial than ever to have a properly functioning justice system. It takes centuries of experience to create an effective legal and judicial system. And individuals who find themselves face-to-face with officials have nowhere to turn for a judgment "according to justice" if not "according to law". And when morality and good morals are not defended by justice, they become depraved. Any country deprived of justice leaves the field open to individuals devoid of any morality to prosper, enrich themselves and take power. This leads to a devaluation of ethics and an even blunter sense of justice.

Moral consciousness in Russia[63] has always prevailed over *political conscious-ness* or the *notion of law* (but not always over economics). This can be summarized as follows: every act is considered by the Russians from the moral point of view as long as it is *fair*. The notion of law is not very developed in Russia; it is compensated by moral relationships between individuals.

What conclusions can we draw from this? In Europe, for example, you can work in science or do research with someone you don't like or don't like. In Russia, for any activity to be successful - including business - people have to establish personal relationships based on trust, due to the lack of precise professional rules and criteria, whatever the type of activity. In business relationships, unfortunately, you have to convince yourself that the most important thing to succeed in your project (signing a contract, obtaining a major order, etc.) is to find the right key people and "get along with them" (using bribes).

This principle fuels the corruption of today's officials, parliamentarians, judges, generals, etc. The Russians have not yet acquired true professionalism in the European sense, with *impersonal business relationships* based on the obligations of each partner. In Russia, the human, emotional factor is decisive in business relationships based on subjectivity and motivated by self-interest or enthusiasm. For this reason, a "good", trusting relationship with the "right" partner is far more important than the rules and behavior to be adopted during such relationships. Above all, "paperwork" (contracts, agreements, etc.) is particularly unreliable.

When establishing business relations with Russians, there's no point in relying on the country's legislation, documents, supervisory bodies, laws and so on. The only thing that counts is the personal contacts you make with people, while making sure you always keep them under control.

In recent years, with the end of Soviet legislation, the Russians' notion of the law, which was not very developed, has even weakened, and moral (personal) relationships have only become more important in their eyes. But this morality also has a conservative character: it is based on a tacit

---

63. K. A. Aboulkhanova, "Russian mentality: cross-cultural and typological approaches", from *Russian mentality: questions of psychological theory and practice*, Moscow, published by the Institute of Psychology of the Russian Academy of Sciences, 1997, p. 23.

relationship between partners according to the principle: "You give me something, you get something." And this formula works in all areas of relationships. Reluctance to make mutual concessions can lead to a total breakdown in business relations.

How can we explain this lag in the Russians' notion of right? According to analysts[64], it is psychologically linked to the *absence of a developed sense of self-respect*. Most Russians don't feel that they are the architects of their own lives or in control of their own destiny; they always defer to the state, to their hierarchy, when it comes to solving their problems, making choices and acting on them. Let's not forget the Russian's innate *fear of* the state and power. Of course, this is less true of young people, who were raised with perestroika.

Take Europeans and Americans, for example, with their well-developed sense of personal dignity. They have not had the experience of the Russians. This confidence in themselves and their abilities creates initiative, self-assurance and an entrepreneurial spirit that annoys the Russians; they may even perceive these qualities as arrogance and stupidity!

With Russians, in situations where their personality (their "self") is crushed, protest can take the form of deeply wounded self-esteem, creating complexes within them. When dealing with Russians, you need to bear in mind their particular self-esteem, their exacerbated susceptibility and mistrust. Because of their impulsive and explosive nature, you need to show them as much thoughtfulness and tact as possible. Wounded self-esteem, coupled with inner freedom, can lead Russians to actions totally unforeseeable to a European, even to the point of resorting to violence and the desire for revenge.

---

64. See note 60.

9. Relationship to property

"Everything that belongs to the kolkhoz belongs to me".
(proverb from the lyrics of a Soviet folk song).

"You won't take anything with you to your grave".
(popular Russian saying).

Historically, *the* Russian peasant's relationship to property was, it could be said, highly unusual. Indeed, the Russian cultural archetype has no well-established notion of ownership capable of distinguishing "what is mine from what is not (and belongs to others)". Historically, the Russian peasant did *not differentiate between the right of ownership, usufruct and the right of disposal.* This is probably due to the direct influence of peasant community traditions, which determined all questions of private property.

In the observations of foreign travelers, the lightness with which the Russian peasant could, without unnecessary remorse, appropriate something that didn't belong to him was often noted. Poverty, in this case, morally justified theft. What's more, the good-natured peasant considered theft to be only a *material and not a moral* injury to the victim.

It used to happen (and may still happen) that when the Russian borrowed something, "borrowing" was understood in the sense of "simply taking", with no intention of returning what was borrowed. The collectivist consciousness, the constant gaze on "what others have", favored this state of mind: the individual did not consider it a sin that the rich "shared", as it were, with those who needed it most. However, even with this conviction, if you're caught red-handed, it's shameful to steal. But more often than not, it's just a case of "no harm, no foul." Because philosophically speaking, there's nothing shameful about it, and in fact, it's quite right.

The lack of distinction between what's mine and what isn't has historical causes. The vast majority of Russians had no concept of personal autonomy, having so often worked for "foreigners": Tatars, the royal treasury, the tsar, the *barin* (master), party bureaucrats and so on.

The inability to plan one's life out of habit leads to a desire to "live in the moment", "here and now", before what you've earned is taken away from you. The logic is simple: "There's no point today in making plans for tomorrow: a new master will come and give new orders." It's for this reason that the ant-like patience required to build a home, work for oneself and accumulate wealth is something totally absurd and pointless for Russians, since, in any case, "You won't take anything with you to your grave". Which explains why they like to be so generous when they spend money, even if it hasn't been earned easily. Russian tourists are renowned and appreciated the world over for their extremely generous tipping, and during the years of Soviet rule, the profligate nature of the Soviet economy only reinforced this stereotypical behavior.

Remember that entire generations of Soviets were brought up with the idea that public interest took precedence over personal interest. Asking for a pay rise privately was considered "greed" (one "appropriated" a share for oneself without thinking of the general interest). The worst thing you could be accused of in those days was "putting your personal interests above the public interest". It could get you fired, and your reputation damaged forever.

This inability to distinguish between what's theirs and what's someone else's should not, however, be misinterpreted as "a Russian penchant for thievery" (which sometimes gives rise to such claims). This practice calls for a much more open mind. Of course, the Russian is capable of borrowing money and "forgetting" to pay it back, on the pretext that the lender doesn't really need the money at that moment, he has "enough as it is": for example, "he's rich", "he's lucky", and so on. In this way, you can take someone else's property without any problems of conscience, simply because "I need it more right now" than "my victim".

But at the same time, Russians have the opposite inclination. Always without hesitation and without thinking, they are capable of giving you everything they have left in order to share with the person who finds themselves in a difficult situation. It's a Russian tradition to "give away your last shirt". The literature is full of accounts of this Russian "generosity" that so strikes Westerners[65]. Although things have changed somewhat in today's Russia.

---

65. Memoirs of participants in the Second World War: *The Germans about the Russians*, collection, Moscow, Stolitsa ed., 1995.

It's interesting to note that theft is rarely condemned in Russian sayings; on the contrary, many expressions such as "what's lying around belongs to the thief" and others of the same style express contempt for the carelessness that made the theft possible. Clearly, popular wisdom does not so much condemn the thief as the fool and careless person who gave him the opportunity to steal.

This peculiarity of the Russian mentality reflects, if not a hostile attitude, at least *an unreceptive, indifferent attitude towards positivism and practicality*, and a lack of interest in civilization and material values. This explains other Russian "idiosyncrasies", such as their love of grand gestures, which leads them to spend lavishly, the poor upkeep and dirtiness of Russian homes and toilets, and the neglected state of gardens and parks. The Russians' special relationship with property is further proof that all our faults are merely an extension of our qualities.

Moral principles therefore do not exist in a pure state, but are always the *result of history, of economic, political and other relations between the individual and society*. The Russians' nascent sense of property, its destruction, the absence of it or indifference to it, the lack of distinction between what is yours and what is someone else's, are constant features of the Russian archetype. They haven't disappeared over time, but have taken root in the mind and can be observed right up to the present day.

10. Relationship with hierarchy

Let's not forget once again that the traditional relationship between ordinary people and those with power was quite democratic in ancient Russia. We know that in the northern cities of Novgorod, for example, there was a *vetche* (people's assembly in old Russia) - the prototype of parliament. Only the cruelty of Ivan the Terrible was able to put an end to this democratic institution.

It was only later, from the 16th century onwards, that another trend, brought by the Tataro-Mongols, prevailed in the Muscovite kingdom. And it was under their influence that a type of social relationship between "master and servant", in its Asian version, was reinforced in Russia. The behavior of an individual in public and private life came to be judged according to his *tchin* ("rank") - in other words, his place in the social hierarchy.

And so, little by little, new patterns of personal behavior took shape: a particularly *servile psychology* and a morality reinforced by the repressed Russian sense of self-respect (see *above*). The same individual can be scornful and haughty towards an inferior and, one minute later, completely change his behavior and be servile towards a superior.

This gave rise to the Russian saying, the cynicism of which aptly reflects the relationships still prevalent in every work collective: "You're the boss and I'm an idiot. I'm the boss, you're an idiot." In practice, this means that the powerless individual must not consider himself a person. His only value is to be a cog in society, a part of the machine. He has no right to discuss or defend his opinion before a superior. In any case, even if he's right, the attempt will end badly for him. For centuries, the Russian has been told: "Don't argue with your superiors: they know better than you. And if you start arguing, it will cost you dearly."

This slavish psychology is to be condemned. But we can also try to understand it as an imposed model of behavior, the result of a fatalistic attitude to life and Russian conformism.

Why, despite the appalling working conditions and unfair way of life, the wages unpaid for months on end and the obvious deterioration in relations between workers and employers (all things the Westerner has no idea about), do people so rarely demonstrate in protest?

At the beginning of 2002, Argentine citizens, panic-stricken by the 50% devaluation of their currency, organized nationwide demonstrations and deposed *five* (!) of their presidents one after the other. In Russia, after the 1998 crisis, the rouble was devalued by 400%, and millions of people saw all their savings melt away, lost their jobs and the hope of regaining their previous material status... It would never have occurred to anyone, however, to set up barricades or legally resort to the instruments of democracy in place: The liberal press, for their part, trot out the old clichés about the Russians' long-standing submissiveness...

As sociological studies show[66], from 1995 to 1998, most Russians offered passive resistance to the indolent course of reforms. This was evidenced

---

66. See note 63.

by the production of goods and services, which continued despite unpaid wages or their considerable decline. People continue to work for derisory wages! This is hardly conceivable in market economies.

This form of passive opposition, experienced by many generations, leads to the *habit* of *putting up with things*. The worst consequence is that people lose their sense of danger. Analysts[67] call this the "boiled frog phenomenon". We know that the frog is a cold-blooded animal and that its internal temperature corresponds to its external one. If plunged into boiling water, the difference in temperature signals danger and the frog leaps out of the water. But if you put it in water that you heat up gradually, it has time to bring its internal temperature into line with its external temperature while it cooks.

The Russian aspires to create a *stable situation*: living conditions in Russia are often extreme, but there's always a desire to live. And everyone tries to adapt to all living conditions, to endure, to "tighten their belts" in the hope that, one way or another, "luck will smile on them" and they'll get by... The fatalism and conformism typical of Russians has taught them that there's no point in resorting to brutal actions, otherwise "things can get worse".

Finally, the apathy and lack of concerted action of today's Russians can only arouse pity and gloomy forebodings for the future. But, at the same time, one cannot help but feel respect for the Russians' stoicism, infinite patience and sensible calm. What kind of riots can be organized in a country where atomic reactors and a number of other particularly dangerous chemical and radiation products are worn out? And can we forget the harsh Russian winter? All it takes is a power failure or a rupture in the heating pipes during the bitter January cold for the population of an entire city to be condemned to die in silence... So much for riots and revolts! At 30°C, crowds can go on a nightly rampage, robbing stores without risking freezing to death. Comparing Argentina and Russia makes no sense, just as it's wrong to resort to hackneyed myths about Russian submissiveness.

Stoicism, infinite *patience*, the ability to create a *stable situation*, *sensible calm*, the *ability to survive* in the most incredible conditions, the ability to

---

67. Facts taken from A. Gorianin, *Myths about Russia and the Spirit of the Nation*, Moscow, ed. Pentagraphic, 2002, pp. 138 and 249.

find a way out where another would give up, the inability (lack of desire) to defend one's own interests, the ability to submit to difficult circumstances without getting worked up. In our opinion, the combination of Russians' training and motivation creates the right conditions for any employer in Russia to collaborate in business.

11. The traditional attitude of Russians towards foreigners

"Tell me who you haunt, I'll tell you who you are" "What makes the Russian healthy causes the German to die".
(Russian folk sayings).

As far as relations between nations are concerned, the whole history of Russia shows that the structure of a multinational state has taught Russians to be *tolerant of* other customs and mores. The Russian is neither a nationalist nor a racist. His history, with its many contacts with foreign countries, has only enriched him.

Moreover, it has always been able to appropriate and transform original ideas from abroad to the point of making them unrecognizable. Without China, for example, the "Russian shirts" with embroidered collars, the painted and lacquered boxes of Palekh (a school renowned for its lacquer boxes) and the tea mania would not exist. Without the Tatars, the structure of the Russian state, "Russian toques", coarse swear words, boots, coachmen, the "knout" (whip), the "Russian troika" and many other things would never have come into being. Without Peter I's delicate attraction to Dutch porcelain, there would be no *Gjele* (Russian white and blue porcelain), so cheerful to look at. Without Japan, we wouldn't have our famous Russian *matryoshki* (dolls). And without the Middle East, we'd have done without the "Russian samovar" in Russia. As for our form of Christianity, our writing, our church architecture, our original painting and the double-headed eagle, they all came to us from the Byzantine Empire. And all of Russia's contemporary civilization (with its material, technological and legal cultures, as well as certain elements of spiritual culture) has developed in close contact with - and to a large extent under the influence of - Western Europe.

However, all these examples of openness to foreign cultures are not so much about tolerance as they are about flexibility, practicality in business and the Russians' *gift for imitation*, catching on the fly and turning into good anything that might be of practical use to them. Contacts with foreigners enriched Russian material civilization, philosophy and language. But to be more precise, rather than *tolerance*, let's talk about resourcefulness, purely material advantages and interests.

Throughout history, Russians have always been open to newcomers. In the 18th century, Russia was home to many Germans. The Russian word for "German", *nemets*, literally means a "mute person" (*nemoi*), unable to express himself or make himself understood. Poles, Dutchmen and Frenchmen could all be considered *nemtsi*, and at the time they were all quite happy in Russia. Ruined Hanoverian aristocrats, craftsmen, professors and merchants came to Russia to "remedy their affairs" and then return home or stay in this wild but rich country. 200 years ago, Germany was dismembered and overpopulated, while Russia offered vast open spaces, a wealthy and prodigal aristocracy and a cordial and submissive people. This made it easy for foreigners to put down roots, especially after Peter I forced Russia back into Western civilization. After Peter I, the main feature of Russian culture became *openness and receptiveness to all things foreign* - for three centuries. And it's only now that this Russian quality has begun to change, to be transformed into something new.

Just as the *nemtsev* ("foreigners") saw the Russians as savage barbarians living according to incomprehensible laws, the Russians saw foreigners as semi-legendary figures with whom they had a complex relationship of curiosity and hostility. Foreigners rarely mingled with Russians, settling in separate "suburbs" such as Kukui in Moscow. We put up with each other - we derived practical benefits from each other, but we had no particular mutual attraction to each other.

The relationship between Russians and foreigners, who are extremely numerous in Russian literature, is interesting to observe. Foreigners portrayed *with a satirical note* by Russian writers are, generally speaking, obvious evildoers who nonetheless attract sympathy but, in a way, have been "corrupted" by Western civilization. Foreigners in Russian literature are very rarely positive characters.

This is not just because nationalism was virulent among Russian writers. Their philosophical orientations diverged widely, and their description of foreigners was a *literary device* for observing the Russian people as "outsiders" and comparing national mentalities with other cultures. Russian writers generally described the Germans, French and English with their own national traits. For it is precisely these peoples who have had the greatest influence on Russian culture.

Germans are the most frequently portrayed. Already under Pushkin, they were traditionally portrayed as individuals for whom economic interest, "prudence", a penchant for hoarding and self-assurance were of great importance. Their excessive reliance on reason, on the "arithmetical" spirit, clashed with Russian reality and often put them in ridiculous situations, going so far as to cause their bankruptcy and downfall. The gallery of German characters in Russian literature can be off-putting because of the satire they are subjected to.

The Russian attitude towards the French was original. For two centuries, the finest members of the Russian nation spoke French, ashamed of their mother tongue. This may seem vexatious to Russians, and even ridiculous, as if, for example, the court of Louis XIV spoke Chinese. Even Alexander Pushkin, the "Russian phoenix", only learned Russian from his nanny. In Russia, there were many French people who had fled the horrors of the 1789 revolution. And in Russian literature, the character of the sympathetic Frenchman is an exception. The vast majority were governesses invited into wealthy homes to educate young children. They often neglected their duties, were uneducated and foolish, prone to adultery with the master of the house, and treated Russians badly. They had come to Russia with a single aim: to earn money and put it to one side. After a few years, they left the country without having learned the language or understood anything about a country that inspired only annoyance, dislike and weariness.

Throughout Russian history, however, foreigners have successfully integrated into the Russian nobility. In high society, blue blood was so mixed that, for example, Felix Yusupov, Rasputin's notorious murderer, happened to be both the great-great-grandson of the King of Prussia and the descendant of a Mongol warlord.

A glance at the genealogies of the nobility of Russian origin in *The Velvet Book* will be enough to convince you of the large number of foreigners and the success of their integration in the country. Until the Revolution, this book was kept in the Heraldic Department of the Russian Senate[68]. Reading it shows that almost all the old Russian nobility had foreign ancestors who had come to serve the princes or the tsar.

Presumably, not all these genealogies corresponded to reality. Having a foreign ancestor in Russia was prestigious then as it is today: this particularity in the family tree distinguished the aristocrat from the masses.

Since ancient times, people in Russia have had a favorable opinion of France as a *country of culture* par excellence, unlike other countries associated with history, politics and economy. Even in the 19th century, representatives of the Russian nobility and intelligentsia were fluent in French. Russians often describe France as the "crossroads of the world" and this opinion about French culture is often based on their detailed knowledge of art monuments and architectural sights. For 33% of the respondents, France evokes the names of writers, painters, musicians, singers and composers, world famous museums and other sights (the Louvre, Notre Dame, the Eiffel Tower, etc.).

This cultural approach to France makes Russians benevolent towards other aspects of French life, such as the French. The following opinions prevail: "In France, women are pretty and men are elegant", "It is a peaceful people", "It is a country of independent and temperamental people". Russians are quite familiar with famous Frenchmen: they consider Charles de Gaulle "a great politician" who "liberated Algeria" and "strengthened ties with the Soviet Union". And a third of the Russians surveyed said that they sympathize with Jacques Chirac as a politician and that the concordant positions of Russia and France in foreign policy in recent years were a good thing.

At the same time, many analysts note that although Russians are well-informed about French history and culture, their conception of today's France doesn't always correspond to reality, just as the French idea of Russia needs

---

68. Facts taken from the book by S. Valianskiï and D. Kalujnyï, *Une autre histoire de la Russie: de l'Europe à la Mongolie*, Moscow, ed. Vetche, 2001, p. 402-405.

serious "updating". They need to go beyond the old stereotypes, because Russia is not only the country of corruption and mafia, with *bears*, *balalaikas* and other nonsense, it is also a country with a market economy and a huge domestic potential. And the way citizens perceive each other often has an impact on the relations of their respective states.

So, in external contacts, in *relations between nations*, the Russians have been indulgent. Other nations have always exerted a certain attraction on them, drawing them in like a magnet. Russians have always tried to gain maximum benefit from their contacts with strong and "civilized" countries: to learn from them, to borrow technical or cultural novelties from them, to enrich themselves through advantageous trade.

This *openness to the outside world*, this *gift for assimilating the most attractive features of other developed cultures* (while retaining its own archetype) created the conditions for a highly original and rapidly expanding culture in Russia.

This magnetic attraction also benefited small, weak peoples, and enabled Russia to keep almost *200 other peoples* (!) on its territory. It's true that this "magnetism", as academician D. C. Lichaëv, "constantly repelled other peoples sparkling with life - notably the Poles and the Jews".

It is more difficult to speak of *Russian tolerance at the level of individual conscience*, as there are no documents or historical testimonies other than personal observations on the attitudes of contemporaries.

And under Soviet rule, relations were governed by the "iron curtain". The state propaganda machine was in full operation, presenting foreigners as an enemy force entering the country with evil intentions. Of course, this machine often worked empty-handed, as "brainwashing" had inculcated in Russians, in the absence of animosity towards foreigners, distrust and a basic fear. And the authorities monitored the slightest contact between Russians and foreigners, whether in meetings, correspondence or telephone conversations. Anyone who naively violated this tacit prohibition risked jeopardizing his career, his position and even his freedom.

In those days, foreigners felt "like kings" in the USSR, despite the stressful feeling of being spied on and the restrictions on movement: they had access to special stores, the *Beriozka* ("the birch tree") and, for a derisory sum, could buy items and services that Russians couldn't even dream of in their own country: beautiful editions of books, the best shows and ballets, sightseeing tours to the most exotic corners of the country - in a word, everything that was best in the country was reserved for them.

This state policy of the USSR (humiliating for its own citizens) was motivated by the desire to "extract currency" from foreign tourists.

Naturally, throughout this period, this policy could only pervert foreigners' relations with the local population: they could be neither sincere nor on an equal footing. For the citizens of the USSR, every foreigner, especially from the "West" (this included all developed capitalist countries, including America), was a "dweller of the heavens": rich, free, self-confident, carefree in everyday life (this appeared to be an inconceivable happiness), beautifully dressed and perfumed, in short, "civilized".

Comparing himself to a foreigner, the Russian could not help but develop inferiority complexes and a critical attitude towards those around him and those in power, so striking was the contrast.

And although contact with foreigners was limited, this in no way diminished the Russians' natural curiosity for foreign cultures. A solid classical education and a taste for knowledge encouraged Russians to rub shoulders with them, even passively: foreign literature was translated and published, films were shown, artistic and theatrical troupes toured the country.

But this "long-distance relationship" had perverse effects in that the Russians' imagination attributed a fairy-tale life to the foreigners: they were, it is said, all incredibly rich, living like "Hollywood stars": in luxury, without problems, without the dull routine of Soviet life, free as air...

When Soviet propaganda "edited" documentaries about poverty, drugs, crime and filth in Western cities, nobody paid any attention: it was "just propaganda"! And the clichés forcibly imposed had the opposite effect: people believed that all these evils were fabricated by Soviet power, and that paradise awaited you abroad.

As a result, when the "Iron Curtain" collapsed for good, many Russians became convinced of the illusory nature of their ideas about "Western life", and made no secret of their disappointment.

Nonetheless, respect for Western material civilization and technology persists. These "innovations" in the Russian language: *inomarka* ("foreign brand") and *evroremont* ("European-style repairs") - see chap. 2, § 1 - show that Russians have a deep respect for Western material civilization.

At the same time, the huge disparity between Russian and "Western" lifestyles is obvious. And this dissimilarity is reflected in the stereotyped behaviors of Russians and Westerners. For example, the Russian cannot imagine that the French can differentiate between a hundred wines by taste, color and aroma - how can they? This science of the French makes them even more enigmatic and refined than they were in their own eyes. And this impression is further reinforced by the hundreds of cheeses and perfumes that exist in France...

In addition, because of their superficial knowledge of "Western" life, Russians still have in mind old stereotypes such as: "Germans are neat freaks", "English are distinguished gentlemen", "French are the most gallant people alive", and so on.

If we take into account the traditions of Russian hospitality and the Russians' benevolence towards guests (foreigners included), your Russian interlocutors, in your dealings with them, will know how to show you attention and make you feel at ease (as long as you behave correctly). But don't expect them to trust you completely: after all, you're not "one of them". God knows what you have in mind. And you shouldn't take offense.

12. Russians' relationship with time and its management

"A lot of water under the bridge in an hour of Russian time".
"Don't anticipate the future".
"He who hastens too much stays on his way".
(Russian sayings).

Many of the character traits and stereotypical behaviors of Russians have already been described in the literature. Some of these traits, however, have never been addressed, because they remain misunderstood, even though they disconcert the foreigner who encounters them. Specifically, I'm referring to the Russian *notion of time.*

First peculiarity: for a long time now, it has been noted that the Russian is more inclined to look *back* than to plan for the future. As the writer

Chekhov put it, "the Russian likes to remember without being satisfied with the existence he has been given" (story *The Steppe*). It's not for nothing that the Russian feels contempt for those who don't remember their past, those who "are as forgetful as a cuckoo clock".

The proof is in the classic Russian literature. The subject matter of many famous novels or tales is built around the memories of storytellers (occasional drinking buddies), the incredible story that happened to them and how it "turned" their lives upside down.

The past is very important to the Russian. *Nostalgia* for childhood, adolescence, first love and the places where they once lived characterizes them. Of course, this explains why Russians find it hard to acclimatize once they've emigrated: nostalgia is too strong for them. And this psychological trait is also found in today's Russians, old and old alike, nostalgic for "Atlantis", the USSR, the homeland of their childhood and youth.

Why is the past so important to the Russian? Precisely because he looks to the past for the secret reason behind his future actions, for moral support, consolation, justification for his own conduct, the reason for his choices. It's not in vain that it's said that "the Russian has the spirit of the staircase".

But don't interpret this saying to mean that the Russian is foolish or slow-witted. It means that they are *more circumspect than far-sighted.* In other words, they are better at registering consequences and results, better at analyzing the past than at setting goals for the future and organizing themselves to achieve them. You need to take this Russian archetype into account in your business dealings with them.

The second particularity of the Russian archetype is that it's not so much logic as *mood, emotions,* personal experience *and* the very course of life that will decide the priority of tasks to be accomplished.

This applies above all to *time in private life*: here the Russian can really throw the foreigner off guard, changing his plans unexpectedly (depending on the circumstances of his private life, his mood, etc.) - being late, cancelling a planned appointment at the last minute, not fulfilling his obligations, etc. And what often strikes the foreigner is that after this, he won't even try to explain himself and apologize. And what often strikes the foreigner is that, after that, he won't even try to explain himself and apologize. This behavior on the part of the Russians (as well as that of other peoples on Russian territory) is quite bewildering to Westerners, who are used to behaving in a rational, logical and pragmatic manner on all occasions. These discrepancies do have their drawbacks, especially in business relations, and these must be taken into consideration.

These Russian traits can, of course, be interpreted as lack of discipline, instability and even falsehood. And this is how they are most often interpreted - in an extremely negative way.

But they can also be seen in a different light - as the result of the Russians' particular relationship to life, their ability to go beyond the usual, narrow framework of existence. The individual may well have made you a promise in all sincerity, believing he could keep it. But new circumstances in his life are now taking over his mind. And his priorities have changed as a result... Previous obligations seem less important under the pressure of new events. "To live life, let's avoid crossing the field": this saying implies that it's impossible to avoid all problems. For this reason, we must "live the present moment now", and for the rest, "as God sees fit"...

In this respect, the Russians are reminiscent of the Greeks who, as we know, equated punctuality with zeal for work, and valued above all their leisure, their private life and all that was emotionally associated with it.

Russians have a different relationship to *working hours*. The vast majority of the country's population, from generation to generation (especially during the Soviet era), perceived their work as a public fee which, generally speaking, did not correspond to the person's real contribution. The same applied to wages, which had nothing to do with the individual's contribution. People had become accustomed (especially those not involved in direct production) to disregarding work schedules: arriving late, leaving earlier than scheduled, taking long lunch breaks, drinking tea and chatting during working hours were all part of the way of life. And the many films, shows and stories written by contemporary writers bear witness to this.

This behavior comes as a shock to outsiders. They have to be prepared (even if the scheduled meeting is to clarify a few technical details) for a variety of eventualities: if, suddenly, the indispensable person is missing, and no one is there to replace him or her... Today, fortunately, people in private companies are paid a salary commensurate with their contribution to the work, and professional behavior is changing for the better.

Thirdly, for Russians, as for all Orientals, *time is cyclical*. Every day, the sun rises and sets, the years follow one another. People grow old and die, and their children start all over again. For this reason, the past is omnipresent in Russian thinking. This idea is confirmed by the etymology of the word *vremia* ("time" in Russian): it comes from the Old Slavic word *veremia* and is related to the words *vertet* ("to turn"), *vereteno* ("cattail"). In the Russian unconscious, the perception of time is cyclical and linked to the idea of repetition.

Compare this word with its German equivalent *die Zeit* ("time"), which comes from the verb *ziehen*, meaning "to draw". As we can see, in the German language, the idea of "time" is based on a linear mode. This is reflected in the stereotypical behavior of Germans: it's hard to compete with them when it comes to their constant striving towards a goal, their rigorous punctuality. And if the Russians lack these qualities, it's because they "look at life through different eyes".

The difference in perception of time has important practical consequences. Westerners solve problems "linearly", "step by step", taking into account today's advantages and getting straight to the point. It doesn't matter what happened yesterday or in the past: it's all about the future.

But with the Russians' cyclical perception of time, decisions are made differently in business. It's as if Russians are unconsciously *always looking to the past*, never losing sight of it. The past is, for them, the hidden reason and foundation of every decision. They are not so presumptuous in their plans for the future, insofar as they are convinced that the latter cannot be mastered, it is fate that decides: "Don't anticipate the future." You can only sweeten your destiny by living in harmony with nature and, above all, with the people around you.

For this reason, according to Russian logic, there's no point in making decisions in the minute; it's better to reflect, "weigh up", "turn your tongue seven times in your mouth" before deciding on something. And, generally speaking, it's better to postpone the final decision, because "sleep is best".

This is a far cry from the Western rule of "don't put off until tomorrow what you can do today". In Soviet times, we had fun transforming it into "Don't put off until tomorrow what you can do the day after tomorrow".

In addition to "Russian fatalism", the refusal to plan for the long term can be explained by the brutal reality of Russian life: the decline in the standard of living of the vast majority of the population over the last ten years, the lack of guarantees offered by the state, day-to-day survival, the sudden change in the country's political and economic situation - all of this puts a brake on and makes nonsense of forming long-term life plans.

13. Confessional particularities of Russians

The special character of the Russian people has been the subject of a multitude of works by philosophers such as N. O. Losski, N. A. Berdiayev, N. Ilyin, L. P. Korsavin and others (see Bibliography). All agreed that "the Russian spirit is imbued with religiosity"[69].

Let's agree with them that, for almost 1,000 years, religiosity has been at the heart of the Russian archetype. In Soviet times, however, the Russian Church was virtually wiped out, plundered and humiliated when the popes were forced to cooperate with the KGB, providing it with information. Miraculously, however, it survived and retained a spark of life. And since the beginning of perestroika, we can even speak of a revival of the Russian religious spirit.

Russia is a multi-faith state, with Christianity, Islam, Buddhism and Judaism all represented. N. Margelova, Director of the Institute of Religions, on the TV program "Voice of the People" in winter 2001, reported that 11,000 *Orthodox* parishes, 4,400 *Evangelical* parishes and 258 *Catholic* parishes were active in Russia. Of course, the Orthodox, by tradition, predominate.

A study of religious life in today's Russia is, of course, beyond the scope of this book. All we know is that the Orthodox Church plays an important role

---

69. L. P. Korsavin, *L'Idée russe: l'Occident et l'Orient*, in N. Losskiï, *Le Caractère du peuple russe*, book 1, p. 5, ed. Posev, 1957, p. 5 and others.

in the life of the community. It has, of course, lost some of its influence, and is unlikely to regain in the future the role it had before the 1917 revolution.

However, unlike other national institutions, it enjoys a high level of public confidence. In any case, according to the results of public opinion polls, 54% of those questioned (more than half) declared their attachment to Orthodoxy, while 46% declared themselves to be atheists.

We're not in a position to give you any more precise data; after all, freedom of conscience exists. For this reason, we can only convey an atmosphere of...

In this respect, we can recall the television reports broadcast around the world showing the politicians of the first democratic wave, B. Yeltsin, Khasbulatov and Zhirinovsky, awkwardly signing themselves with a candle in hand. It's now fashionable to go to church, get baptized, marry religiously and stoically endure very long liturgies. Perhaps these acts are intended for the media, where leaders appear more human, closer to the people.

However, we cannot speak of a revival of religious awareness, even though more than half the Russian population claim to be Orthodox and wearing a cross has become fashionable. True faith is passed down from generation to generation from an early age, not by decision of the old political nomenklatura.

However, even if we assume that the deep religious spirit that once animated the Russians has disappeared as a result of cruel persecution, it has not done so without leaving traces in their consciousness, and this spirit has been preserved at least in the language. For example, every individual (whether believer or atheist) utters the word *spasibo* ("thank you") all day long, unconsciously asking God to help and "save" them. *Spasibo* in Russian is formed from the verb *spasti* ("to save") and *bo* (for *Bog*, "God"). In the Middle Ages, people gave thanks by saying *spasi (tebia) Bog* ("I ask thanks to God"). Similarly, the expression *Gospodi, Bojie moï!* ("Lord, my God!") is frequently used in Russia to express enthusiasm, awe or rapture under strong emotion - especially in the mouth of a woman. To a Westerner, however, it would appear somewhat archaic.

Without entering into theoretical considerations, we can note certain confessional particularities of the Orthodox Church.

Firstly, compared to Catholicism, Orthodoxy is more intimate, a popular religion. Cases of fundamentalism, opposition or religious warfare are comparatively rare. When they converted to Christianity, Russians received the Holy Scriptures not in a foreign language (Latin, Greek or Hebrew) but in the accessible translation of the Slavic apostles Cyril and Methodius - unlike many other proselytizing nations.

In "Rus" (ancient Russia), there was no European-style monastic erudition (with knowledge of Latin, philosophy, Roman history and literature). Yet it was on the basis of this knowledge that universities were founded and the arts developed in Europe. The popes and monarchs of the Rus were not obliged to study ancient languages and the sciences. This explains Russia's gradual backwardness in science and technology - an obvious gap in its historical heritage, at least from a materialist, Cartesian point of view.

Secondly, under present-day conditions, Russian Orthodoxy appears to be a more archaic and traditional religion. Prayers are said in Old Slavonic, a language artificially created by Bulgarian librarians to translate the holy books. It is incomprehensible even to educated individuals. The Russian does not always understand word for word the meaning of his prayer.

Thirdly, Orthodoxy contains some rather strict injunctions: women are forbidden to enter a church wearing make-up and improper attire, pants are forbidden, they must cover their heads with a scarf or scarf and their bodies must be completely concealed from view, whatever the outside temperature.

In addition, Russians are required to fast *voluntarily for* almost *half the year*, *i.e.* they must not eat meat or animal products. And during the six weeks leading up to Easter, they must follow a particularly strict and severe diet. Many Russians follow these traditions not so much for religious reasons as for dietary reasons.

Generally speaking, you'll need to respect and follow the injunctions of the Russian Church, even if you're just a foreign observer or tourist.

Fourthly, attending a Russian liturgy is an out-of-the-ordinary experience for a foreigner. On the one hand, the warm atmosphere, magnificent icons and extraordinary chants will plunge you into rapture. On the other hand, it's impossible to sit comfortably in a Russian church. For hours on end, you have to stand, bow all the way to the ground, get down, kiss the icon, even if many others have kissed it before you... It's not the icon itself, however, but the edge of the icon or its silver coating that needs to be kissed. In short, liturgy is an unforgettable experience, but it can also be a trying one!

Fifthly, it's worth recalling the tense relations between Orthodox and Catholics. And this tension, far from diminishing, is only getting stronger. We need only recall, for example, the outcry triggered by the Catholic Church in the Russian media in early 2002: the Ministry of Foreign Affairs - in other words, the government - was even obliged to intervene. The dispute began with the question of a live TV broadcast between the Pope of Rome and Russia's Catholics. Patriarch Alexei II described the project as "interference by the Catholic faith in Russian territory".

And *last but not least*: Orthodox traditions dictate that everyone, including those who have succeeded in business, are obliged "as a matter of conscience" to sacrifice a portion of their income to Church works, orphans and the needy.

Herein lies the secret to the radical transformation of Russia's major cities. Over the past ten years, countless churches (not just Orthodox) have been covered in gold and richly decorated, palaces have been restored... And this splendor is not the fruit of the generosity or excessive patriotism of the government and its officials. It exists thanks to the sacrifices, funds and prosperity of a multitude of individuals.

14. The phenomenon of alcoholism

The *Izvestia* (national newspaper) of February 22, 2002 and the Internet circulated a piece of information that caused quite a stir. It referred to "a Russian banquet which caused the death of a French expert". Three years ago in Nalchik, a 44-year-old Frenchman died of alcohol poisoning: he had spent the night drinking vodka with Russian colleagues. His widow was refused a pension and took legal action with the help of the Social Security system. The court ruled that the widow was entitled to the pension, as the accident had taken place "in the workplace", and that the deceased's employers should have taken into account the "Russian specificity"; they were therefore responsible for their employee. His mission was to establish relations with colleagues in Russia, which were accompanied by traditional libations.

The idea of "having a drink to get over a hangover" was totally unknown to the Frenchman. The employers were aware of this aspect of Russian life, but had not taken it seriously and had not warned their employee, for which the latter paid with his life. They would have to answer for their thoughtlessness. To avoid a repeat of this case, we need to know more about the phenomenon of alcoholism in Russia than just hearsay.

The penchant for strong drinks - a long-standing tradition - was already known in the "Rus".

Firstly, it's linked to the cold climate: alcohol warms up significantly in cold weather. Wine doesn't grow in Russia. That's why honey, beer and wine made from bread were used at first. Vodka appeared only in the 15th century.

Secondly, laughter and drink are inseparable in the Russian mind. In the 10th century, the great prince of Kiev, Vladimir, chose to convert to Christianity also because it didn't clash with the old tradition "The joy of Rus is drinking... you can't live without it."

This tradition has been carried on from ancient times to the present day. Statistics show that Russia is the world leader in terms of alcohol consumption per capita, ahead of traditional "heavy drinkers" such as France, Portugal, Italy, Germany and Hungary.

According to medical opinion, the consumption of strong beverages in Russia exceeds accepted norms. To avoid irreversible damage to health, this consumption should not exceed 10 liters of alcohol in a year, yet it reaches *13-15 liters* per individual *(including women and children)* in Russia.[70] Russians remain the leaders in alcohol consumption, even though they are aware that they lose between 9 and 22 years of their lives as a result of alcohol-related illnesses.

"Do-it-yourself" alcohol wreaks even more havoc, claiming the lives of around 35,000 people every year, particularly in the Russian province. In small towns and rural areas, where it's hard to find work, alcoholism takes the lives of young men - the most active and employable population.

---

70. "Vodka burned as arsenic". - *www.utro.ru* - November 28, 2002.

It's indisputable that alcoholism is also the primary reason why women live 13-14 years longer than men in this country, and this gap remains stable; men drink infinitely more and more frequently.

This situation is catastrophic for the whole country. How can we explain this calamity, which is silently killing large numbers of people without a war?

There's also the long-standing tradition of Russian *hospitality*, according to which it's unthinkable to sit down to dinner without a strong drink. And finally the *climate*, which of course plays an important role.

The *third reason is* purely *physiological*. You have probably already noticed that alcohol acts differently on individuals. For some, all it takes is one mug of beer and they show all the signs of drunkenness: red face, extreme agitation and so on. This depends not so much on the quantity and quality of alcohol ingested as on the activity of the ferment that oxidizes alcohol, acetic aldehyde. Depending on the individual, the rate of activity of this ferment can be multiplied *by ten*! Among Mongolian populations, for example, this rate is very low, which explains why a mug of beer is enough to intoxicate them. Europeans generally have a high level of activity of this ferment. This is why they tolerate alcohol better than Mongolian-type populations, and don't fall into heavy alcohol dependency. People's behavior, paradoxical though it may be, depends not only on their education or common sense, but also on the physiological composition of their blood. In this respect, Russians occupy an intermediate position (as in many other respects) between Europeans and Mongoloid populations.[71] On the whole, Russians have a high level of "alcoholic" ferment in their blood, which means they tolerate alcohol well, can drink a lot of vodka and remain "lucid": even when consumed in large quantities, alcohol does not make them ill. These physical qualities, positive at first sight, are at the same time their downfall. Because they tolerate alcohol well, Russians quickly become accustomed to it and fall into addiction.

There are also other reasons for the current Russian alcoholism. The *psychological* factor, for example, through which alcohol plays both a devas-

---

71. Commentary by Vladimir Noujnii, Director of the Toxicology Laboratory of the Ministry of Public Health of the Russian Federation - *AiF*, April 16, 2001.

tating and positive role with its anesthetic action. For centuries, alcohol has served as an outlet for Russians, enabling them to "forget" the despotism of the master, the arbitrariness of the authorities, and the anguish and sadness of everyday life. This form of outlet has been preserved during the fifteen years of "shock therapy" recently carried out in Russia. Many more Russians (47%) who abstain from alcohol say they "can no longer bear their difficult situation", while only 20% of drunks say the same.[72] Which just goes to show that endurance and submission are not just traits of the national character. More prosaically, they come from alcohol.

In today's Russia, alcohol also has an *emancipating* role: it frees the Russian from daily worries, social obligations and state authority, and reinforces his "love of freedom". This enables them to adapt to difficult living conditions.

But there's also a not insignificant reason for widespread Russian alcoholism, and it's purely economic. Vodka is very affordable in Russia, both because of its price and because it's easy to get. There's always a stall or store open 24 hours a day, 7 days a week, selling it near a metro station, bus stop or other popular spot.

What conclusions can be drawn from the above?

Firstly, the Russian penchant for beverages should not be seen as a manifestation of "barbaric mores". There are many reasons for this phenomenon: historical, physiological and economic. Taken together, they are further reinforced by dissatisfaction with life in Russia today.

Secondly, this ancient Russian drinking habit will inevitably concern you if you are preparing to do business in Russia. It is unlikely that you will be able to escape the "Russian banquets" where vodka is drunk. It is known that people who do not drink with others have little success in business and other areas. And that's nothing new.

This tradition has been preserved to this day. To succeed in business, you have to know *where, with whom and how to drink*. You have to keep this in mind at all times.

But you may well also meet a Russian who can't stand vodka and only knows good wine. A new generation has grown up, which has experienced

---

72. Public opinion poll - *Ogoniok* magazine, June 1997.

a golden youth, studied at foreign universities, has multiple life experiences and has adopted a new stereotyped behavior pattern modeled on that of the "Westerner".

It's not out of the question that you'll come across this type of individual in the upper echelons of power and in serious businesses, especially in Russia's major cities.

In conclusion, it's worth noting that, according to the statistics, vodka consumption has fallen somewhat in recent years, while champagne consumption (for New Year's celebrations, weddings and other official occasions) has risen, and beer consumption even more so. The latter has become incredibly popular, as is obvious to TV viewers, for example: a program is regularly interrupted by a beer commercial. Russia's youth are drinking so much that it's becoming alarming. According to experts, a penchant for this beverage can only lead to true alcoholism.

And so, the traditional Russian penchant for "strong drinks" has evolved somewhat, without disappearing altogether...

Conclusion of the second part of the book on the traditional ethno-cultural characteristics of Russians

A comparison of Russian and Western mentalities has shown that Russian mass consciousness is more interested in the *human* than the practical *side of* things.[73] Russians are above all interested in the individual and his or her development, historical subjects, creative problems, politics and people's social relationships.

The Western mentality is more rational: it places greater emphasis on "common sense", logic and the problems posed by the construction of society, while insisting on terms such as "tolerance", "equality", "law", political institutions and so on.

Russian consciousness, on the other hand, is more idealistic: it more often uses expressions such as "world view", "relationships between people"...

---

73. *La Mentalité des Russes. The Consciousness of Large Population Groups in Russia, op. cit.* p. 98.

The Russian is marked by the traditional principles that govern society and influence his training, his endearing qualities and his "vices".

On the one hand, it is his hospitality, his frankness, his spirit of comradeship and mutual aid, his willingness to help someone in misfortune, his trust, his patience and his lack of resentment...

Someone who knows Russian culture and Russians well, and has befriended them, will always regard them with sympathy. What's more: under their influence, they may even become, over time, more generous, more serene about their career and success, more open-minded, less petty and less busy in the pursuit of material goals.

Russians, on the *other hand,* are also characterized by their lack of practicality, their lightness in the face of serious problems, their lack of diligence at work, their lack of discipline, their inability to plan for the future and to consistently carry out their projects, their lack of true professionalism (more evident in their inability to consistently carry out their professional obligations than in their "ignorance"), the overly "personal" and emotional nature of their relationships, their puerile hope in "luck", in the "miracle along with their penchant for alcohol and exuberant partying, their desire to find someone to blame in a difficult situation... All these shortcomings complicate their relationships with others and contribute, unfortunately, to the poor reputation of Russians in the business world, where they are perceived as Oblomovs and unreliable partners.

This is not entirely true, however. The Russians themselves openly admit that they are not seasoned businessmen. Until such time as the business really interests them...

Russians are *enthusiasts.* They need to have a goal, an interest, not necessarily a financial one. And if they're interested in "business", if you've been able to dangle prospects in front of them, and if you've managed to establish a relationship of trust and friendship with them, you won't find a better partner in any field of activity.

PART THREE - CONTEMPORARY RUSSIAN SOCIO-CULTURAL VALUES

1. New realities and values in contemporary Russia

It has become commonplace to think that, over the last ten years, Russia has changed as the consciousness and behavior of Russians have changed.

After taking stock of the "revolutionary" changes in Russia, many analysts[74] note that the main one concerns the *deterioration in quality of life. There are* objective reasons for this.

After the collapse of the USSR, Russia was deprived of its southernmost regions to the south and west, losing half its population, 40% of its gross national product and a quarter of its territory. Its natural resources are located in areas with a very harsh climate. Extracting 70% of Russia's oil and gas requires infinitely more effort than in other parts of the world. Russia's gross domestic product ranks it among the *bottom two hundred countries in the world.* According to Interfax experts' calculations based on official Russian statistics, gross domestic product has fallen by 27% over the last ten years, while consumer prices have risen 10,139 times since November 1991 (!). Industrial production has fallen by 35%, and capital investment by 3 times. Russian real incomes, taking inflation into account, fell by almost 2 times (47%) between 1992 and 2001.

---

74. S. Valianskiï and D. Kalujnyï, *Comprendre la Russie par l'esprit,* Moscow, ed. Algorithme, 2001, p. 232-233.

Rapid population decline and deteriorating health are often discussed in the media. Russia's population is shrinking by almost 1 million a year. The Russian mortality rate is 2.5 times higher than world indicators.[75] Road accidents play a crucial role: half of them result in the death of pedestrians. The average lifespan of a man is less than 58 years, and that of a woman less than 73. These averages are lower than those found in Mongolia, Vietnam and Egypt... and for men, it's equivalent to that of Botswana or Lesotho![76]

The opinion of academician I. Arnold, published in *Izvestia*[77], is even more frightening: according to him, the drop in average life expectancy over 10 years, on a Russian scale, would be equivalent to the simultaneous passing under arms of almost 40 million citizens. These facts and figures are exploited in many media, but journalistic "business" is not our purpose.

At the same time, how can we fail to notice the radical changes to which Russian society is beginning to become accustomed? It now often takes them for granted, easily forgetting the terrible realities of the Gulag, severe ideological and political control, party bureaucracy in all areas of private and social life, general scarcity, ration cards, endless queues for basic necessities, etc.

Today in Russia there are institutions and freedom unthinkable for several generations of Russians: a liberal constitution, free elections, multi-party system, opposition, parliament, free media, uncensored film production, freedom of movement in the country and abroad, freedom of conscience, freedom of entrepreneurship, personal initiative, full cultural freedom, theatrical and editorial boom, etc. These realities must be seen as a real leap forward. Unfortunately, these are not facts that journalists are particularly interested in. Just 10-15 years ago, many generations of Russians could not have believed in their advent!

Journalists and politicians rarely mention the fact that, since 1998, *one family out of three* already owns a car (in other words, the number of private cars has multiplied by 5!); that 32,000 kilometers of highways have been built in recent years (which does not prevent permanent traffic

---

75. Website SMI. ru - *Megalopolis - Express*, n° 58, 2002.
76. www.Cronicle.ru/2002/10/sac/01opinion/index.html
77. *Izvestia* of January 16, 1998.

jams on the roads); that the number of telephones has increased by 40% in private homes and that the number of international telephone calls has increased by 12.

The mortality rate, which had been on the rise in recent years, has now fallen back to 1990 levels. Young people who, 3-4 years ago, refused to study and preferred to "take care of business" (selling alcohol in kiosks) are now rushing to the institutes and taking competitive exams in which fifteen people compete for one place! Today in Russia, there are 264 students per 10,000 inhabitants, 20% more than the best scores of the Soviet era.

When asked whether their *well-being* has improved in recent years[78], the majority of Russians are not too alarmed: for half of them, the answer is "yes"; for 20%, "nothing has changed". Only 11% admit that "things are much worse" and 15% that "their situation has deteriorated a little". As we can see, even Russians, who are not known for being great optimists, lead us to draw some not too pessimistic conclusions. What's more, the political and economic situation in Russia changes constantly and so abruptly that the figures have to be updated every 2-3 years.

Looking at the new realities of Russian life over the last 10-15 years, the "rollercoaster" model comes to mind again, with its unpredictable turns and precipitous changes. For although Russia has suffered immense losses in all areas of life, it has not succumbed, it has risen and, like the phoenix, is rising from the ashes.

In order to describe the present-day life of the Russians, we shall endeavor to set out the facts objectively, using the study "Ten years of reform as seen by the Russians". This work was carried out by the Russian Academy of Sciences (Institute for Advanced Social Research) and the Independent Russian Institute for Social and National Issues, in cooperation with the Friedrich Hebert Foundation (Germany). The use of concrete figures will allow us to understand what the people think and how their opinions reflect those of the elite who have access to the public forum. The polls were conducted throughout Russia between 1991 and 2001. They show how, in ten years of reform, people's opinions have changed on a very wide range of

---

78. See note 67.

issues - from attitudes towards free enterprise to sexual taboos. With results that analysts themselves find surprising.

On the whole, it should be noted that the majority of Russians feel burdened by the *deterioration of* the country, which is reflected in almost all indicators. It's no coincidence that they take a largely *negative view of* the current period their country is going through: they mention "crime and banditry", the "uncertain future", "national conflicts", "corruption and embezzlement", the "absence of spirituality", the "difficult economic situation", "social injustice", etc. They also worry a great deal about the fact that Russia is no longer seen as a country with a high level of social cohesion. People are also very concerned that Russia is no longer considered a developed country.

However, these pessimistic responses from Russians must be viewed in the light of the peculiarities of their national character: *fatalism,* a tendency to exaggerate and fixate on the *negative aspects of everyday life, and a* tendency not to closely associate a sense of *happiness* with the *material* aspects of life (see Part 1, § 5; Part 2, chap. 2, § 1; chap. 3, § 1).

The average Russian's *negative assessment of the* decade of reforms implies a search for a culprit. And for the first time in their history, 30% of Russians[76] believe that "they themselves are guilty".

The hardest thing for the Russians is that the transition to a "market" economy and democracy has been accompanied by the collapse of the previous social system, its political, economic and social structures, and the stereotypical citizen behavior associated with them. The society that seemed to be united has literally split into groups with different orientations on almost all political, economic and social issues.

The questions arise: How exactly has the consciousness of Russians changed in concrete terms? How have traditional patterns of consciousness and social behavior changed? How are they integrated into the new social relationships? Which Russians have adapted to the new conditions of life and which ones have not? And why not?

According to current criteria, today's Russian society is a *transitional society, in the process of change.* Analyzing the mood of individuals in this society is not an easy task, just as it is not easy to identify and explain transitional phenomena that are not yet fully structured, but only sketched out.

2. Safety and legality in today's Russia

The problem of personal security arises for anyone planning to visit Russia.

Firstly, the media don't spare us any details on the subject. To the point of sometimes giving the impression that every Western journalist makes it a point of honor to unearth some tragic or abominable subject from Russian reality. As a result, Westerners are so frightened by Russia's apparent criminality that they almost jokingly wonder whether they need a bullet-proof vest to visit the country.

Secondly, legality in today's Russia is cause for concern. Not only the newspapers, but also radio and TV talk about it openly. For the first time, the Prosecutor General of the Russian Federation publicly addressed the seriousness of the situation in his speech to the National Assembly.[79]

Rampant crime around the world is a growing concern for ordinary citizens in the countries concerned. The events that unfolded during the spring 2002 election campaign in France bear witness to this. However, the specific situation in Russia over the last ten years has only reinforced this general trend.

The speech delivered by Russia's Prosecutor General in April 2002 is alarming. Here are a few figures: 1 *murder*, 4 *burglaries* and almost 40 *robberies* occur *every 10 minutes* in the country; 2 million citizens were the victims of criminals last year and, according to various estimates, almost 600 billion dollars have left the country over the last ten years.

What's most appalling is not the figures themselves, but their tendency to keep rising. The number of crimes[80] recorded last year did not fall, on the contrary - it rose by 0.5%. Premeditated murders also rose by 5.5%. Crimes are increasingly pre-planned and well-organized. It is horrifying to note that gangs of delinquents are often teenagers who cannot even be seriously convicted under the law, and who therefore receive symbolic punishments.

However, most murders (almost 80%) take place as before, as part of *everyday life.* The classic case, for example, is when two "friends" who were business associates got drunk, lost their tempers, and the argument

---

79. Journal *Vremia Novostei*, May 5, 2002.
80. V. Kostikov, "Anatomy of corruption", *AiF*, nos 22 and 24, 2002.

ended with a knife - a common occurrence in Russia, hardly conceivable in Europe. There are many variations. Deep disillusionment, dissatisfaction and bitterness, impulsiveness, feelings taken to extremes combined with poor-quality "doctored" vodka are enough to create the incident.

According to analysts, the violent social divide has only served to reinforce social aggression: after decades of general poverty, Russia's population has suddenly split into social strata previously known to Russians only through books and films. Human consciousness hasn't always had time to adapt to new realities. It's hard for people to accept that someone is getting rich very quickly before their very eyes, and often illegally too. This break with the past is causing great social tension.

It also explains changes in life orientation, particularly among young people. It's no coincidence that 10% of all crimes are committed by teenagers under the age of 18. The latest public opinion polls show for the first time that, for a new category of people, it's not so much *traditional* Russian values (e.g. "family", "health", "friends", "respect for those around us", etc.) that are important (cf. part 2, chap. 3, § 2, and part 3, § 7) as *personal well-being* and *material affluence.* Nor does it matter how the latter was acquired.

Drug addiction has taken on worrying proportions. The number of crimes linked to the drug trade increases every year. From Afghanistan, drugs quickly invaded the Russian market after transiting through Tajikistan, and today, alas, there is not a single inhabited place in Russia, even in the most remote province, where this poison is not known. As for the police, they only manage to catch small-time dealers or consumers, but there are still no known cases where the organizers of drug trafficking have been arrested.

The number of crimes is, of course, impressive. But even more worrying is the loss of confidence in the State to find the culprits in the country; Russians believe even less in the possibility of a proper conviction or compensation for damages. 90% of citizens have no confidence in the public prosecutor's office.[81]

Russians don't trust the police any more, to the point of not even reporting crimes to their officers. In the fight against crime, the police are more

---

81. *AiF* survey, n° 21.

concerned with showing their "good results" to their superiors than with concentrating their efforts on protecting the citizen. The common practice is to conceal certain non-obvious crimes. As can be seen, the Russian relationship with the police is totally different from that in Europe or America.

Corruption has traditionally been the weak point of law enforcement agencies. The practice of bribing civil servants does not date from today or from Soviet times, but its origins go back to the earliest times. The Russians have an ancient saying: "If you don't grease the paw, you won't get far." And no one has ever found fault with it. Whatever the object sought (a court decision, a certificate or a copy of a notarial deed, etc.), the Russian was not accustomed to arguing and "seeking justice" at every step, but to shut up and pay: it was less stressful and less risky, and the matter was "dispatched" that way.

And so it has been for centuries. And it remains so today. It is even continuing on a large scale, as *the number of civil servants in Russia has increased by 1.8 times* in 10 years.[82] The "Informatics for Democracy" foundation has carried out a study showing that almost *half the* country's population and 60% of businessmen believe that "bribery is an essential part of our lives". From time to time, newspapers leak information about corruption at the highest levels, and everyone is outraged.

More often than not, however, people prefer to turn a blind eye to everyday corruption. Wherever you turn, you'll find yourself confronted by it. The range of bribes is limitless, but there are some big favorites: a bribe for "free" medical assistance, for example, costs $600 million a year, entry to prestigious higher education establishments $520 million, rigging files with the automobile inspection or the police $465 million, "restoring" justice in court $275 million, awarding or completing all the formalities required to buy an apartment $123 million. Roughly speaking, the Russian population spends around $3 billion a year on bribes. And it's possible that this sum is 3 to 5 times higher.[83]

---

82. V. Lobanov, "Who's at the helm of the state machine?", *Komsomolskaia pravda*, August 28, 2002.
83. See Note 80.

The sectors of the economy where corrupt "networks" get their palms greased in particular are: oil, gas and metal exports, electric power, rail transport, communications, the national defense procurement service, army stewardship and wholesale trade.[84] Of course, the production and trade of petroleum vodka and the production and distribution of medicines are also corrupt. In some regions, the "leaders" in this field are the fish industry, the logging and timber trade, and the mining and processing of gold, diamonds, aluminium and precious metals.

The spheres where corruption is most rampant are public health and education, making life particularly difficult for families with sick children or parents. Managers of small and medium-sized businesses have a particularly hard time of it.

Compared to the corruption that reigns in the upper echelons, the average amount of a bribe is not so high: 2,000 to 4,000 dollars "in all". But the crooks won't let any businessman through without asking for "retribution". And it's control and inspection that "cost" the most. The issuing of documents of all kinds and the concealment of tax errors account for approximately 60% of the total corruption market. Expenditure on "unofficial state action on the business world" accounts for a total of 15% of GNP, or almost 1.4 trillion rubles.[85]

The highest bribes are paid to customs officials. An ordinary customs officer can easily "demand" $4,000 or more. The absolute leaders in bribes to control bodies are[86]: customs (18.3%), fire inspection (5.9%) and health and epidemic prevention services (5.6%).

The breakdown of the corruption market between the different branches of government is interesting: executive branch 98.97%; legislative branch 0.17%; judicial branch 0.86%. This means that accusations that the legislative and judicial branches are mired in corruption and are thus preventing the establishment of the rule of law are unfounded. As we can see, their role has diminished and merely reflects the arbitrariness of the executive branch.

---

84. *Ibid.*
85. Article "The shadow economy thrives and spreads", *AiF*, n° 18-19, 2002.
86. *Ibid.*

The main winners are, of course, the civil servants who impose their rules of the game on the business world, especially SMEs. And they don't just take bribes in cash. A civil servant may demand as payment for his services that his son or wife get a good job in the company he is controlling; or ask for a "share" of shares or a large donation to the "charitable foundation" he has set up; or ask to be provided with a luxurious apartment. The cost of these gifts can range from tens of thousands to $1 million.

It goes without saying that corruption puts pressure on the development of start-ups in Russia, reducing their chances of success. It reinforces monopolism, weakens competition, and makes life easier for "its companies" without making them lucrative in the long term, since its sole aim is to extract maximum profit quickly and without delay, while ensuring that "the grass doesn't grow there".

A country's level of corruption depends on its level of economic development and democracy: the more developed the economy and democracy, the lower the level of corruption. Today, as the institutions of power are weakened in Russia, corruption is "running the show". According to the Prosecutor General of the Russian Federation, the police have information on the corruption of "people in the highest echelons", but they don't even try to fight it. 70% of the *lawsuits filed for bribery have been* against doctors, professors, employees of commercial organizations - in other words, the poorest, most defenseless citizens. While representatives of state administrative bodies and senior civil servants account for no more than 1% of those caught "red-handed" in bribery cases, we simply don't dare go after them.[87] This situation is often explained by the fact that the police, public prosecutors and courts are themselves corrupt.

Another serious reason is the low level of development of the Russian market and economic legislation. In its own way, corruption helps to overcome the superfluous "regulation" of the *economy* inherited from the Soviet system.

The essential reason for "indifference" to corruption lies, of course, elsewhere: in stereotypes that have been ingrained in people's consciousness

---

87. See note 80.

for centuries, in the lack of control by special forces, and in the presence of a "shadow economy".

What is the "shadow economy"? The Accounts Chamber of Russia recently checked the taxes paid "on vodka". And it made a startling discovery. Every year, 185 million decalitres of vodka are sold in Russia, and 215 million are drunk. How is it possible to drink more vodka than is sold? The reason is simple: the difference lies in the illegal production of "firewater". And there are even more staggering figures: the fact, for example, that Russia exports *1 million tonnes less gas* each year than is imported into the countries where it is sold.[88]

What do these figures mean? That part of this economy is "underground", enabling it to evade taxes, that it is illegal production, and so on. According to estimates by the Sociological Center of the Russian Academy for State Service[89], the underground (non-state-controlled) sector has increased 5-fold over the last ten years, and now accounts for 50% of Russia's total production volume. Of course, this is not a specifically Russian problem - it exists in all countries. But whereas in Europe the underground economy accounts for only 6-8% of overall production, in Russia it accounts for *half* (!).

The important thing is not so much the scale as the original situation of this "shadow" economy, which leads the authorities to accept it and turn a blind eye to it, making any attempt to combat it futile. In the West, things are clearer: the trade is either legal (the company is registered) or illegal, and there is no in-between zone.

In Russia, the so-called "shadow business" is practically inseparable from the legal business. Every business has its shadow component. And 81% of Russian business leaders admit that they could not conduct their business successfully if they did not break the law. Only 15% claim to be able to succeed without having to circumvent them.[90]

The whole Russian life consists in evading taxes and statistics, in hiding production. However, one should not think that data on the "underground"

88. Presentation by the Institute of Experts, "La charge de l'État et la politique économique" (October 23, 2002), in the journal *Finansy* ("Finances"), November 2002.
89. V. Ustinov, *Our main task: the defense of the individual,* Rossiskaia gazeta, May 5, 2002.
90. See note 88.

economy are kept secret in Russia. When the State Statistics Committee calculates its indicators, it always takes into account the shadow economy. However, the government has no plans to combat it in the near future.

At first glance, it would seem that the *underground economy does* not offer any advantages, especially for ordinary Russians. Producers, for example, evade taxes, and as a result, old women receive a miserable pension, there is a shortage of textbooks in schools, medicines in hospitals, and so on. Analysts, however, see things differently. The "parallel sector" enables the population of Russia to survive. The income of those who work is extremely low and the *parallel economy* offers them cheap goods and services. What's more, it offers a wide range of ways to earn money. The lower strata of the population aspire to well-being and do not have the possibility to access it legally. If this sector is destroyed, people's lives will become untenable. That is why it is not in the interest of the state to end it quickly. It's better to turn a blind eye to the shadow sector, in order to reduce social tensions and avoid marginalizing people.

Analysts at the Sociological Center[91] have calculated that a *third* of official Russian household expenditure does not find its way into official coffers. What's more, the lower people's salaries, the more they spend in the informal sector. The "turnover" of the parallel economy in Russian family budgets totals *40 billion* dollars a year, or as much as the country's budget. And according to experts, nothing is likely to change in the next 10-15 years.[92]

And last but not least. It's in the *food industry, trade and services* that the "shadow trade" thrives, i.e. where there's no need for large production areas, big machines and a large workforce.

These are the riskiest sectors of the economy, but also the ones that attract the most profit.

---

91. See note 89.
92. See note 85.

3. Different generations of Russians

The transition to a market economy and democracy meant the break-up of the old economic structure and its links: scientific centers, companies, production centers, design offices, planning bodies, etc. Educational diplomas, qualifications, seniority, honors, decorations and the profession itself lost all meaning in the new Russian context. Educational diplomas, qualifications, seniority, honors, decorations and the profession itself lost all meaning in the new Russian context, dealing a heavy blow to the morale of many citizens. Generational differences played an increasingly important role in social differentiation, particularly in the perception of the Russian past and present.

The positions taken in opinion[93] polls reveal three different *groups of* people. Older and younger people often express opposing ideas and judgments. And when it comes to middle-aged individuals, the responses of the two extremes are often more measured. In this way, they act as a transitional link and social buffer, with their balanced worldview.

And as paradoxical as it may seem, the "middle ground" is not necessarily linked to a given age group. Different generations think that "Western democracy, individualism and liberalism are values that do not suit Russians", but to different degrees. Thus, 24.4% of 16-24 year-olds, 40.7% of 25-35 year-olds, 49.4% of 36-45 year-olds and 62.9% of over-55s are of this opinion.[94] As we can see, rejection of the values of Western democracy increases with age.

But when people are asked *whether trust between individuals was a feature of the Brezhnev period,* the ratio is reversed: 27.4% of young people under 25 consider this question outdated, while 71.8% of people over 56 - an overwhelming majority - disagree with the young people's position. The older people are, the more tolerant they are of their past.

So, when it comes to *moral and ethical values,* some things mean nothing to the young, while they endure for people of a certain age. You need to bear

---

93. See note 64.
94. See note 63.

this in mind when dealing with Russians of different age groups. That's a first conclusion.

A *second conclusion* is that the middle-aged people who responded to the various questionnaires often have fluctuating answers, sometimes close to those of young people, sometimes close to those of older people. This age group plays a *stabilizing role* in the country, preventing total misunderstanding and the splitting of society into generational groups. It's as if they cement society together, albeit not on every issue.

Here are the opinions common to almost all generations of Russians.

First and foremost, an overwhelming majority of Russians are proud of the country's victory in the Second World War (over 80%) and its post-war reconstruction (70%). 75% of Russians are proud of their great poets, writers and composers, as well as their achievements in space conquest and astronautics. 50% of Russians admire Peter the Great and his reforms. Don't forget that.

Secondly, the traditional way of thinking has not changed in Russia. The majority of Russians continue to believe that "the individual must strive to keep his conscience pure and his soul at peace" (69.3%) and that "the most important thing in life is equal opportunities for all in all spheres[95]" (56.8%). Despite the recent upheavals in the life of the country and the different assessments of events by different generations, *the Russian socio-cultural world has not changed.*

And more than ideology, common interests, values and goals, it is shared trials and emotions that bind generations together. This unity of the nation is, of course, fragile and can collapse in the course of sudden historical reversals... At the same time, it serves as a psychological bulwark for people in these uncertain times, and enables Russians to retain the sense - important to them - of a *common destiny* and concepts such as "nation".

In recent years, the succession of values in the evolution of society has not been normal. The traditional respect for the elderly has been shaken.

---

95. "Public opinion monitoring by the Independent Russian Institute of Social and National Problems in N. Thikhonova's article 'The general state of society and the values of Russians'", in the newspaper *Izvestia*, 1997.

Nowadays, the "young" go ahead and dominate, concerned only, according to the "old", with their own personal well-being.

However, there is every reason to believe that the link between the different generations has been maintained in Russia.

It's true that young Russians, born in a different context, are more *pragmatic* and sometimes more *cynical* than their elders of 40 and, even more so, 60. They've been dubbed the "perestroika generation" and even the "Pepsi generation". Not having experienced the genetic fear of their elders, they are more dynamic. What's most important to them[96] is "interesting work" (42%), "friends" (37%), "money" (32%), and, of course, "love". Today's youth are culture- and education-oriented, but tempted by wealth. They are particularly characterized by their entrepreneurial *spirit, willpower, desire for wealth, indifference* and *laziness. Hard work, selflessness* and *patriotism* are less developed qualities. This is the most "pro-Western" generation, devoid of any nostalgia for the USSR. *On the whole,* their way of thinking and their values are no less close to those of their older brothers and fathers. At least they do not oppose them.

Representatives of the *"in-between" generation*[97] - or, as they're known, the "stagnation generation" - are now aged between 40 and 50. These individuals are oriented towards values such as *family, health,* but also *work* and *money.* The dominant character traits of this generation are *honesty, diligence* and *kindness,* although to a lesser extent than in the older generation.

In turn, the *older generation*[98] (over 55), who sometimes call themselves "60-somethings", are nostalgic for the period of "stagnation" and have a negative perception of the current situation. They idealize pre-revolutionary Russia to a far lesser extent than younger people, and generally perceive it as a society of crime, lack of spirituality and corruption. As with other generations, their main values are *health* and *family.* But unlike the other generations, it is *justice* (45%) that comes third, rather than *money,* which comes last (seventh). This generation is oriented towards "high spirituality" and "social justice". Its main character traits are *honesty, diligence, kindness,*

---

96. See note 63.
97. *Ibid.*
98. *Ibid.*

responsibility, selflessness, patriotism and *collectivism* - the traditional qualities of the Russian archetype.

So, although the different generations of Russians have different traits, they nevertheless share *qualities and values that form the core of their consciousness.*

This unity of values is also apparent on another level. According to analysts[99], the *historical period of reference* for all generations of Russians is the Soviet period. This period, well known to virtually all Russians today, provides them with the stock of ideas, notions and direct life impressions that make up the social experience of each generation. Added to this, of course, is the experience of the new Russia. But this new experience appears "secondary", grafted onto the Soviet experience. The consciousness of Russians is still imbued with the Soviet past, whatever their relationship with it. This explains why individuals, in their character, actions and reactions, remain "Soviet".

In practice, this is reflected in the tendency of Russians to judge the present and assess the country's development trends according to specifically "Soviet" "positions". These positions, moreover, are not necessarily pro-communist, but they remain "Soviet".

Despite the anti-Soviet tone of the influential media, Russians are not inclined to systematically blacken the Soviet period. Only 18.4% of people agree that "there is little in the history of the USSR to be proud of", compared with 75.5% who take the opposite view.[100] The stereotype of the class struggle also seems to concern Russians less and less. They feel they would be much better off today if it hadn't been for the 1917 revolution. Despite the "romanticism of the White Guard", which enjoyed great popularity in film and theater, they were not always enthusiastic about the struggle of the White officers against the Bolsheviks...

Russians, of course, no longer have a sense of the "exclusivity of the Soviet regime", no one proudly calls it "Soviet", but the feeling of having personally participated in "Soviet life" remains, even if tinged with bitterness.

---

99. *Ibid.*
100. *Ibid.*

One more important point. In the consciousness of all generations of Russians, a completely new trend is clearly emerging, unknown in previous decades: *patriotism.* Despite the country's difficult situation, most Russians want to feel that they belong to a rich, free power that enjoys the respect of the rest of the world. Notions such as "fatherland", but also the two-headed eagle, the anthem and other symbols of the state have not lost their meaning for Russians.

The new trend has practical consequences: first-name fashion, for example. In the past, Russians gave their children exotic names (Marianne, Cruz, Iden), whereas today the trend is towards traditional Russian names such as Egor, Pakhom and Anfissa. Fans of easy reading have long since noticed that national crime novels now dominate the shelves. If Russian Simenons and Chases are well on the way to overtaking their Western masters, it's because it now seems more interesting for Russians to immerse themselves in national realities. Foreign TV series have suddenly lost their appeal. Just ten years ago, Russians had an all-consuming passion and interest for overseas exoticism, and overnight they've become totally indifferent to it.

What's more, Russians are increasingly annoyed by the negative things they read or hear about their country. It's not so much the point-blank truth as the negative, arrogant, ironic or critical tone used towards their country that gets on their nerves.

In this way, the civic sense of Russians, their patriotism, the feeling that their destiny is inseparable from that of the country are widespread and today depend neither on age nor on the material situation of citizens.

4. Russians and entrepreneurship

"I sell while laughing, I do the accounts while crying".
(popular Russian proverb).

Economists, sociologists and other theorists have written a great deal on the subject: can entrepreneurship take root in Russia after several decades of oblivion, prohibitions and severe sanctions? It seemed that the most active, inventive and enthusiastic Russian individuals had been put out of business... Life has belied these assertions.

First of all, it's surprising to find that the entrepreneurial spirit is not so foreign to Russians, despite their aforementioned indifference to pragmatism and the material side of life. 52.6% of Russians have already set up a business or would like to do so.

At the start of the reforms over 10 years ago, they were even more numerous - 63%. The number of those who actually run their own business today (5.6%), compared with those who did so ten years ago (12.6%, or 1 in 8), *has roughly halved.*[101]

The reasons for this decline are obvious: none of the past ten years has been favorable to entrepreneurs. SMEs are particularly affected. By way of comparison[102]: in the USA, 7.3 million of the 7.5 million businesses are small and account for 50-52% of America's GDP. In Russia, there are just 844,000 small businesses out of a total of 3 million, and they account for just 10% of Russia's GDP. They employ just 8.3 million people (compared with 70.2 million employed in US small businesses), almost *10 times fewer than in the USA.*

Why are there so few SMEs in Russia? What prevents them from growing?

First of all, there are the numerous bureaucratic hurdles. In order to start a business, you have to fill out all kinds of documents, register with the trade and tax authorities, complete all the necessary formalities with pension and social security organizations, etc. In terms of money, the cost is 2,500 rubles and the wait is at least a month.

But this is nothing compared to what awaits them once the business is up and running. The entrepreneurs are regularly solicited by the most diverse authorities: police, tax department, fire department, health and epidemiological center, governmental inspection organism, etc. And they have to be paid every time...

It's easy to see why the number of those planning to trade in the near future *has fallen by almost 4 times.*

So we can conclude that *capitalism has not yet become a national affair in Russia during these ten years of reform.* Not at all because it is alien to

---

101. *AiF* survey, n° 16.

102. M. Tchijov, "Les particularités du monde russe des affaires", *www.AIF.ru* - n° 40, October 2, 2002.

Russians, but because all the reforms undertaken have failed to make it a mainstream type of activity. It's still a hassle, and remains a marginal activity that can only be undertaken by active people who aren't afraid to take risks.

What's more, 4.5% of Russians *would never want to be entrepreneurs*. These are generally people who have always had a traditional approach to business: for them, it can only be a dishonest activity. In their view, wealthy people are usually criminals who owe their freedom only to the "chaos" in the country. These Russians would gladly give up their business if they had a choice, but fear of unemployment *forces* them to continue.

Finally, the reasons increasingly given by entrepreneurs to justify their choice of activity are *material well-being* and the desire to *show what they are capable of*. This is a far cry from the motivations of the early years of free enterprise: the reasons given by entrepreneurs then were "independence", "the usefulness of their work for others", "their authority within their entourage", etc.

These answers better reflected traditional Russian values, which are clearly disappearing.

5. How do Russians rate their material situation and social status?

It's extremely difficult to deal with this issue seriously and accurately. On the one hand, the media are full of figures on the appalling poverty of Russians. For example, the leader of the Yabloko (liberal) party recently announced on television to anyone who would listen that 97% of Russians live in *destitution*, on the verge of poverty. And nobody challenged him. Perhaps because it is not the Russian way to be optimistic, while moaning and complaining is "in fashion", especially during a political battle.

On the other hand, any foreigner cannot but be seized with astonishment when taking a look, even superficially, at today's Russia. The most striking impression comes from the countless new houses and buildings, not so much in the city as in the dacha districts. These are not even the palaces of the "new Russians" (there are not that many of them), but one- and two-story houses, often of brick.

A senior official of the State Construction Committee[103] claims that over the last ten years, 15 million unlisted dachas have been built to avoid taxes. And if you think for a minute that half of all landowners are, in spite of everything, law-abiding and don't wish to shirk their obligations to the state, then the number of new suburban homes has reached 30 million! And in each house lives a family of at least three people. Under these conditions, talk of "impoverishment" and population extinction in a "starving" Russia seems somewhat misplaced.

The figures usually given by the media can be puzzling to anyone, as they contradict the daily reality that everyone is able to observe.

For example, it's hard not to notice the huge markets and "shopping malls" that invade the country and never empty; they operate day and night, and even on public holidays. The crowds in the streets are well-dressed, the traffic in Russian cities is jammed, and the number of stores selling building materials and furniture is beyond comprehension. Why do *tens of millions* of Russians travel abroad (according to data from the Federal Tax Service)? How is it that Russians keep nearly 140 million dollars in their stockings (according to a study of the population's economic and social problems conducted by the Russian Academy of Sciences)[104]?

There are many more facts that contradict the media's pessimistic assertions and for which no logical explanation can be found. *Russia's inner workings are still a mystery* to many people. Nobody knows how they work. It will be up to the future to solve them.

To return to the reality of concrete facts and figures, however, we have to agree that the material situation of Russians today is extremely difficult. Statistics show that *a third of* Russians earn between $100 and $150 a month, and that the very rich (over $5,000) make up only 7% of the population.[105] The overwhelming majority of Russians are not satisfied with their situation. And there are good reasons for this.

It's already ten years since the creation of the Council for Foreign Policy and Defense, which brings together quite a few "brains". In 2002, according

---

103. See note 81.
104. *AiF*, March 13, 2002.
105. See note 14.

to the organization's calculations, the average Russian had just $4,500, *15 times less than the* US standard of living. In other words, the average Russian is *15 times poorer* than the average American.[106]

How much do Russians earn on average? At first glance, this question makes no sense. According to the State Statistics Committee, it's around $100-150. However, these figures do not take into account what is known as "hidden labor remuneration", i.e. the amount that, according to the State Statistics Committee, is paid in the black (cash) and on which the citizen pays no income tax.

There are huge regional differences in wages: the lowest are in Dagestan (around $30, *three times less* than the national average) and Buryatia (*2 times less*). And the *richest* regions are the centers of the oil and gas industry: the Yamalo-Nenetskij and Khanty-Manskitel districts (respectively *3 and 4 times the* Russian average).

Salary costs in Russia were only $1,926 in 2002.[107] By way of comparison: in 1996, this figure was $57,009 in West Germany and $47,076 in France. The cost of skilled labor in Russia is therefore almost *25-30 times lower* than in Europe! The cost of rail freight across Russia is *14 times lower* than in Europe.[108]

This difference in *production costs is* bound to attract the attention of those who have decided to do business in Russia.

But let's leave these statistics aside. Russians are divided into several groups according to their standard of living. This group is determined according to these elements: type of company where they work (private or public sector), profession, age bracket and place of residence.

Those working in the private sector are better off than those in the public sector: the average level of income per family member for a private-sector employee is *twice* that of a public-sector employee ($160 and $95 respectively!).

Social and professional differences are not so obvious between different groups of people.

---

106. Article "Dynamics and evolution of the political climate in Russia", message from the President to the National Assembly, *Moskva* magazine, June 27, 2001.
107. See note 81.
108. See note 67.

On the whole, it's clear that among the *rural population,* there are 1.5 times as many poor people and 2 times as few affluent people as among the *intelligentsia.*

The poorest are rural dwellers (with an income of around $60); the unemployed, pensioners and workers have slightly higher incomes ($70-86). Career military and police officers don't earn much more ($105.20). Employees, teachers, doctors and scientists are in a difficult situation, with salaries ranging from $110 to $128.2.

The main factor differentiating the population is *age.* The level of satisfaction with one's life and material situation drops sharply from one age group to the next.

The "new Russians" are *no older than 45.*

Among the *middle-aged,* only 25% have an average standard of living; 33% are poor. While only 3% of young people under the age of 25 feel they live below the poverty line.

To generalize, we could say that all the reforms undertaken since the start of perestroika have penalized first and foremost those who, at the time, were *over 40* and mainly those *over 50.* They are the victims of perestroika.

The Soviet model of wage distribution took into account seniority, which gave different advantages and privileges. The Soviet regime therefore favored the old. But since then, there has been a reversal of social roles that "disadvantages" those of the older generation, even if they receive the same salary as the young.

What's more, Russians assess their level of affluence differently: they evaluate their situation in *relation to the opinion of those around them,* and then only *in relation to their salary.* Let's remember the most important principle of the Russian archetype: the aspiration to "live like everyone else".

Can we compare the impact of this principle during the USSR and after? Has the Russian perception of the world changed over the last ten years?

In 1990, the majority of the population (61.3%) lived "like everyone else", 25% "better than everyone else", and only 7% "worse off". Today[109], this majority is virtually unchanged (53.7%), but what's even more frighte-

---

109. See note 63.

ning is the number of those who live worse than everyone else: up from 7% to 29.6%!

The most dramatic change concerns those who once lived in poverty. With the decline in the standard of living, they now live in deepest poverty.

Conclusion

Taking into account the changes in the standard of living of Russians during the reform years, we can distinguish 5 groups of Russians:

1) The "new Russians", whose situation during the years of reforms improved (10.5%).

2) The "old rich", who once lived better than those around them and now "live like everyone else" (4.7%).

3) "Those who had an intermediate situation" and now "live like everyone else" (39.2%).

4) "Victims" who feel their situation has worsened during the reform years (27.1%).

5) The "new poor" who feel their standard of living has fallen catastrophically during the reform years (14.1%).

According to experts[110], a *middle class is gradually* emerging in Russia: it now comprises around *10 million households*. Its representatives also differ from the middle class in developed countries. Middle-class Russians have a certain socio-professional status: they are generally well-educated people - managers, mid-level executives, high-level experts - who earn $300-600 per person. There are *7.5 million households* belonging to this group in Russia.

2.5 million households belong to the "privileged" of this class - with a salary of around $2,000 per household: these are the heads of SMEs, lawyers and doctors who have prospered.

What's important is how the middle-class Russian spends his money: 30% goes on food, the rest equally - on services, leisure and clothing. They usually have a cell phone and a car. Every middle-class Russian family has

---

110. V. Sivkova, "Comment la classe moyenne a changé en une année", *AiF*, July 2002.

$4,000-$4,500 in savings, which they save for "lean times", for holidays abroad, to buy a car or a fur coat for the wife.

It seems that these dry figures do not reflect the full reality. Yesterday's engineer now trades on the market, and the man who was once regarded as a speculator and despised by society has now acquired the status of "capitalist shock worker".

Psychologically, Russians assess their situation differently, and this assessment is not necessarily directly linked to their material wealth. For example, we must not lose sight of such important psychological factors as, on the one hand, the loss of confidence in tomorrow, the loss of a sense of security, etc., and on the other, the acquisition of personal freedom, freedom of conscience, freedom of movement... Certain factors can complement or neutralize each other.

Overall, judging by the data obtained, *upward* social mobility concerns *one in ten Russians*, while *downward* mobility concerns 41.2%, or almost half the population. In other words, only *10% of the population have been able to adapt to the new conditions, and have emerged as winners from the reforms* after fighting off the competition, which is not the case for almost half of Russians.

And if most Russians would like to become rich, it's not for the wealth itself, but for the opportunities it offers: "an education, an interesting job, etc.".

The growing gap between rich and poor is perceived by Russians as a crying injustice.

Only 7% of Russian citizens like to live and work under competitive conditions: they prefer chance, risk and forward movement. And these are precisely the people who drive Russian society forward.

As we can see, progress is not the work of the majority.

6. Who are the "new Russians"?

"He who has dared, he has devoured".
(popular Russian proverb).

Who are these so-called "new Russians"? The shadow economy seems to have contributed to their emergence. They form two groups of people.

The first is made up of *business leaders* who are active in finance and the economy. The second is made up of property *owners* who secretly took part in the privatization of large state-owned enterprises in the early 90s, using their dominant position in the nomenklatura during the USSR.

Overall, it's fair to say that it's the previously relatively privileged sections of the population - such as teachers, cultural workers and researchers - who have *suffered* most from the transition to a market economy.

In the course of the reforms, there was a succession of leaders and "outsiders". Those with prestigious professions lost their advantageous (or comfortable) material situation and their leadership role, to be replaced by modest "little engineers" and "lab managers" who emerged from the shadows and were treated with haughtiness by the intelligentsia. It's fair to say that the scenario of the 1920s has virtually been repeated in Russia: "He who started from nothing became omnipotent."

The first group, *entrepreneurs, is* the most interesting and the most promising. They are generally individuals of 45 years of age or less, with high intellectual faculties. As they have to act in a relatively uncertain and unstable economic context, only particularly energetic, brilliant and efficient individuals can assume the role of pioneers in an economy in transition. *They owe their position solely to their personal qualities and determination.*

The emergence of an entrepreneurial class has yet to be fully appreciated. The speed with which this class has emerged in Russia is astonishing. Just ten years ago, everyone was lamenting the loss of the business class, an irreversible loss of pre-revolutionary Russia.

How do these people know about tax law, the stock market and shares? Nobody ever taught them. None of this was included in the USSR legislation that was still in force when Russia switched to a market economy.

The pioneers of the business world, breaking all the laws, were advancing on a minefield. Not surprisingly, the first cohort of entrepreneurs was made up of the fittest, fastest and boldest individuals, those who, as the saying goes, "know all the tricks". In record time, they set up the country's infrastructure: they acted as "shuttles" (in trade), opened stores, created stock markets, banks, holding companies, started exporting goods, opened advertising and production agencies, issued shares and bills of exchange, went bankrupt and got back on their feet. At first, they learned to trade and act as intermediaries. Now they're learning to produce, grow, build and mine.

Admittedly, a criminal undercurrent has existed in the Russian business world from the very beginning. However, those who have entered the legal economy no longer wish to find themselves in conflict with the law. Their ability to adapt and learn, and their desire for respectability, should not be underestimated. Running a dubious business is a dangerous and time-consuming exercise. This reassures us that Russia's economic situation can only stabilize in the future.

The anecdotes about the "new Russians" (of which there is a whole series - see Part 4, §4) describing them as primitive, savage and dreaming of just one thing - transferring their capital out of the country and "taking it easy" somewhere in Cyprus - are gradually becoming a thing of the past. They've probably already realized their dreams.

As for mature individuals who have consciously chosen their path, they are certainly not inclined to spend their money indiscriminately. The presence of a category of responsible people, motivated to build, is increasingly apparent. Far from "flaunting their wealth", they secretly support orphanages, for example, with private donations.

Who are these individuals who make up the class of Russian entrepreneurs who have been able to make their way?

Over the last 10-12 years, objectively speaking, those who have *gained* and moved on are, above all, those who have been able to go to work in the brand-new *private sector* companies. This depended on age, profession and place of residence. In the depressed regions, it was of course less feasible to work in the private sector than in Moscow, St. Petersburg or Nizhny Novgorod. Previous *position* was also an important factor: managers retained their privileged position on the whole, while middle managers lost it. This group is mainly made up of *men*. Women, who are mainly active in the *social sphere of the public sector* (doctors, teachers, scientific researchers, engineers, etc.), have suffered more than men. In short, the *losers* are those who have remained outside the "market sector".

In addition to objective factors, there are *subjective factors that* have influenced the growing well-being of Russians. Let's remember the Russian conservative syndrome of "being like everyone else" and "not standing out from the crowd". Only the brilliant, non-conformist individuals who aspired to the individualism of Western societies came out on top by occupying leading positions, while the others - the losers - remained on the bangs of society. The sudden change of leaders and outsiders is not due to chance, it is linked to the mentality and behavior of the individual.

How do Russians view the rich? According to sociological studies, the most widespread stereotype - that Russians feel distrust and hostility towards wealth - is rather contradictory. On the one hand, more than half of Russians (58%) make no distinction between those who have become rapidly wealthy over the last ten years and others, and even regard them with respect and interest. On the other hand, 30% of Russians feel distrust and hostility towards them. More than envy, this attitude is a reaction to the behavior of the rich, their arrogance, their need to flaunt their success and wealth.

The "American dream" of getting rich quick doesn't really catch on in Russia. Even those stimulated by income differences and the presence of the rich are not totally indifferent to how these differences translate materially. Research carried out by the Institute of Psychology shows that Russians are prepared to accept a 5-7 times *difference in income* between the richest and the poorest. Beyond that, it is perceived as an injustice. However, according to Natalia Rimachevskaya, Director of the Institute of Demography at the Russian Academy of Sciences, this gap is 14. This compares with 7-8 in the USA and 4 in Europe[111]. These data give cause for concern.

The *way in* which money is earned is very important in the Russian mentality: the individual must have *worked hard and made an effort*. It is no less important to spend money "intelligently", not to throw it away, but to use it "for the good of society".

The clashes and huge differences in the social situation of Russians do not promote social harmony, but encourage poor people to achieve well-being by any means possible, even if they are illegal or even criminal.

As for the *middle class,* which is supposed to consolidate and stabilize any society, *it is weak and few in number* in Russia. This is why Russian society,

---

111. V. Sivkova, "Le salaire : stimulation et démotivation", *AiF*, n° 49, 2001.

unlike French society, is in a precarious equilibrium, constantly subject to change, and any harsh conclusion or long-term prognosis may prove inaccurate over time.

7. What moral values are important to Russians today?

For a long time, Russians considered themselves "part of the Soviet people". The official hierarchy was identical, whether in Tsarist times or in the USSR: the people - the collectivity (the production collective or the village community) - the family - the individual.

This is the Russians' symbolic representation of the world: a solid pyramid with the leader (patriarch, tsar, party general secretary, etc.) at the top and the people at the base. Russian citizens had a high opinion of their belonging to a powerful community, which is why the fall of the Soviet Union was so painfully felt by them.

Perestroika not only changed everyday life, but also many values and principles in Russian consciousness. Under the Soviet regime, the most "prestigious" professions were: *diplomat, cosmonaut, ballerina, actress, scientist and teacher, writer, poet or musician - in other words, the professions of the intelligentsia, which included the creative sphere.* And this despite the fact that a blue-collar worker's salary was 4-5 times *higher* than that of a young doctor or university professor. Despite all the inequities in the remuneration of work, "social success" depended on obtaining a higher education diploma, the opportunity to create or realize oneself.

Today, judging by the ranking of the most sought-after professions, *bankers come* first, *entrepreneurs* second, managers third and *top models* fourth. The officer corps *ranks* only *12th*, while the professorial and teaching corps *rank 14th and 15th* respectively.

Today, the individual is assessed not so much on the basis of his or her intellectual abilities, potential or services to society or the state (as was the case in the past), but rather on the basis of the goods and money at his or her disposal. The "obsession with success", previously unknown to Russians, is gradually spreading.

How do Russians see themselves today: as a "fragment" of the great community that used to be the "Soviet people"? Or as an ethnic group? In what circle of people do they experience this traditionally important sense of community? Who do they prefer to associate with?

Analysts' data[112] show that *health and family* (79.9%) and *friends* (74.4%) play a decisive role in Russians' lives. In the event of a general crisis in the community, people take refuge in their closest circle to escape the storms and upheavals shaking the outside world.

The *second* largest *group is work and school mates* (51.3%), people with whom one shares the *same outlook on life* (52.9%), people of the *same generation* (51.9%), and people *of the same profession* (50.7%).

"National affiliation", "political opinion", "neighborhood", "material affluence and wealth" play a far less important role in the dating habits of Russians: only 25-40% take them into account.

Notions such as "national power", "progress", "prosperity" and "democracy" no longer have the same value as they once did.[113]

A value like "probity" is making a comeback. Given weakened social protection and the almost total lack of state control, the unlimited development of individual freedom has both positive and negative aspects. In this context, people are particularly fond of anything that can regulate their lives, first and foremost "probity, honesty, honor and dignity".

The so-called "New Russians" form a very special group. In their hierarchy of values, "freedom", "property", "prosperity", "stability" and "wealth" occupy first place. Values such as "understanding", "justice" and "spirituality" count for much less. They are more selfish and more concerned with their personal well-being, and their value system means they are moving away from traditional consciousness.

It's paradoxical that work has disappeared from the list of important values for Russians.[114] Especially when you think of the place it occupied in the

---

112. See note 64.
113. *Ibid.*
114. See note 63.

days of the USSR. Refusing to work for the good of society was considered a crime against the socialist state, with all the consequences that entailed. The slogan "If you don't work, you don't eat" was rigorously enforced.

It's interesting to compare the differences in the choice of values between men and women. While men prioritize "freedom", "legality", "order", "professional success" and "ease", women more often choose "family", "charity", "health", "love", "spirituality", "peace", "compromise". Young people, on the other hand, give priority to "love", "success" and "professionalism". But these values lose importance with age. As people age, they place more importance on "spirituality", "stability", "peace", "order" and "legality".

An important feature of Russia in recent years has been the emergence of a large number of economically enterprising people. For the first time in decades, we're dealing with *people who have something to lose* (and not just in the material sense). And there are enough of them to rule out a return of the Communists to power in future elections. Regardless of their economic situation, most people understand where the range of new possibilities comes from, including the ability to "see the world". As for those in intellectual professions - *no less than a third of the population* - regardless of their material situation, they have ideas and values that are characteristic of the *middle class*. The intelligentsia, on the other hand, value their freedom and want to preserve it for their children and grandchildren. As a result, no one is in a position to put society back on its old tracks.

As a result, Russians find themselves enmeshed in a highly complex system of social relations. For them, the old definition of this community as the "Soviet people" has lost its meaning. 40% of Russians no longer identify with the ideal of the Brezhnev period: "Keep quiet, don't stand out from the crowd, wait for a better fate. Today, Russians essentially rely on their own strengths and have no confidence in anyone but themselves.

8. The morals of Russians past, present and future

Moral principles are always the result of history, of political, economic and other relationships in society. For this reason, debating the morality of a nation is a difficult exercise. Indeed, the same event can be judged differently depending on one's point of view.

From a moral point of view, the Russian of yesterday seemed equivocal, to say the least. In general (at least in appearance), he showed contempt for commercialism and pragmatism, categorically condemned prostitution (even if he practiced adultery), observed the traditional rules of family life (inherited from *Domostroy*), jokingly repeated that "you can't catch fish without effort" and was secretly proud of the "great power" that was his country. Apart from that, the deceitful duplicity of Soviet life taught him not to be sincere all the time, and even to lie, to simulate, to get by, to feign "enthusiasm for work"; it also taught him contempt for wealth, hatred of the petty-bourgeois spirit and of the speculators who had prospered, as well as to agree with the regime... And who could afford to argue with the powers that be anyway? It was a matter of survival...

In post-Soviet Russia, it's not just the political system and essential values that have changed, but imperceptibly, morality itself, the notions of morality, probity and non-probity of the individual. The criteria for assessing morality are no longer the same.

For example, a Russian characteristic such as disregard for the material aspect of things may seem, at first glance, to be totally naive. And this particularity can, today, prove dangerous in your business relations with the Russians.

Let's ask ourselves the simple question: "Why do Russians rarely pay their taxes?" Unlike Europeans, *Russians don't obey the law in this area*. And not just because it's a habit that dates back to Tsarist Russia: laws were replaced by the decisions of the master, then in Soviet times, the party official, the leader and so on. And this stereotype of behavior, unconsciously ingrained in people, has been reinforced and re-emerged in all kinds of situations. As a result, today we have the most unruly pedestrians and car drivers in the world. When it comes to taxes, we find the same stereotyped behavior.

The Russian may be surprised by the behavior of the Frenchman who, in addition to his income, goes so far as to declare his company car or apartment on his tax return. Convinced that the taxman knows everything about his material situation, since everything is computerized these days, he prefers not to hide anything and to sleep easy. This behavior is unusual for Russians.

First of all, it's worth noting that *taxes in Russia are the lowest in the world*, at just 13% of income. At the suggestion of the President of the Russian Federation, these taxes are constantly being simplified - especially for those who might set up a business in Russia today. Small businesses (with no more than 20 employees and annual revenues of 10 million rubles) are particularly indulged: they are exempt from profit tax, sales tax and the one-off social tax. The government is working hard to legalize business and gradually *get* citizens *used to* paying taxes.

But this enterprise is not successful, as people try to conceal their income and it is very difficult for the state to collect taxes. The population's *economic ignorance* contributes in no small measure to this situation.

For decades, under Soviet rule, the population was not given even the most elementary notions of economics, which would have been useful if only to manage their own affairs. Everyone waited painfully for a paycheck and somehow made ends meet. Economics was the preserve of professionals: economists, planners and accountants. This system engendered an exaggerated respect and even fear of individuals who were erudite in economics. In Russia, the accountant became the key figure in the company, "running the show", whereas in the West, he or she is merely a cog in the whole machine.

According to the testimony of foreign and even Russian businessmen, standards of business behavior in Russia differ from those generally accepted around the world.

Naturally, attitudes towards taxes are beginning to change for the better. Russians are slowly and painfully beginning to realize that cooperation between business partners cannot be regulated solely by economic and legal provisions. It must also obey the culture of the business world, the generally accepted "rules of the game". Russian businessmen are the first to take an interest in this. It was precisely on their initiative that codes of business ethics were drawn up and the "Charter of Business in Russia" adopted.

The codes exist, but they are far from being observed and respected... For the Russian, "rolling over" the State is, by tradition, a good thing. For the State, in the person of its officials, was for decades always hostile to the interests of the citizen, and never defended them.

We know that Russians are unanimous in noting *a decline in morality as a result of* the changes that have taken place over the last ten years. It would be more accurate, however, to speak of a *shift in priorities* under the influence of Western trends and culture. This is particularly evident among young people, with their "obsession with success", pragmatism and desire for material well-being.

But a Moscow-based American journalist[115] has noted the emergence of a "completely new" behavior, different from the past and from new "Western trends". This recent phenomenon runs counter to the "morality of success". The national star Massiana is the most striking example. Created by the artist Oleg Kuvaev in his web-site studio in St. Petersburg exclusively for his own pleasure, she became popular on the Internet and then even made her place on the TV show "The other day" in Russia... Everyone talked about her enthusiastically, because "she was the proof that you can do your favorite activity and make a lot of money with it, which is something you can only dream of." This "I'm not ashamed to be unemployed" philosophy of life is very much in vogue in Russia today, where the important thing is to "make money", no matter how you do it. Nowadays, work in the traditional sense is rapidly losing its value among Russians, especially young people.

In short, claims about the moral decline of today's Russian are not unfounded. This truth does not need to be demonstrated by extensive sociological research.

Sociologists have succeeded in highlighting a no less interesting paradox: over the last few years, Russians' moral criteria have regressed in the sphere of *social behavior*. For example, far fewer people now condemn the purchase of stolen goods, speculation, the non-repayment of a loan or credit, the

---

115. Gaï Tchazan, Moscow correspondent for the *Wall Street Journal*, "La réponse à la BBC et à Batkhed", in *Moskovskie Novosti*, no. 45, November 19-25, 2002.

appropriation of found money and even political murder - in other words, acts that fall within the sphere of social conduct.

But when it comes to *private life,* Russians have become harsher, at least in words. In public opinion polls, Russians have harshly condemned: moral laxity, failure to meet family obligations - particularly towards children - insincerity and betrayal towards friends, the arrogance of individuals who have rapidly enriched themselves. Far from reflecting the cynicism and growing immorality of Russians, these responses confirm their attachment to traditional values in private life.

And even if Russians have a special relationship with property (see part 2, chap. 3, § 9), they would consider it particularly shameful if they were taught to steal and be dishonest.

If we apply the problem of morality to the field of business, we find that the most interesting results are obtained by comparing estimates of certain amoral acts and whether the authors of these estimates *have won or lost* from the reforms.[116]

It turns out that, despite the generally accepted decline in public morality and the corruption of the economy and the state, attachment to traditional moral values remains *the economically advantageous model of behavior* for Russian businessmen.

Thus, among those who consider it normal to *give bribes, one and a half times fewer* people have improved their material status than those for whom this practice is unacceptable.

Among those who don't condemn not paying taxes, there are half as many successful people.

The success of those who agree to engage in *sexual relations for their own benefit* is virtually nil.

Only those who accept that *deception is a* means to an end have been slightly more successful in life than those who reject this moral choice.

---

116. See note 63.

9. Russians' relationship with the state

One of the most contentious issues in the transition period from Soviet rule to a market economy is the role of the state in the economy and in the social sphere. An analysis of the traditional principles of the Russian archetype (see part 2, chap. 3) is enough to convince us of the close relationship between the individual and the state. However, these relationships have changed over time.

Thus, only ten years ago, the state was still perceived by certain social groups (notably the country's cultural and techno-scientific elite) as a "monster", the "evil empire" and so on. The hysteria manifested at rallies organized at the start of perestroika demanded that the "monster be put to death" and that the country "rejoin the civilized world". For many, this was the natural reaction of a generation that had grown up without freedom in a totalitarian state that permanently repressed personal initiative. It's no coincidence that all the transformations begun in the country were carried out under the banner of the "divorce" between state and society, and minimal state interference in the realm of private interests.

The majority of the population, however, were well aware that the state necessarily had a *social role to play*: social protection, free public health and education, regulation of the economy at various levels. In their struggle against the state, the Russians nonetheless recognized its "fatherly" *obligations* towards them. Thus was born the current conflict between state and society. The only way out seems to be a "return of the state", mainly where its presence is largely lacking, i.e. in the regulation of socio-economic processes.

Having abandoned their ideas of destroying the state, today's Russians are beginning to understand that the "market" is a social institution like any other, and that its existence requires certain rules that the state is able to control. This is why representatives of almost all political parties and groups (and to a lesser extent "liberals") are in *favor of*[117] *state control over the main*

---

117. See note 101.

---

sectors of the economy: communists (45%), socialists (40%), nationalists (43%), and even centrists (30%).

The Russians still believe that *the state should play a predominant role in the economy*.[118] And neither the (currency) exchange of the early 90s nor the economic crisis of 1998 could shake them from their convictions.

For example, 88% of Russians believe that the state should manage electrical energy, and 63% also "return" the *management of housing to* the state. In 1998, only 42% held this view.

72% of Russians think that *metallurgical and machine-tool* plants should be under compulsory state control.[119]

Nearly *half of* Russians share this opinion when it comes to *transport*. But when it comes to *food production,* 2/3 of those questioned have no hesitation in entrusting it to the private sector.

The majority of Russians are dissatisfied with the fact that the state has virtually disappeared from the *social sphere*, having transferred all its concerns about health, education, training, etc. to the individual. Under Soviet rule, people had become accustomed to the state being responsible for the timely payment of pensions, the payment of all work being guaranteed, the disabled and visually impaired being socially protected, and criminals being compulsorily unmasked and punished. It was all self-evident. And when this well-functioning system collapsed, the public didn't understand: either the state was shirking its responsibilities, or it was unable to function normally. Which explains the huge number of demands and the deep resentment towards the state.

Most Russians tend to blame the state for all the misfortunes that befall them. The state is, as in the past, seen as the only body responsible for everything that happens in the country. They are not yet ready to see the other side of the problem - the *weakening of* the Russian state as an institution. And it is precisely Russian doubts about the state's ability to function normally that influence public opinion's move towards authoritarianism.

---

118. Figures taken from the Institut d'experts' report «La charge de l'État et la politique économique», *op. cit.*
119. *Ibid.*

The weakened state has now lost much of its *deterrent power*. Russian citizens say that many no longer trust the state, especially the law enforcement agencies: only 11% of the population trust the police, compared with 71%; for the judiciary, the figures[120] are 12.5% and 64% respectively.

Crime, to which the corruption of officials at all levels contributes, is rampant. Unfortunately, this is an indisputable fact of life in Russia today. In this situation, citizens are demanding protection from the State, and are in favor of strengthening the State's law enforcement agencies.

Given the different approaches to the role of the state, it's only logical that, when asked the general question: "What is the most advantageous political model for Russia?" 37% of Russians favor a *mixed economy with strong state involvement*, 18% favor *centralized planning (socialism)* and only 8% favor a *liberal model* with minimal state interference. Interestingly, the latter figure reached 12.5% in 1994. So the popularity of the liberal model in the economy is plummeting.[121]

But what's most astonishing is that the percentage of those in favor of strong state involvement *is not age-related*: the responses from 18-55 year-olds are more or less the same. This may reflect a certain *conservatism* in Russian consciousness.

According to analysts,[122] the ideal for the majority of Russians would be a "social state" based not so much on individual freedom as on the *idea of solidarity* as a "common good". This model would combine an active role for the state in the economy and strong social protection, with non-interference by the state in private life and political and civic freedoms.

This model does not seem to them to be a projection into the future or something unachievable in the long term. Russians have the impression of having already experienced this system of government in the USSR, especially under Brezhnev.

More than *half of* all those questioned were convinced that "the USSR was the first state in Russian history to ensure justice for simple people and give them a decent life". Such a paradoxical idea is not the result of

---

120. *Ibid.*
121. *Ibid.*
122. See note 63.

ideological "brainwashing" during the Soviet period. It's the very situation in post-perestroika Russia, which hasn't offered people any positive models to structure their lives. As a result, they are driven to idealize their past.

What *social development goals* are the Russians aiming for?

Out of almost two dozen development goals, *half of* the Russians surveyed chose only two: *increasing the quality of life* and putting *the country back in order*. Other objectives, including moral renewal of society, preservation of Russian traditions, creation of an efficient market economy, take a back seat. Russians believe that the state should give priority to the first two objectives.

In keeping with Russian traditions, the State takes on the burden of social obligations, and this burden is growing: in 1998, budget spending reached 37% of GDP (41% of GDP in 2002). By way of comparison: in countries with strong economic growth (China, Malaysia, Taiwan), such expenditure does not exceed 15-20% of GDP, as the governments of these countries refuse to pay pensions and other social protection schemes. But in Russia, such spending is the rule, and it's impossible to avoid it. This places an additional tax burden on Russia's booming corporate sector.

After perestroika, Russian society adopted essential democratic values: equality of citizens before the law, freedom of speech and of the press, independence of the judiciary, free elections of the organs of power, etc. However, these instruments of democracy have not yet been sufficiently appropriated by citizens. However, these *instruments of democracy* have not yet been fully embraced by citizens. The right to freely choose one's profession, the right to travel throughout the country and the right to strike still seem to have no particular significance for Russians. And the media rarely raise this issue.

That's why, given the context, Russians aren't paying too much attention, for the moment, to legitimate forms of political and economic self-organization. Instead, they hope that, for some obscure reason ("a miracle?!"), the country will finally experience "competent power", a "good president" who will "do everything", and that everything will return to "normal". Remember that the traditional Russian archetype is based on the *paternalistic* state (see part 2, chap. 3, §7 and 8).

In any case, Russians categorically reject any revolutionary means of reorganizing society. Only 12% of those questioned were in favor of a *radical transformation of the system*, while 62.4% opted for gradual, evolutionary reforms.

Thus, the widespread myth that Russians have a particular state of mind that causes them to "revolt" is not empirically confirmed. On the contrary, Russians are increasingly united in their *aversion to social experiments*.

They reap the rewards of the bitter road they have travelled.

10. Russians' relationship with capitalism

How do Russians rate the country's economic reforms? They consider them "bad", "mediocre" and even "totally unsatisfactory". Only *1 in 8 Russians* feel they *have benefited from* these ten years of transformation. *1 in 2* think they've lost out and been cheated. The rest either consider that they have lost their previous status, or are hesitant.

As we have seen, the Russians have a paternalistic conception of the state, and their consciousness is still largely imbued with it today. For this reason, a weak state is impossible in Russia.

94% of those surveyed expect the State to guarantee them remuneration for work that is commensurate with its duration and quality. However, half (50.3%) believe that it is up to each individual to look after his or her family's welfare, without relying on the State. It is true that more than a third (36.5%) of citizens do not share this view and still rely on the state to take care of them in a market economy.[123]

It's interesting that, in the opinion of the Russians, the *private sector* cannot operate completely autonomously and independently (28.1%).

Moreover, we should not be disconcerted by a certain contradiction in the figures, as this same contradiction reigns in the consciousness of Russians in this period of transition. There are two models in the minds of Russians: 1) a *paternalistic model*, inherited from the past; 2) a *new, individualistic model*, imposed against their will by today's reality.

This antagonism in Russian consciousness was clearly expressed in their relationship with the private sector. It seems that 47.8% of the respondents

---

123. *Ibid.*

would defend the "freedom of choice" in the restoration of the economy and 47.9% the "freedom of enterprise" of the private sector. That's almost *half* the population! But if this free, competitive market economy is *not regulated by the state*, only 30% would support it!

Of course, business leaders are in favor of the market economy, and they don't accept pressure from the state. Teachers, engineers, the scientific and literary intelligentsia, representatives of trade and the service sector are also in favor.

Among those who are *categorically against* the private sector are: pensioners (57.7% are for a strong influence of the state on the private sector) as well as workers, rural people, army and police (almost *half of them*).

People's positions also change with age. Among Russians under 35, supporters of an independent private sector are *twice as numerous* as among older individuals. However, in all age groups (except for 16-24 year olds), the number of supporters of state intervention in the private sector is higher than the number of opponents.

For example, there are far more supporters of a *strong social state* than of a liberal model, and there is far more support for state regulation of the economy than for a free and competitive economy. On the whole, Russia's citizens aspire to a *mixed economy with strong state regulation*.

It's interesting to see which areas and sectors are involved.

Analysts' data show that, for Russians, the *strategic sectors* (raw materials, energy, communications, rail transport) and the social sphere guaranteeing the health and well-being of the nation (pensions, public health, education, science and culture) must be under state control. For the majority of Russians, however, this predominance of the state does not mean a return to the former planned economy with total state control.

Russians do not accept the *predominance of the private sector* in any sphere. Half of them prefer a mixed economy, with the private and public sectors working side by side in non-strategic sectors. This applies to construction, the media, housing, agriculture, railway construction, finance and the light and food industries. In Russian consciousness, this economic model is called "state capitalism". It provides for the following functions to be performed by the state: elements of *state planning* in strategic areas, and the provision of *subsidies* to companies that have an important social role to play.

The result is a model of the relationship between the individual and the state that is essentially different from that in Western Europe. In the West, the state is first and foremost the guarantor of the rights of the individual in his or her relations with society. In Russia, the traditional model of state-individual relations, but also society-individual relations, has been preserved: society, in other words the "people" represented by the "state", is the starting point.

This information is interesting not only because it shows how Russians feel about the current situation, but also because it gives a clearer picture of the country's prospects.

It is of particular interest to those preparing to do business in Russia. It is precisely in those areas where the private sector and mixed economy predominate that their intentions can best be realized.

11. Russians' relationship with different social groups

So Russians are not opposed to the market economy (capitalism), but they prefer its mixed variant. This opinion is confirmed by their answers to the question: "Who contributes to and who hinders Russia's development today?"

Russian opinion is roughly as follows[124]:

The workers, peasants and intelligentsia (i.e. "the active") are "the most useful" to Russia.

Young people and entrepreneurs are "relatively useful".

Television, newspapers and big banks are "on the whole useful".

The Church, regional authorities, unions, the Federation Council and pensioners are "of little use".

The government, the Duma and the political parties are "not at all useful" and are actually holding back the country's development.

So, according to the locals, today's Russia is held together by its working population, together with entrepreneurs and young people, with the support of the media.

---

124. *Ibid.*

The main "parasites" in today's Russia are politicians with dirty hands who are involved in scandals (75% of those questioned) and who want only one thing: to send their capital and their families abroad, and to come to Russia only occasionally - for their business and to earn fabulous incomes. Russians also see the lack of professionalism among those in positions of power as detrimental to the country.

And that's not all. Among the factors hindering the establishment of normal life are: non-payment of taxes by oligarchs (35.3%), the strongly negative influence of Western states on Russian power (31.1%), environmental degradation due to the activity of industrial enterprises (22.4%).

Particular attention should be paid to the mutual relations between the provincials and the federal centers (Moscow and St. Petersburg). The very strong mistrust of the provincials towards the federal center is all too evident today. Moscow is considered to be "fattening up" without paying any attention to the misery and problems of the provinces, taking credit for everything that has been earned, and so on. This is nothing new in the Russian mentality. Remember the Russian proverb we all know: "Moscow doesn't believe in tears".

Not all provincials are unanimous in their hostility to the center. It depends on the region. Overall, a few years ago, 1 in 3 Russians trusted local authorities more than the center. However, this trend seems to be a thing of the past, as Russia's new president has the support of almost 70% of Russians.

Finally, the idea of dismantling Russia as a united whole is categorically rejected by the majority of Russians.[125]

12. Russians' relationship with freedom and democracy

"Each people has its own conception of freedom, which it distributes and shapes to its own taste…"

(I. Ilyine, On Future Russia, p. 189).

We have already mentioned (part 2, chap. 3, § 4) the *duality of Russians in their relationship to freedom.* Traditionally, they have been ascribed anarchy as well as a capricious temperament and the humility of slaves.

---

125. *Ibid.*

This statement takes on its full force when we consider the totalitarian system the Russians experienced for several decades, the fact that they adapted to mass terror during the civil war and later (under Stalin) never organized mass protests.

This assertion is unjustified: without getting into unnecessary discussions, let's just remember that the number of victims of Stalinist terror was frightening. It's clear that the state used repression not only to break down opposition as such, but to annihilate the very idea of opposition.

Faced with the brutality of terror, the people's opposition to existing laws took a passive form: they circumvented them wherever possible. In the nineteenth century, the Marquis de Custine was already indignant that "Russians obey orders like good soldiers", and even noted that "Russia would be absolutely despotic if all existing laws were observed".

And, more recently, the Communists were unable to overcome the people's passive resistance. Repressed resistance took the form of unconscious sabotage: refuge in private life instead of "building a bright future", indifference to politics, contempt for careerists (especially party members), distrust and even mockery of state propaganda, sustained interest in Western culture, etc.

Bolshevism gradually putrefied over the course of a few decades. And finally, in a matter of days, it was not foreign armies (as in Germany, Japan, France and other countries) but precisely this *permanent internal resistance* and the sabotage of citizens that returned to Russia the freedom so long confiscated.

Of course, the unexpected regaining of freedom brought with it its share of problems for the ordinary citizen, including that of survival. They may even complain of being "tired of freedom" and nostalgic for the "order of yesteryear". It's no coincidence that, as sociological surveys show, the number of Stalin supporters is growing year by year. 50 years after his death, only *a third* of Russians *disapprove of his role*, and 45% of the population (these are people of modest means) are convinced that he played "an absolutely positive role" in the life of the country (GZT.ru - March 7, 2003).

The reasoning of these people is understandable: the new "freedom" is perceived by them as freedom of behavior in society, which is almost tantamount to "acting as one pleases" and may come close to anarchy. For the

242

Russians, freedom is, to a large extent, understood as *social freedom* (the will!), *freedom of decision, freedom of choice and action*, the possibility of living for oneself without taking into account the opinion of those around one, without conforming to anyone.

In this context (associated with the harsh economic conditions of survival), values such as the *expression of the will* and *freedom of conscience, freedom of the press, freedom of movement, free elections* and other *democratic institutions* are no longer as essential, since a more vital problem arises: how to adapt to the new conditions of life, how to survive, how to get back on one's feet and preserve one's children.

However, the intellectually active (31.2% of Russia's population[126]) express middle-class values and cherish freedom, appreciating the absence of censorship, editorial and theatrical boom, freedom of press and conscience, the ability to move "wherever they please", entrepreneurial freedom and so on.

An interesting psychological study was carried out a few years ago in Russia. People were asked to explain *their conception of freedom, and whether they would be prepared to accept a restriction of it.*[127]

As it turns out, almost half of Russians are still prepared to accept restrictions on their rights, provided they receive guarantees of state protection in return. For example, 43% of Russians believe that certain categories of working people do not have the right to strike, whatever the conditions; 42% are in favor of maintaining *propiska* (registration of the individual at his or her place of residence); 31% agree that the media should reflect only those points of view that are useful to the state; and 22% agree that the state should oblige all able-bodied individuals to work as they did in Soviet times.

This study totally destroys the myth of Russians as individuals for whom freedom means "anarchy", "doing as one pleases". For Russians today, the most important aspect of *democracy* lies in the very foundations of the democratic state: the "equality of all before the law" and the "independence of the judiciary". And the importance of these two principles has only increased

---

126. *AiF* survey, n° 18.
127. See note 35.

over the years, from 54% to 83% for the former, and from 41% to 46% for the latter.[128]

The possibility of free political expression ("freedom of the press", "free elections of governing bodies") and democratic forms of social organization, etc., come second for many Russians, unlike Europeans, for whom they are values of prime importance.

It would be naïve to believe (although we often hear it) that Russians are only "learning" democracy and have not sufficiently "assimilated" its norms and rules. The liberal media like to repeat this myth, which is widespread in Russia and abroad. In fact, it's not a question of "learning", but rather of "adapting" the notion of democracy to the Russian experience and traditions.

2/3 of Russians believe that "democratic procedures are just window-dressing and that the country is run by those with money and power".[129] For the majority of people, the interests of the community (society, the people), the social problems to be solved and the defense of national interests against the oligarchs are far more important than problems of democracy and freedom. Only in this sense can we speak of the collectivist spirit of the Russians.

Note that for the majority of Russians, the collective is not the herd instinct, but *a voluntary sacrifice of their rights for the benefit of the community.* In this sense, it is right to speak of the "spirit of sacrifice" as a distinctive feature of Russians.

A poll on a highly controversial issue was conducted among Russians. To the question: "What do you prefer: total democracy with weak guarantees for your personal security or strong power that fully guarantees this security?", only 10.5% of people chose freedom, while 58.7% of Russian citizens favored *personal security* and 30% had difficulty answering.[130] As we can see, in the event of an alternative, democracy loses its importance.

Security is one of the most important demands of the individual, and it's clearly not being met in today's Russia. What's astonishing is not that 58.7% of citizens chose security, but rather that 41.3% did not. This means that

---

128. See note 34.
129. See note 36.
130. See note 63.

for half of Russians, *democracy* is an *essential value,* provided that personal security is already guaranteed.

The choice between democracy and security reflects not so much one's relationship with democracy as the price placed on human life. This is very clear when we analyze the responses of Russians with higher education. The educated and the intelligentsia are more market-oriented than other segments of the population. At the same time, however, they take a very firm stance on "total freedom". Given the country's growing crime rate, they unhesitatingly prefer a strong government capable of guaranteeing the individual's right to security. Even if this means sacrificing certain democratic rights.

And when asked whether they prefer *a society of individual freedom* or *a society of social equality*[131], 26.6% of Russians - young people under 25 - gave priority to individual freedom (i.e., the American "market society" model). More than half of Russians (54%) chose a society of social equality, and 19.4% had difficulty making up their minds.

This clearly shows that the "American" model of society is perceived in a negative light with age. 61.8% of the over-45s are *against it*, and this figure rises to an overwhelming majority (71.8%) for the over-55s. But beware! *Social equality* among Russians is not understood in the sense of *equality of income* or *living conditions*, but in terms of *equality of opportunity*. Even the 25-35 year-old generation, totally converted to the "market", prefers the *idea of equality* to that of individual freedom. And these answers do not reflect so much the "anti-market" consciousness of Russians as the specificity of their culture (see Part 2, Chapter 3) in the broadest sense of the word, i.e., in the sense of their own values and goals in life.

In keeping with the famous motto of the French Revolution, *equality* and *fraternity come* first for Russians. *Freedom* - understood by them at the individual level and not at the level of political institutions - comes only afterwards. Moreover, the *state*, not political forces or parties, should express the general interest: it should first take into account the interests of each

---

131. *Ibid.*

individual, then those of social groups, and in this way conduct a policy for *the good of the whole people.*

13. Russians' relationship with money

The Russian relationship with money is ambivalent. On the one hand, *we avoid talking about money in society*, and insisting on this theme makes Russians feel embarrassed and even ashamed. To persist on this theme is as indecent as talking about sex. This is particularly true of previous generations.

The majority of Russians have a strong prejudice against very rich people, considering that they got rich illegally or with money stolen from the public treasury or from the national wealth. And for those who work hard and can afford the life they deserve (apartment, car, rest in the South Seas and so on), insults like "speculator" are numerous and they are not soft on them.

Certainly, for decades Russians were taught that it was "improper to make money" because money must be earned in the form of a salary set by management. Even in Soviet times, anyone who tried to show initiative and autonomy (such as sewing and then selling their work) was severely punished by the state.

At the same time, today's market laws are dictating new rules of behavior and new values in Russia. The desire to earn money, to become wealthy and materially independent is increasingly openly expressed, especially among young people. 84% of young people believe that "it's better to work more in order to earn more". They are convinced that "money offers freedom" by giving access to education, culture, travel and other things.

The cult of success grows stronger every year, and people are more and more proud to flaunt their wealth and pragmatism. A growing number of Russians admit that "there is nothing shameful in being rich", on the contrary: money is becoming more and more the criterion and even the key to success in life. The desire to get rich is increasingly overt (or covert). Class warfare has become somewhat obsolete, and owners of Mercedes cars or beautiful apartments now annoy only 21% of the population. "Those who know how to make money" are regarded with growing *respect* (by *more than half the population).*

However, the number of those who remain stuck in Soviet positions remains considerable. The motto "work less and earn less rather than overwork" remains true for a *quarter of* Russians. Money can be coveted and earned, but it's indecent to flaunt it. This shows the profound difference between Russia and the West, as well as Russians' ambivalent attitude to money.

How do Russians spend their money?

We know that people in developed countries prefer to live on credit and don't like to carry cash. Russians may seem stingy by comparison, as they spend their time saving: for the purchase of a home (36%), a car (34%), children (25%), education (23%), vacations (21%) and older people (17%), despite the unfortunate experience they've had - with their savings going up in smoke - continue, as in Soviet times, to hoard "for a rainy day", "for a funeral".

Of course, not everyone is able to save the required amount. Most Russians live paycheck to paycheck. Most of their money is spent on food and a modest wardrobe, as well as on children's education (13%), health care (8%), and only 2% on vacations.

What does money mean to Russians today?

Just a few years ago, the Russians captured the imagination of the French with their huge bundles of dollars, which they brought in cellophane-wrapped packages. Those fabulous days are long gone. Russian businessmen have become more civilized and no longer bring huge sums of money in cellophane packages, but simply transfer their money to their foreign accounts via offshore havens.

The shocking differences in behavior between Western and Russian businessmen have all but disappeared, but not for good. A closer look reveals a few more.

Russians, for example, don't like to use checks, checkbooks and credit cards, unlike the French, who often use their credit cards even for everyday purchases.

For Russians, there are several reasons for this. First of all, it's hard for Russians to fill out a check in a foreign language!

Secondly, in Russia itself, a corrupt system prevails where any document can be easily fabricated, while real "securities" can, in the space of a minute, have lost their value forever. So it's hardly surprising that Russians have a sarcastic attitude to cheques, bonds, shares and so on. How many times in life has a Russian found himself stripped of every last cent of everything he had! That's why, in today's Russian "economic jungle", people have no faith in securities. Cash, on the other hand, is psychologically reassuring and reassuring.

These are roughly the same reasons why Russians don't trust their credit cards. Not just for lack of habit. Rather, the reason is that it's not as secure there as it is in the West. The way the card works in Russia is behind the Western standards. There is, for example, no secret code (or "pin code") to issue to gain access to your account (mandatory in the West). To pay with a credit card in Russia, a simple signature is enough. This means that any purchase can be paid with a stolen card. The risk of being robbed considerably reduces the interest of Russians for the card. Therefore, they usually use it when they are abroad.

For the Russian, there's no substitute for cash! It's the only way to feel secure.

14. How do today's Russians see themselves?

Many myths have circulated about the character of Russians, including that of the "enigmatic Russian soul", beyond Russia's borders. Today, as Russian society changes, these myths are multiplying even more. And the unresolved secrets of the "Slavic soul" are being joined by new ones. *How do Russians cope with the new reality? How can they succeed in this context? What impact have the new living conditions had on Russians' traditional qualities? How do they see themselves?*

According to analysts' data[132], Russians, in their self-assessment, focus mainly on their qualities and much less on their shortcomings. If we try to draw a general portrait from these elements, we get the following picture. Russians are warm and welcoming, generous, trusting and courageous. They are characterized by joie de vivre, kindness (27.6%), modesty, honesty, patience (22.1%), hospitality (28.9%), benevolence (18.5%) and piety.

---

132. A. Karmin, *Étude des civilisations, op. cit.* p. 116.

They are as active as they are inert, as lazy as they are hard-working, as submissive to authority as they are self-assured, as carried away as they are balanced. But that doesn't stop them from admitting to a lack of punctuality and discipline, a tendency to drink, carelessness and slovenliness.

It's not hard to see that the "sociological model of today's Russians" is almost identical to the one anchored in mass consciousness, even among other peoples. Russians seem to make objective judgments about themselves.

However tragic and complex the last 10-15 years have been for the Russians (it's a short period in history), *the traditional traits of the national character have withstood the changes.*

If we compare the traits of the Russian character with, say, those of the American, we can deduce that they differ considerably.

American culture is more brutal, business-oriented: individuals are motivated by commerce, calculation, success and career.

Russian culture, even in today's context, appears less aggressive, with informal, "cordial" relationships playing a key role. Russians don't have the toughness, dynamism and entrepreneurial spirit of Americans, but they do have patience and great adaptability. And while American relationships are built on *individualism* and the *rule of law*, Russian relationships are built on *sociability*, *trust* and *mutual aid.*

However, under the influence of recent processes, Russians have begun to acquire traits hitherto unknown to them.

In Soviet times, for example, Russians attached virtually no importance to their national identity. With the collapse of the USSR, however, they were reminded that they were Russians, sometimes in the most brutal terms, as in the Baltic republics. This was the starting point for Russian nationalism as a social and political movement.

The crystallization process of this movement is becoming increasingly visible. For example, Russians no longer see themselves as a state, but as a nation. Until 1991, they saw themselves as "Soviet". Today, they prefer to refer to themselves as members of an ethnic group.

Awareness of a national identity unites and unites today's Russians. One possible explanation for this is that Russians find it humiliating to see their country belittled in comparison with the recent past. According to surveys,

64.7% of Russians are ashamed of the country's current state, 73.6% feel a sense of injustice about everything that's going on, and 49.5% think that "it's impossible to go on living like this". Only 11% are "satisfied" or think that "we just have to wait a little longer and everything will be all right".

Nowadays, Russians find it important to emphasize their membership in the "Russian ethnic group" - especially abroad - to form a diaspora or simply a circle of acquaintances. These consolidation factors are not yet firmly in place. Particularly noteworthy here is the role of the Orthodox Church, which enjoys great confidence among the population. In the past (before the 1917 revolution), membership in the Russian community was determined by the Orthodox faith. This does not mean that it will be the same in the future. In this period of transition, many principles and concepts are not yet fully structured.

It's also important to emphasize that "Russian specificity is a value" for the majority of the population, who believe that *Western values and economic recipes* for Russian renewal are alien, inappropriate and even harmful to the country. Only 15% of the population, comprising the intelligentsia of the humanities and technical sciences, are still in favor of transforming the "evil empire" into a Western-style "civilized country".

However, in parallel with this *process of Russian consolidation* (importance of ethnicity), Russians on the whole do not discriminate on the basis of nationality: inter-ethnic marriages are as well tolerated as before. 70-75% of young people do not place any restrictions on them. More than 60% of Russians see Russia as a "common home" for many peoples with the same rights. But at the level of government, 48% of Russians believe that "all people have equal rights... but the President must still be Russian". For the other half of the population, "this question is indifferent to them. As for the Tatars, Bashkirs and Ukrainians who live on Russian territory, 34% disapprove of the choice of a Russian president.

Thus, the majority of Russians traditionally hold to the model of bene-volent relations with their neighbors. And Russians today are more inclined towards *self-awareness* than confrontation with other nations. However, should inter-ethnic conflicts worsen, should other ethnic groups increase their expansion (including economic expansion) or put pressure on Russia, a different evolution of Russian consolidation cannot be ruled out. The ethnic factor as a mode of self-defense could then play a part in this process.

There are already signs of this turnaround on the political horizon. For example, many Russians are currently worried about unfavorable shifts *in the ethnic balance of the* country's population, which is *shrinking by almost 1 million a year.* Individuals with a pronounced oriental physique do not always have access to elite establishments after *face control.* There is also a nationalist electorate (of the "Lepenist" type), some 9-11 million strong, who believe that "Russia must be a state of Russian individuals". Parallel to similar trends in Europe (in France, for example), extremist nationalist demonstrations were particularly active a few years ago (in memory of Hitler). And their aggressiveness is growing with each passing year. So much so that, for the first time in years, the country's President referred to "skinhead" demonstrations as "a serious threat to the country's stability and security" in a letter to the National Assembly in April 2002. He also pointed out that this was "one of the factors that could inconvenience citizens and make the country inhospitable to foreigners".

Other "softened" forms of nationalism have become even more popular: according to them, "since Russians make up the majority of the population, they bear the main responsibility and should therefore have more rights". This position, held by 13.1% of the population ten years ago, now attracts over 20%.

The foundations for the political progression of Russian nationalism have thus been laid in Russia in recent years. According to analysts, "today's rapidly expanding nationalism is a *quest* ideology in Russia. It experiments with different models of political mobilization, which sets it apart from both communist and liberal ideologies.

15. What is the Russian attitude towards other countries today?

The relations of Russians with foreign countries have changed dramatically in the last 10-15 years: during perestroika, the "democratic wave" encouraged them to shout slogans about "making Russia a civilized country" (as in the West), but these slogans are no longer relevant today. What's more, Russians have recently become more convinced that foreign recipes for getting the country out of its acute economic and social crisis are *unacceptable to* Russia. Favoring the enrichment of certain oligarchs and capital transfers abroad, they serve, in other words, only to enrich the West.

This seems even more paradoxical when you consider that the majority of Russians view Russia's current situation very critically, and even compare it to a developing country.

It is interesting to see how Russians perceive themselves... Are they *closer to the West or to the East*? There can be several answers to this question because of the different aspects it presents: is it about the proximity of culture, mentality or economic system?

In cultural terms, 26.3% of Russians feel they occupy *an intermediate position* between the West (America, France and Germany) and the East (China, Japan and India). However, they feel closest to Germany (17%) and France (14.9%). *In economic terms,* 25.9% of Russians feel that they are halfway between the West and the East, but the economic systems of countries like China and India seem much closer to 10-12% of them, and those of America the most alien (2.4%). As for *national character,* almost 40% of Russians see themselves as halfway between the West and the East, while feeling slightly closer to German (10%) and American (7.1%) character.

Russians are clearly more *aware of the European aspect of their culture,* especially when it comes to the national character. On the economic front, however, *less than a quarter of the country's population* believes that a Western-style economy can develop in the country. Competition, individualism and non-interference by the state in the economy are contrary to ancient Russian traditions.

Given the topicality of the Eurasian theme in political discussions, it's worth taking a closer look at the *Eurasian* trend. It is least expressed in culture, and somewhat more pronounced, albeit at roughly the same level, in the economy. A further 40% of Russians do feel Eurasian when it comes to national character. So we can't talk about Russians being "purely *Eurasian*". They themselves see Russia as "a European-Eurasian country". The Asian component of their consciousness is too weak, and should not be understood as a particular attraction or sympathy for Japan, China, India or the Arab countries, but rather as their feeling of being "almost European, but not quite". The best proof that the Orient doesn't particularly appeal to them is that they never think of emigrating there. Instead, they choose the USA or Western Europe.

However, despite their belief in the European origins of their culture and the relative proximity of the European and Russian mentalities, Russians do not really aspire to be part of the "European house". There is nothing even remotely reminiscent of the euphoria for Europe in Eastern Europe or the Baltic States. Just a few years ago, the question of whether Russia was part of Europe was hotly debated in the media. "Scientific" conferences were even organized on the subject on several occasions. Today, looking at a map of the world where Europe appears as a small peninsula in the immense Asian continent, the Russian simply shrugs his shoulders in response to this question. The way Russians look at themselves is changing rapidly and significantly.

The Russians understand that the prospect of Russia merging with a "united Europe" in the near future is impossible for both political and economic reasons. At the same time, this eventuality has little appeal for Russians, who do not see it as an objective to be achieved at any cost in the near future. In any case, only 2 per cent of Russians said they were in favour of Russia's integration into the European Union, even though the latter enjoys a much higher degree of confidence among Russians (20 per cent) than they have in their own government. Russians are progressively *distancing themselves from* the "Western world" in spirit, and this trend is only getting stronger. Their mindset can be summed up as follows: "Do whatever you want at home, and we'll do whatever we want at home too."

The Russians' attitude to the possible integration of the former USSR republics bears witness to their growing skepticism about this prospect. The once popular idea of creating a "Ukraine + Russia + Belarus" troika has suffered a serious setback. Today, only 12% of Russians are in favor (20% less than in 1995). What's most interesting is that young people under 25 are the most hostile to the idea of such a union. The older generation (over 55) is in favour of the creation of the CIS (Confederation of Independent States) and the "restoration of the USSR". We can therefore assume that, as the generations change, the *trend in favor of* Russian *independence* will only grow stronger. The *isolationism of young people is* particularly in line with the idea of expanding borders in the field of business, work opportunities abroad and tourism. In this, young Russians are reminiscent of Americans, who are content with superficial, partial and purely practical information about other countries and peoples. This information only scratches the surface of their consciousness, without penetrating deeply or transforming their mentality. For the moment, it's hard to say just how deep-rooted this tendency towards isolationism among young people really is. If it continues to develop, it will in principle change the parameters of Russian culture and mentality.

Today, Russians no longer seek to identify themselves with the rest of the world, let alone aspire to "save it", as they did in the past. And it is not excluded that in the future, the transformation of Russia into an "open" economic system will be counterbalanced by cultural and psychological "enclosure", reinforced autarky and the opposition of its "specificity" to the rest of the world.

It should be stressed, however, that this does not mean a decline in economic relations with other countries. This is merely a psychological shift in Russian consciousness. In the Russian perception, the relationship with the Western world is divided between two extremes. On the one hand, the general model of the "West" is *negative* for them: Russians (especially the elderly) are against foreign geopolitical influence, pressure on them from outside, interference in their internal affairs, pragmatism and the "unspiri-tuality of consumer society". They are suspicious of the good intentions of Western politicians towards them.

At the same time, in terms of material and technical culture, the economically developed countries are viewed *positively,* thanks to cultural proximity, shared history and the Russians' traditional ability to take on new things. Germany is viewed very positively: it was on the basis of its experience that the state was established after the reign of Peter the Great, and the education system was set up. Italy, with its refined culture, usually appears as a spiritual homeland for half of nineteenth-century Russian artists and writers. Even England appealed to them, with its conservatism, respect for the monarchy and the seductive manners of English gentlemen. For

Russians, however, France is the beacon of Europe. It has a rich history and architecture, refined cuisine and, above all, cultural affinities with Russia. Here, as nowhere else in the world, there is a particular interest in Russia and all that is linked to its roots and culture. And it's not likely to disappear any time soon... And it's no coincidence that, according to data from the ARN Institute for Social Studies, when asked "Which country do you like best?", Russians cited France first (68.1%), followed by Germany (64.1%) and England (62.8%).

PART FOUR - BUSINESS COOPERATION WITH THE RUSSIANS

"It's time that teaches us.

1. Western involvement in Russian industry

Many Russian companies are now in foreign hands. The state owns 100% of natural resource monopolies such as *Gazprom*, the energy and gas sectors and metallurgical combines. It also owns the Ministry of Communications, sea and air transport, and national defense enterprises. All these companies are virtually inaccessible to foreigners, since participation in them brings extremely high profits and a great deal of influence. In general, the Russian business elite has long been involved in all export-related industries.

Even where there is the greatest influx of foreigners - in the *food industry* - Russian companies are working successfully alongside foreign firms.

In the *cosmetics industry,* the share of Russian manufacturers has shrunk by 40%. There are still a few major Russian cosmetics factories (*Nevskaya Kosmetika, Svoboda, Novaya Zaria*) producing low-cost products. But they are being overtaken by the French, who take the cake in this sector and are particularly appreciated by the wealthy and fickle clientele.

Patriotic-minded Russian manufacturers aren't really looking for foreign capital, contrary to the claims of government experts echoed by the media. The financial manager of the *Nevskaya Kosmetika* factory, for example, is adamant that the factory's profits are sufficient to finance increased production, training and advertising. And if money ran short, he would ask the bank for a loan, but under no circumstances would he resort to foreign loans, interest or guarantees.

The same applies to the *meat industry*, where virtually all companies are Russian. And there is no foreign capital in the *wheat* industry.

Competition on the Russian labor market has intensified, there is a shortage of good marketing and management experts, and companies are willing to pay a premium for their services. Employers are scrambling to find good employees. *Lawyers, technical support specialists and personnel managers have seen their salaries rise sharply.* Their salaries reach six figures (in dollars).

2. The style of business relationships

How can mutual understanding be achieved in business collaboration between the French and Russians?

First of all, you need to analyze the specifics of your own culture. It's very important to be aware that Russians perceive the French as haughty individuals who like to "blow smoke". This behavior repels them and arouses their hostility. And this is not just the "superficial tourist look".

"Why do Russians prefer to build long-term relationships with Americans, Germans and representatives of other countries rather than with the French?" To this question posed by the book's author at the Chamber of Commerce and Industry in Moscow, the General Director of the national foundation "Russian Business Culture" Galina Konstantinova gave us the following answer.

She told us that, in addition to purely economic reasons, psychological aspects also play an important role. In her opinion, the French, in addition to their condescension and apparent coldness, give Russians the impression of being stuffy, insincere and uninterested in the development of Franco-Russian trade.

Compared to the French, representatives of other nations seem to the Russians to be more welcoming, sincere and dynamic. And the contribution of other countries to joint affairs seems to them to be out of all proportion to that of the French. Can we really compare the activity of the French with, say, that of the Americans, Germans or Italians on the Russian market?

Today, the huge Russian market attracts the attention of an extremely varied number of countries, giving Russians an embarrassment of riches when it comes to selecting a partner. On equal terms, they will choose the country with which they feel most comfortable establishing business relations. And the French are not the best placed in this respect.

According to intercultural management expert D. Luce, "formalism in business relations" is a peculiarity of French mores. This is expressed, for example, in the fact that the French arrive at business meetings in suits and ties, cannot stand the casualness of someone taking off their jacket, and cannot stand being addressed familiarly by first name. They also show no interest in personal and family life.

They arrive at the meetings with heavy files prepared in advance, which annoys the Russians who are not used to this and even despise all this "paperwork".

Logic prevails in French argumentation during trade talks; for this reason, talks with them seem too long to the Russians, who resort to intuition. As far as the Russians are concerned, the French, with their long speeches, want to divert attention and mislead their partners.

To formulate a logical argument takes far more words and time than to resolve an issue with one's intuition. The French, moreover, habitually "quibble" over any non-logical statement made by the other side, clinging to it and dragging out the discussion, painstakingly probing the other's weaknesses. In a questionable situation, they are obstinate, wanting to impose their logical conclusions.

This way of studying files at length, point by point, can exasperate the Russians, who have a fiery temperament. This "nitpicking" over details can be perceived by them as "pettiness" and end up tiring them.

In addition, the Russian usually has a ready-made solution that has often been decided by his boss. And if, during the talks, a problem arises concerning the choice or modification of certain points of the contract, the Russians can interrupt the talks without further discussion. Because sometimes it is not the participant in the negotiations who makes the decision, but someone above him who may not be present at that moment.

For this reason, you are never sure that you can solve a concrete problem in one stroke.

Blame and disappointment in business cooperation can be mutual. Because the Russian habits annoy their business partners enough.

First of all, Russian businessmen do not yet have well-developed patterns in conducting business. There are many reasons (including historical and economic) why many Russian businessmen simply do not have the right experience yet.

All the more so as the less-than-stellar qualities of Russian businessmen - already discussed in previous chapters - are nurtured by the peculiarities of their mentality. Doing business with Russians can sometimes prove extremely difficult and disappointing. Even such a basic rule as replying on time to letters and requests for information is not customary among business leaders!

Secondly, for Russians, business is often a gamble, not a long-term activity. Russian entrepreneurs expect their foreign counterparts to make large profits quickly, without which they lose interest in the business. These two facts do not reassure Western businessmen.

Russian entrepreneurs generally expect their foreign partners, "on their territory", to conform to their business habits, rather than the other way round. It's not easy for them to build something to European standards.

In this respect, we recall the well-known (and already discussed) aspects of the Russian character such as lack of precision and punctuality, rigor, pure professionalism and - on the other hand - unnecessary emotionalism, over-dependence on mood and personal relationships with colleagues.

Despite all the difficulties and temptations, the trend today is *inexorably* towards *reinforcing ethical standards of business conduct* in the Russian business community. The publication of texts such as P. N. Chikharev's "Rules of Business Conduct in Russia" (Moscow, 1998), as well as *National Program: Russian Business Culture* (Moscow, 1997) and others, speak volumes in this regard.

Even more symptomatic is the new trend among Russian business leaders towards openness and transparency. As soon as *Youkos* announced its transparency in 2000 and promised guarantees to its partners, its shares immediately shot up by 30%.

I guess it's simply becoming worthwhile to be honest in Russia.

3. The problem of punctuality and precision in Russian business relations

When we discussed the ethnic peculiarities of Russians in the second part of the book (see Part 2, chap. 3, §12), we referred to their *singular* - or rather *subjective* - relationship with time, reminiscent of their "southern" character.

In this, they differ greatly from Europeans, and in particular from Anglo-Saxons with their *linear perception of time*. Time, for the latter, is focused on "business", on the successive accomplishment of a given task, step by step. For them, time not used for action is an irretrievable "waste of time".

Unlike Europeans, time for Russians is linked not to fixed goals, but to events and people. What's more, "active" temperaments prefer to do several things at once, making life seem more interesting and fuller. Russians divide their occupations not according to their usefulness, but above all according to the importance these encounters can have on their lives on a personal and emotional level. Emotions, rather than business, determine how Russians divide their time.

That's why "professional" qualities such as punctuality, precise execution of a schedule or project are not so important to them. More to the point, they may sometimes pretend to observe schedules or follow a plan, but deep down they're convinced that real life, which is constantly changing as circumstances dictate, is infinitely more important than any agreement or timetable. They respect the punctuality of others, but they're not overly enamored of it.

The French - albeit to a lesser extent than the Anglo-Saxons - are also distinguished by their linear orientation to time. And it's very difficult for them to forgive someone who simply "forgets" to keep an appointment, changes it at the last minute, doesn't complete the work plan on time and - an important detail - doesn't even apologize afterwards. The interruption of the established program through the fault of the other person, the fact of not being able to go through with the goal set, makes them angry. They see it as a waste of time.

And sometimes serious friction arises between Russian and French partners. Even French people with experience of working in Russia admit that it's better to have alternatives in case the planned meeting is cancelled without even a call to apologize. Or it's the Russians who change their plans at the last minute without apology or explanation, despite firm and precise agreements. It is better to be psychologically prepared for these reversals and to plan alternatives to your stay, other options in your schedule.

When conducting talks, it is necessary to take into account the peculiarities of Russians. Since Russians are more focused on the people they're dealing with than on the business itself, they can't stand it if the partner abruptly interrupts the conversation on the pretext that "time is money", and the partner fears being late for his next appointment. For them, the most important thing is that the meeting ends in a dignified way, even if they do not get any material benefit from it. Besides, the conversation can be as personal as it is professional.

When meeting a foreign delegation or colleagues (department, service) for the first time, Russians immediately look for the key man, the one with significant power and the mandate to decide on a matter. In this, they are realistic: almost everything depends on the boss.

With their linear conception of time, Westerners see life as a road to be travelled at a set speed, pursuing one goal after another. For them, the future is not an enigma, it's programmed and planned. And to get there, all you have to do is work conscientiously and methodically.

But the Russians, with their cyclical representation of time, believe in destiny and are not so presumptuous in their plans for the future. They consider it impossible to manage the future. And they don't see life as a straight road leading to the goal they've set themselves, but as a winding path in an unknown land where you don't know what's around the bend.

Now we understand why Russians avoid making long-term plans for the future. They're not sure enough about the future, and even have a superstitious fear of it. Even if they make big plans, they're never sure they'll be able to carry them out. And that's not just because they're fatalistic, or because of the radical changes that have recently taken place in the life of the country.

It's clear that this divergence in the perception of time between Russians and Europeans in business relations is causing major inconvenience and mutual annoyance.

It's true that it's debatable which of the two positions is more respectable. In the end, the two do not have the same meaning. The Russians can and should be criticized for not knowing how to concentrate on the essentials, for being undisciplined and unreliable in business dealings. In any case, they need to be checked when cooperating, and every step of the way.

However, we shouldn't try to eliminate or argue about this particularity of the Russian character, which consists in knowing how to go beyond the limits of its routine daily life, refusing the "race behind the leader" just as much as success "at all costs". It is necessary to take it into account in order to act with tact.

4. Russians' relationship to work

The original relationship of Russians to time influences their behavior towards work. When dealing with Russians, foreign partners are often annoyed by their casualness and, even more so, by their approximate execution of tasks when work is done, in a way, "under the table" and hidden defects are discovered too late with extremely unfortunate consequences.

Often, foreign partners mistake these "peculiarities of the Russian mentality" for "laziness", a lack of interest in successful cooperation, an absence of real professionalism. And, as foreigners note, the most striking thing is that it's impossible to eradicate these aspects of the Russian character. Rather, it will be the Europeans who will change their relationship to life and work under the influence of Russian partners, comical though this may seem.

It's easy, of course, to counter the various conjectures about Russians being "naturally lazy". It's not fair, since we know that Russians themselves regard lazy people with contempt.

It's true that Russians are fast learners and acquire new professions, making rapid progress in IT and new technologies, and are trained in European organization and management. But their work psychology remains unchanged. This is not because they are stubborn, but because their ethno-cultural particularities, formed centuries ago, influence their psychology. It is only after the radical break of recent years that a change in stereotypical business behavior can be observed in Russia.

So it makes more sense to invest time not so much in fighting these Russian idiosyncrasies as in trying to become familiar with them, accept them and, ultimately, make the best use of them.

If a Russian isn't interested in his work, he'll do anything he likes during the day except work - organize cigarette breaks, drink tea, chat with colleagues - or pretend to work until the signal to leave finally rings.

But if his work interests and pleases him, he will invest himself more than anyone else, forgetting about time, family, his private life, his plans for the evening... and will be ready to work until morning if need be. Besides, material satisfaction is not the most important thing for him. If his work gives him satisfaction, he's ready to accept a modest salary and won't look for another job.

A public opinion poll showed that half of all employees were willing to work for a high salary, regardless of whether or not the work was very demanding. But for the other half of those surveyed, the most important things were "a caring atmosphere within the work group", "opportunities for development" (vocational training, qualification courses, etc.), "health protection", "unregulated work and working hours", etc. All these preferences are based on *personal motivation*, not on the lure of high incomes or the hope of a fast-track career.

But if the work isn't interesting, if it's monotonous, uncreative and lacking in prospects, if the working relationships between the members of the collective are conflictual, even a decent salary won't be enough to keep the Russian in his job.

When you start working in Russia, you need to have a clear idea of not only the economic problems, but also the national problems linked to the psychology and stereotypical behavior of Russians. Not only is it very difficult for someone who knows nothing about Russian psychology, culture or language to work in Russia with Russian partners, it's downright unrealistic.

5. Information gathering

Interestingly, even the means of obtaining information differs between the Russians and the French. "The French get their information from reference books, the Internet, statistics, databases, reviews and so on."

In short, they arrive at the business meeting "armed to the teeth" with a voluminous dossier under their arm, including a preamble, columns of figures, arguments based on statistics and forecasts. In this way, they *impress* the Russians with facts and figures.

Of course figures are important. However, for the Russians, they represent only one aspect of reality, as they do not reflect customer relations. And yet, according to the Russians, customer relations are the key to business success.

What's more, information from the press and databases quickly becomes outdated. Whereas information that does not circulate in the press can be obtained in the "antechamber of power" or during confidential talks with Russian baths...

Russians are more dialogue-oriented, and information seems more reliable to them if it's first-hand and obtained face-to-face. It is precisely through discussions within their circle of friends, classmates, business relations or relatives, from "their clan" in the antechamber of power, that they obtain concrete information on economic developments, forecasts of currency exchange rates and inflation rates, comprehensive information on personalities, including gossip.

They observe the same events and forecasts as their Western partners, only in a "broader context", as they have an impressive amount of information gathered through their private intelligence channels. In search of information or to solve a problem, the Russians don't hesitate to resort to any means necessary, and sometimes it's simply impossible to follow their logic or mode of motivation.

In a case, Russians call on their most diverse personal relations, find a protector (a sort of "godfather"), prefer to solve a problem "person to person". Insofar as Russian society is built on a clan model (made up of relatives and personal relations), it is very important for a Russian to have loyal and influential relatives, friends or classmates for the resolution of any problem.

As a result, they entrust the most complex and important matters not so much to competent professionals and colleagues - as the French do, for example - but to people in "their network" whom they trust and on whom they can rely without running the risk of being deceived.

267

6. Work style and behaviour at work

There are two modes of development in Europe.

The *first mode*: ethnic groups with natural borders and powerful neighbors set a limit to their territorial expansion and, willy-nilly, resorted to *an intensive mode of production*. They gradually learned to work methodically and smoothly, devised thousands of useful practices and technologies, and were finally rewarded after creating an extremely rich civilization, envied as much technologically as spiritually and socially.

The Eastern Slavs were clearly inspired by the *second mode*. They had no clearly defined borders, except in the south-west with the Carpathian chain and the south with its fearsome wild plain. Virtually unexplored forests extended elsewhere. You could go further and further east and north, and settle along countless rivers. It was easier to clear virgin fields and woods than to fertilize impoverished soils. A week was enough to build a new wooden dwelling on any new site. In the presence of such an abundance of forests and virgin spaces, it would never have occurred to anyone to build a stone house, fixing man to a precise spot.

It is this *geographical* factor that explains the Russians' tendency to spread out, their lack of aspiration to put down roots "for long and for good" in the same place that has enabled them to populate immense spaces. Any people in this part of the world, regardless of language or race, would have done the same.

The Russian state and economy subsequently took advantage of this capacity for expansion, which is characteristic of the majority of individuals. Russia's entire history follows this pattern, punctuated by attempts to escape it. This is one of the factors that have determined the Russians' original way of working.

What's more, Russians often mix *their professional, social and private lives* - unlike the French, who make a very clear distinction between the professional and the private. In the workplace, the French just work. They reveal nothing about their private and social lives to their colleagues.

Not so for the Russian, who also lives *his social and private life* at work. For him, work is not just a means of earning a living, it's also "a means of acquiring greater social status, of gaining social recognition", which can be expressed in a variety of ways: in the form of bonuses, valuable gifts, decorations, front-page photographs, publication in the press, and so on. It's very important for a Russian to be linked to each member of the collective by close ties of sympathy and antipathy - in short, emotional ties.

Russians are also stereotypical when it comes to business meetings: they may interrupt you unexpectedly if an interesting idea has occurred to them. They can easily switch from examining your ideas to judging you and your mistakes. But if they realize they're wrong, they'll apologize without trying to "save face" at any cost.

The different attitudes of French and Russians at work can lead to serious conflicts and mutual incomprehension between representatives of the two countries. The French never cease to wonder: "Why did they suddenly change the scheduled meeting time? Why didn't they finish the work within the allotted time? Why aren't they meeting the deadlines for the order?"

For their part, the Russians are also entitled to ask: "But why stick to this plan if circumstances have suddenly changed? And why get so angry if I'm late for the appointment: if only you could have seen the traffic jams on the road! Don't think you're the only one who wants to do business with me! And what's the point of sticking to deadlines if it's detrimental to quality (or price)! Why not change the price of the product if world raw material prices have changed?"

As long as one side doesn't make the effort to adapt to the other, these mutually incomprehensible conflicts will continue to arise.

The transition from one system of thought to another is not easy, but it is possible if we put our minds to it.

A compromise between the two ways of working can produce good results. You simply have to know how to use your business partners' individual qualities to your advantage.

But to do this, you need to get to know them, accept them without getting upset, and keep their personal skills in mind at all times.

7. Hierarchical relationships

"Like master, like servant
(popular Russian saying).

In Russian society, traditional forms of power and relations *between superiors and subordinates have been* significantly eroded in recent years.

Let's take a look at some of the different management styles being developed in recent times.

1) The leader can influence subordinates "through fear", using shouting and threats, for example, to get the job done. This behavior was widespread in the Soviet era. According to a public opinion poll, the absolute majority of people surveyed still tolerate the severity of a manager in the case of a job badly done.

In the 1960s, norms were introduced into "superior/subordinate" relationships that upheld human dignity. Their influence has been reinforced by the market economy reforms of the last fifteen years. Managing people through fear does not necessarily contribute to the development of competitive production.

We can, however, observe that some European businessmen, although far from imagining the existence of such behavior at home, do not hesitate to resort to a brutal management style in Russia, knowing full well that they will go unpunished as bosses. They don't always realize that this style of management is a legacy of the past, and that Russians don't take kindly to being humiliated.

2) It is also possible to influence subordinates through *tradition*. In a traditional relationship, the subordinate believes that the official in charge has the unquestionable right to give him any order he wants, and that he must comply without complaint. The influence of tradition was once very strong. In the 1970s, the Soviet regime reinforced the power of chiefs, who had to be obeyed regardless of their competence. This practice only consolidated the bureaucratic basis of the totalitarian regime. By tradition, the leader must be severe, hard. An "indulgent" leader is perceived as lacking self-confidence, character and weakness. Rather than being appreciated, his behavior will be condemned and even mocked by his subordinates. We shouldn't systema-

tically condemn the traditional mode of management, since it can "work" very well in a market economy, as the example of Japan shows.

In Russia's transition to a market economy, these traditional behaviours are rapidly eroding and, clearly, are tending to align with European and American models. This evolution is not always easy.

Authoritarian-style business relationships are more often advocated by older or less-educated individuals than by the young and educated. This is obviously due to their age or lack of education. High-level executives, government officials, military personnel and pensioners are all perfectly in tune with this style of relationship. Business leaders, on the other hand, consider them to be in contradiction with the very principles of the market economy.

3) With the development of market relations, we can expect to see the rapid establishment of new standards of behavior, with managers resorting to "material incentives".

However, a public opinion poll has yet to confirm this trend. No doubt the growing hostility of Russians to material inequality has something to do with it.

4) The model of the executive who owes his position to his "expertise" is consolidated. The ideal leader is seen as the one who possesses *the knowledge* related to his or her professional field. And if the worker obeys him, it's because he's convinced of his leader's *great competence*. It's considered normal for the leader to think only about "business", to "work himself to death", and at the same time to be open to criticism from his subordinates. However, this type of leader is more wishful thinking than reality: it is still rare in public companies and many private firms.

5) The Russians have also actively anchored in their consciousness the model of the *charismatic* leader. In a way, this model is opposed to that of the leader who is an "expert" in his field. In this case, the leader owes his power solely to his *will* and *personality*. To be charismatic, an individual must be energetic and capable of "sharing" his passion with those around him. Charismatic action enables those who carry out the work, seduced by the leader's ideas and personality, to identify with him or her.

To lead people, the ideal leader needs to be *energetic*, able to *organize, plan ahead, control* subordinates and *maintain discipline*, make decisions quickly and take responsibility when things go wrong.

Impressive looks, independence of character, the ability to *express oneself well* and *self-confidence* in all situations are also very important. *Sociability* and *politeness* also count. A leader is rarely taken aback and feels comfortable when admired without being arrogant or putting on airs.

If two spouses work in the same company, they should only maintain a professional relationship in the workplace. 69.4% of respondents - more often women than men - disapprove of a woman working under her husband. In the Soviet era, a form of "nepotism" prevailed, which could affect spouses, parents and children. Parental relationships at work were, in the majority of cases, detrimental to the business, and explain the population's strong disapproval of this "scourge".

However, in the market economy, where the income of the company and its manager is directly linked to the effective contribution of each employee, the very foundations of nepotism have disappeared. Family relationships in business, far from being a hindrance, can on the contrary be beneficial to the company. We know that the most effective form of organization for small businesses is the family enterprise - whether it's running a farm, a restaurant, a hotel or a boutique.

In conclusion, let us not forget that the mass consciousness of Russians is still impregnated with the heritage of the past. These are, in essence, the normative requirements that appear in Russia for the leader who wants to act effectively on his Russian subordinates. In a certain sense, this set of requirements for the leader momentarily reflects Russian consciousness at a transitional period in its history.

8. The psychology of today's Russian entrepreneurs

It is interesting and somewhat surprising that the idea of being an entrepreneur has not been perceived in Russia as something totally foreign. 52.6% of Russians are entrepreneurs or would like to become one. It is true that the number of entrepreneurs was even higher at the beginning of the reforms in 1992, when it reached 63%. It's mainly the number of those who run a business that has fallen - there are *half as many of them*. The reasons for this decline are obvious: in recent years, economic and political conditions in Russia have not been favorable to entrepreneurs. In some parts of the country, entire sectors of small (mass) commerce have been outlawed.

For these reasons, the number of those planning to go into business in the near future has been divided by four.

These figures lead us to conclude that capitalism has not become a national affair in Russia. Not because it is alien to Russians, but because reforms have not allowed it to become an activity like any other. There are also 4.5% of Russians who are *forced to* set up a business solely under the threat of unemployment. Nothing would have driven them otherwise.

The slow, contradictory development of small and medium-sized businesses in Russia is characteristic of the period of transition that Russian society is undergoing. This aspect of Russian life has become the subject of intensive research by sociologists, economists, psychologists and even historians. Researchers are trying to gain an insight into the psychological qualities and motivations of entrepreneurs, as well as their relationship to risk, failure and competition; they are also interested in their personal strengths and what entrepreneurs think of themselves.

According to analysts' data, the average age of today's Russian entrepreneur is 35-45. Most are men. At the beginning of the 90s, they made up 96% of the workforce; in subsequent years, this figure dropped to around 80%, indicating a growing proportion of women in their ranks. 85% of them have a higher education, and many have passed through two higher education establishments or hold a scientific degree.

In response to the question: "What attracts you to an undertaking as risky as setting up your own business?", entrepreneurs indicated the possibility of *personal fulfillment* (56%), *independence* (44%), *material comfort* (40%), *authority within their entourage*, the *usefulness of their work for others* (11%), as well as the *novelty* of this type of activity. They have to work in a highly uncertain environment, make risky decisions and take personal responsibility in the event of failure - both materially and morally - for the future of their employees.

Everyone agrees that taking risks is unpleasant and stressful. To live well, it's best to avoid it. The question then arises: what makes entrepreneurs choose this type of activity? Which do they prefer: owning their own business and working intensively, or taking risks to earn big? Or a modest but stable income without risk?

Paradoxically, Russians' responses to this question vary over time. *In the early 90s, 32.9% of entrepreneurs preferred to risk big.* This figure has now fallen to 8.6%. Attitudes to risk have changed, with the majority of people preferring to "look twice before taking the plunge". And 84.3% of individuals now prefer to have a business that requires much less time and effort, while providing them with *a comfortable, stable income.* And only 7.1% of Russians are prepared to accept a modest stable income with no particular risk. In this, they differ from the French who, in most cases, prefer to amass as much as possible without taking unnecessary risks.

In the 90s, the number of Russian entrepreneurs who suffered major business setbacks *tripled.* But a survey shows that this did not shake the determination of half of them (51.5%) to "start all over again". Only 30% would look for a reliable partner in the event of failure. And only 17% would give up their business. *None of them* expressed a desire to *work for a public company or another entrepreneur.* After experiencing failure, businessmen prefer either to set up a new business on their own, or to look for a solid partner.

The entrepreneurs were then asked to assess competition in the country and *their own competitive capabilities.* According to business leaders, competition in Russia is high and has only increased since the 90s. This tense climate has made young businessmen even more dynamic and aggressive: there's no room for the weak.

A quarter of managers are unsure of their ability to compete, yet continue to run their businesses. *A tenth* cannot stand the psychologically stressful competition. But almost *half* (the majority) say they "enjoy competing with people" and "prefer to live and work in a competitive environment".

To sum up, people who are attracted to competition are energetic, self-confident, risk-takers who don't stop once they've achieved their goal. These social-psychological qualities are an integral part of their personality.

Conclusion: Some useful advice for those preparing to work in Russia

Commercial cooperation

1. For small and medium-sized companies, Russia offers the most future prospects in the food industry, cosmetics, trade and service sector.

2. At present, Russia is sorely lacking in Western marketing and management experience.

3. Only *a quarter of the population* believes that a Western-style economy can be developed in the country. The majority have little acceptance of the ideas of competition, individualism and non-interference by the state in the economy. Younger people are more accepting of Western standards, and it's on them that we must rely.

4. For Russians, the economic and the social are inseparable. The success of a company is not seen as the result of the genius of its leader, but as the result of joint efforts.

5. The particularities of the climate have influenced the Russians' way of working, by "quanta" and jerks: intense work, carried out in a fever but of short duration, must alternate with breaks for relaxation. Regular, measured work bores them. Don't try to take them over and control them at every moment: you're wasting your time and energy, and they'll be quick to show you how to work.

6. Russians have different holidays to ours. Taking into account the "bridges" of the Russian calendar (winter and spring) which can last 2-3 weeks, try to avoid the periods from mid-December to mid-January and from mid-April to mid-May before planning any business activity.

7. Remember that in business talks, Russians are not as motivated by money as you are. That's why it's generally easier for them to refuse a deal or business cooperation.

8. Russians have their own notion of "time", they avoid making firm long-term plans and prognoses for the future, because they don't have too much confidence in the future. And if a business meeting falls through, if delivery isn't made on time or if you encounter yet another inconvenience, it's rather

the result of circumstances that have intervened in the meantime and to which they have reacted more quickly than you.

9. Russians are more people-oriented than business and profit-oriented. Do everything in your power to win them over and win their sympathy and trust with your human qualities.

10. The Russian conformism that consists in wanting to "be like everyone else" on an individual level manifests itself in the desire to get along with those around them, in the spirit of solidarity with the work group, and in the habit of putting up with hardship. This can only reassure the employer: the Russian rarely seeks conflict at work, preferring to endure a situation in order to maintain a "good atmosphere" at work rather than "ruin" relations with colleagues and management. And let's not forget the Russians' penchant for group cohesion and their tradition of joint surety if it's in their favor.

11. Try to establish informal relations with Russians in the workplace. Russians "live" at work and are linked to other employees by a complex network of personal relationships in which it is much easier for them to find their way than it is for you. Don't neglect his advice, trust him. Or, better still, entrust him with a business while keeping control of it. No one will know how to solve your problem in Russia better than a Russian.

12. The premises (office, study) where a group of Russians work should be given importance. Russians don't value comfort so much as the idea of well-being, warmth and security. It's very important for them to have a place where they can get together to "drink tea" and chat. It's inconceivable for a Russian to work in an American-style "open space", even if glass walls separate employees from each other in the same area. The same goes for working in an office with the doors open... In all three cases, a Russian would feel watched and humiliated. But this reaction is understandable, given the Russian experience of living in a totalitarian state.

13. Don't expect a Russian to cooperate easily in giving you confidential information about others, as is done in American or German companies. Long experience of tailing and snitching has instilled in Russians a strong hostility to such acts. The words "informer" and "tattletale" are almost insults, and those who indulge in such practices are despised by the community and eventually excluded from it.

14. The collective principle of "being like everyone else" is deeply rooted in Russian consciousness. It breeds jealousy within a corporation and the principle of egalitarian justice. When isolating a member of the group, think of the consequences of your decision. Envy of the success of others is also a trait of the Russian temperament.

TABLES AND RESULTS OF PUBLIC OPINION POLLS CONDUCTED BY THE WEEKLY ARGUMENTY I FAKTY (FACTS AND ARGUMENTS)

1. "Do you have a car?"

I own a car: 42%
No, and I'm not about to buy one: 23%
I'm about to buy one: 17%
I own several: 16%

2. Which fast-food restaurants do you usually eat at?

McDonald's: 54%
Elki-palki: 13%
Rostiks: 6%
Rouskoe Bistro: 5%
Blini: 5%
Kartockka: 4%
Sbarro: 4%
Snack bars in the metro: 3%

3. "Your average monthly income is..."

less than $100: 24%
100-200 $: 7%
250-500 $: 16%
1 000-5 000 $: 21%
more than $5,000: 7%

4. "Where will you go to rest this summer?"

Abroad: 32%
I'll stay at home: 30%
At the dacha: 21%
In a spa: 11%
In a rest home or sanatorium: 4%

5. "How do you plan to spend the long May bank holidays?"

At the dacha, digging in the vegetable garden and resting: 25%
I lie on the couch with a good book in my hands: 12%
I'll be looking for a new love because it's spring: 10%
Drink vodka: 8%
I'll be visiting friends: 8%
J'irai me bronzer sur une plage à l'étranger: 5%
I will devote this time to my children's education: 5%
I'll go and rest in Europe: 5%
I'm about to travel to Russia: 3%

6. "In which country do you often go on vacation?"

In Italy: 26%
In Spain: 22%
In Finland: 11%

In Cyprus: 10%
In Turkey: 10%
In Greece: 10%
In Bulgaria: 7%

7. "Which country do you like best?"

France: 78%
Germany: 68.1%
England: 64.1%
India: 62.8%
Canada: 58.9%
Japan: 55.5%
China: 42.7%
USA: 38.7%

8. "What kind of cinema do you like?"

Comedy: 38%
Melodrama: 20%
Fantasy: 13%
Erotic: 12%
The big blockbuster: 8%
Horror films: 7%

9. "What keeps you from playing sports?"

Lack of nearby disciplines of interest to us: 58%
Price: 33%
Lack of choice in various disciplines: 7%

10. "What is most important to you in life?"

Family: 58%
Health: 29%
Silver: 7%
Work: 3%
The house, the dwelling : 1%

11. "Do you have children?"

Yes, one child: 33%
Yes, two children: 27%
No, but I'm about to have some: 26%
No, and I don't expect any: 12%

12. "Who do you trust with the child?"

Kindergarten: 31%
To grandfather or grandmother: 23%
I take care of it myself: 14%
To the nanny: 12%
To an older brother (or sister): 6%
I take it to work: 1%
To neighbors or other relatives: 1%

13. "Why do men get married?"

For love: 37%
The time has come: 28%
To be like everyone else: 17%
Because of the unborn baby: 9%
By calculation: 3%
For careers: 0%
To meet parents' wishes: 0%

14. "What do you consider to be the most important thing about women?"

The spirit: 27%
Sexuality: 26%
Kindness: 24%
Physical appearance: 11%
Home maintenance: 9%

15. "Which women are you most attracted to?"

Thin women: 66%
Coated women: 33%

16. "Are you living better in the last year?"

Slightly better: 35%
Same as before: 20%
Much better: 16%
Slightly worse: 15%
Much less well: 11%

17. "Who do you believe in most in the world?"

Myself: 45%
In God: 29%
In person: 12%
In my close relations: 10%
In my friends: 2%

18. "What is your dearest wish?"

Living in harmony with myself and those around me: 23%
Achieving success in life: 15%

Improve my financial situation: 12%
to be truly happy in life: 11%
Confidence: 8%
be happily married: 7%
Making the right spiritual choice: 6%
Setting up your own business: 4%
No envy of others: 3%
Career: 2%
Making a good deal: 1%
Don't be envious: 1%

19. "Do you think it's better to pay taxes and sleep soundly or not pay taxes and live serenely?"

It's better to pay them: 57%
Better not to pay them: 42%

20. "Why do you need to earn money?"

To make the most of life's pleasures: 51%
To support the family: 39%
Work is a pleasure in itself, and money is merely a means of remunerating him: 6%
For nothing, but it suits me: 1%

21. "Do you trust the public prosecutor?"

No: 90%
Yes: 9%

Bibliography

A. A. Aboulkhanova and A. N. Slavskaya (eds.), *The Consciousness of the Individual in a Society in Crisis*, collection of articles, Moscow, published by the Institute of Psychology of the Russian Academy of Sciences, 1995.

K. A. Aboulkhanova and R. R. Enakaïeva, "La Mentalité russe: un jeu sans lois? (Études et dialogues interculturels franco-russes)", from the book *La Mentalité russe: psychologie de l'individu. Consciousness. Représentations sociales*, Moscow, published by the Institute of Psychology of the Russian Academy of Sciences, 1996.

K. A. Aboulkhanova, "Russian mentality: cross-cultural and typological approaches", from *Russian mentality: questions of psychological theory and practice*, Moscow, published by the Institute of Psychology of the Russian Academy of Sciences, 1997.

B. Akunin, *Altyn-Tolobass*, St. Petersburg, ed. Neva, 2002.

Les Allemands à propos des Russes, collection, Moscow, Stolitsa ed., 1995.

N. A. Berdiaïev, *L'Esprit religieux russe et l'athéisme communiste*, Paris, ed. YMCA PRESS, 1934.

N. A. Berdiayev, *Self-awareness. Experience of a philosophical autobiography*, Moscow, ed. DEM, 1990.

N. A. Berdiayev, *The Russian Idea. Problèmes majeurs de la pensée russe du XIXe et du début du XXe siècle, from the book Sur la Russie et la culture philosophique russe: les philosophes de l'étranger de l'après-Octobre 1917*, Moscow, 1990.

A. I. Bogdanov, *Trois siècles de bains pétersbourgeois*, Saint Petersburg, 2000.

A. O. Boronoyev and P. I. Smirnov, *Russia and the Russians. The Character of the People and the Destiny of the Country*, St. Petersburg, ed. Lenizdat, 1992, p. 144.

M. Bulgakov, *The Master and Margarita*, Moscow, Khudojestvenaya literatura ed., 1973.

P. N. Chikharev, "Rules of doing business in Russia", Moscow, in the journal *Finansi and Statistika*, 1998.

Les Citoyens de Russie: leur sentiment de bien-être et la société dans lequel ils aimeraient vivre, analysis commissioned by the Moscow office of the Ebert Foundation, Moscow, 1998.

Marquis de Custine, *La Russie de Nicolas Iᵉʳ*, Moscow, ed. Terra, 1990.

N. Danilevskiï, *Russia and Europe*, Saint Petersburg, 1871.

Dictionary of Russian customs, Moscow, ed. Vetche, 2001.

Encyclopedic Dictionary, Moscow, 2000.

Encyclopedic Dictionary of Demography, Moscow, 1985.

I. A. Djidarian, "The problem of happiness in Russian mentality", from the book *Russian mentality: psychology of the individual. Consciousness. Social representations*, Moscow, published by the Institute of Psychology of the Russian Academy of Sciences, 1997.

G. V. Dratch (ed.), *Questions and Answers in the Study of a Culture*, ed. Gardariki, 2002.

Study of civilization. Theory and history of a civilization (as a means of study), Moscow, 1998.

V. P. Felitsina and Iu. E. Prokhorov, "Russian proverbs, sayings and expressions that have become proverbial", Moscow, ed. Russkiï iazyk ("The Russian Language"), 1979.

I. N. Gorelov and K. F. Sedov, *Les Fondements de la psycholinguistique (comme moyen d'étude)*, Moscow, ed. Labyrinthe, 2001.

A. Gorianin, *Myths about Russia and the Spirit of the Nation*, Moscow, ed. Pentagraphic, 2002.

N. Gorin, "La mentalité particulière des habitants de Russie", in *Questions d'économie*, 1996, no. 2.

L. N. Goumiliov, *From Russia to Russia*, Moscow, Ekopros ed., 1992.

L. N. Goumiliov, *Ancient Russia and the Great Steppe*, Moscow, Mysl ed., 1989.

286

L. N. Goumiliov, *Le Recommencement perpétuel*, Moscow, ed. Airis-Press, 2001.

P. S. Gourevitch, *La Mentalité. Vocabulary of a New Form of Thought*, Moscow, 1989.

P. S. Gourevitch, *Civilization Studies*, Moscow, Gardariki ed., 2001.

I. Ilyin, *On Future Russia*: Selected Articles, edited by N. P. Poltoratsky, Moscow, Voenizdat, 1993.

Presentation by the Institute of Experts, "The Burden of Government and Economic Policy" (October 23, 2002), in the journal *Finansy* ("Finance"), November 2002.

V. Jelvisse, *Ces Russes étranges*, Moscow, Egmont Russia Ltd, 2001.

A. M. Zhiguliov, *Russian Proverbs and Folk Sayings*, Moscow, *Moskovskiy rabotchiy* (The Moscow Worker), 1965.

A. L. Zhuravliov and N. V. Kotchetkova, "Dynamics of today's Russian entrepreneurs at the social and psychological level", in the book *Social psychology of economic behavior*, Moscow, Nauka ("Science") Publishing House, 1999.

K. G. Jung, *On the relationship of analytical psychology to poetic-artistic creation, in the book The Phenomenon of the Spirit in Art and Science*, Moscow, 1992.

R. Kaiser, *Russia: the People and the Power*, New York, 1976, pp. 390-393, 482-484.

A. Karmin, *Civilization Studies*, St Petersburg, ed. Lang', 2001.

N. N. Kolesov, *Life Comes from the Word...*, St. Petersburg, ed. Zlatooust, 1999.

L. P. Korsavin, *The Russian Idea: the West and the East*, in the book by N. Losskiy, *The Character of the Russian People*, Book 1, p. 5, Posev ed., 1957.

V. Kostikov, "Anatomy of corruption", *AiF*, nos. 22 and 24, 2002.

L. M. Kulikov, *The Foundations of Sociology and Political Science*, Moscow, in the journal Finansi i statistika, 2002.

R. D. Lewis, *Business Civilization in International Trade*, Moscow, ed. Delo, 2001.

D. S. Likhachiov, *One cannot escape oneself: history of self-consciousness and Russian civilization, in the newspaper Novyi Mir ("The New World")*, 1996, No. 6.

V. Lobanov, "Who's at the helm of the state machine?", *Komsomolskaia pravda*, August 28, 2002.

N. Losskiï, *The Character of the Russian People*, books 1 and 2, ed. Posev, 1957.

The Mentality of Russians. The Consciousness of Large Population Groups in Russia, Moscow, published by the Institute of Psychology of the Russian Academy of Sciences, 1997.

The Mentality of Russians: the particular state of mind of the main categories of the Russian population, Moscow, published by the Russian Academy of Education, Institute of Psychology, Image-contact ed., 1997.

Russian Mentality: Questions of Psychological Theory and Practice, Moscow, published by the Institute of Psychology of the Russian Academy of Sciences, 1997.

"Monitoring of public opinion by the Russian Independent Institute of Social and National Problems in the article of N. Thikhonova "The general state of society and values of Russians", in the newspaper *Izvestia*, 1997.

A. Parchev, *Why Russia is not America (A work for those who stay here)*, Krimskii most 9d, Moscow, 2002.

O. Perepiolkin, "The Russian entrepreneur: outline of a social portrait", in the book *Sociological Studies*, 1995, No. 2, pp. 35-40.

R. Pipes, *La Russie sous l'ancien régime*, translated from the English, Cambridge, Massachusetts, 1981.

L. G. Potchebut, *Introduction to Ethnic Psychology*, St. Petersburg, 1995, pp. 105-106.

National Program: Russian Business Culture, Moscow, ed. Chamber of Commerce and Industry of the Russian Federation, 1997.

The Regions of Russia, Collection of Statistics, State Committee on Statistics of the Russian Federation, Volumes 1 and 2, Moscow, 2000.

R. M. Rilke, *Vorpsvede. Auguste Rodin. Letters*, Moscow, Iskusstvo ed., 1994.

P. Ripert, *Dictionary of French maxims and proverbs*, 2002.

Russians: Family and Social Life, Moscow, published by the USSR Academy of Sciences, Nauka ("Science"), 1989.

Russia and the West: Dialogue of Cultures, ed. Moscow State University, Teaching Center on Intercultural Impact between Nations, Moscow, 1994.

Z. Sikevitch, *The Russians: Image of the People*, St. Petersburg, 1996.

V. Sivkova, "Le salaire: stimulation et démotivation", *AiF*, n° 49, 2001.

V. Sivkova, "How the middle class has changed in a year", *AiF*, July 2002.

A. N. Slavskaia, "Legal concepts of Russian society", in the book *Russian mentality: questions of psychological theory and practice*, Moscow, published by the Institute of Psychology of the Russian Academy of Sciences, 1997.

N. L. Smirnova, "The Model of Intelligent Man: A Russian Study", in the book *Russian Mentality: Questions of Psychological Theory and Practice*, Moscow, published by the Institute of Psychology of the Russian Academy of Sciences, 1997.

H. Smith, *The Russians*, New York, 1976, pp. 139-140, 151-152, 161,163, 332.

A. I. Solzhenitsyn, *Russia Under the Avalanche*, Moscow, ed. Russkiï put', 2001.

N. Tikhonova, "The general state of society and the values of Russians" (results of a public opinion poll on the theme "the directions taken by Russians"), in the newspaper *Izvestia*, 1997.

G. V. Touretskaïa and V. A. Khashchenko, "Social and Psychological Analysis of Different Categories of Women at Work", from the book *Social Psychology of Economic Behavior*, edited by the Institute of Psychology of the Russian Academy of Sciences, Moscow, Nauka ("Science"), 1999.

S. Valianskiï and D. Kalujnyï, *Comprendre la Russie par l'esprit*, Moscow, ed. Algorithme, 2001.

S. Valianskiï and D. Kalujnyï, Another History of Russia: From Europe to Mongolia, Moscow, ed. Vetche, 2001.

V. Volovik, *The Secrets of Gesture*, Moscow, ed. Astrel-Ast, 2001.

V. Vorobiov, *Cultural and linguistic studies. Theory and methods*, Moscow, UDN (Universitet drujby narodov), 1997.

A. P. Zabrovskiy, "The model of the foreigner in Russian literature", in the book *Russia and the West: intercultural dialogue*, published by Moscow State University, Faculty of Foreign Languages, 1994.

T. Zeldin, *Tout sur les Français*, translated from the French, Moscow, ed. Progress ("Du Progrès"), 1989.

Table of contents

Best sellers Max Milo Editions

Hitler's banker, Jean-François Bouchard

Confessions of a forger, Éric Piedoie Le Tiec

The Koran and the flesh, Ludovic-Mohamed Zahed

Governing by fake news, Jacques Baud

Governing by chaos, Collectif

A political history of food, Paul Ariès

Mad in U.S.A.: The ravages of the "American model",
Michel Desmurget

Mondial soccer club geopolitics, Kévin Veyssière

Putin: Game master?, Jacques Braud

Treatise on the three impostors: Moses, Jesus, Muhammad,
The Spirit of Spinoza

TV Lobotomy, Michel Desmurget